GLOBAL WARMING

GLOBAL WARMING

Looking Beyond Kyoto

ERNESTO ZEDILLO

editor

CENTER FOR THE STUDY OF GLOBALIZATION
Yale University

BROOKINGS INSTITUTION PRESS
Washington, D.C.

Library of Congress Cataloging-in-Publication Data

Global warming : looking beyond Kyoto / Ernesto Zedillo, editor.
    p.   cm.
Includes bibliographical references and index.
Summary: "Comprehensive examination of the economic, social, and political context of climate policy in industrialized and developing nations. Calls for a multilateral
approach that goes beyond the mitigation-focused Kyoto policies and stresses the
importance of generating policies that work within a time frame commensurate with
that of climate change itself"—Provided by publisher.
    ISBN-13: 978-0-8157-9714-2 (cloth : alk. paper)
    ISBN-10: 0-8157-9714-1 (cloth : alk. paper)
    ISBN-13: 978-0-8157-9715-9 (pbk. : alk. paper)
    ISBN-10: 0-8157-9715-X (pbk. : alk. paper)
    1. Climatic changes—Government policy. 2. Nature—Effect of human beings on.
3. Global warming. I. Zedillo Ponce de León, Ernesto. II. Title.
    QC981.8.G56G57442 2007
    363.738'74—dc22   2007044850

9 8 7 6 5 4 3 2 1
The paper used in this publication meets minimum requirements of the
American National Standard for Information Sciences—Permanence of Paper
for Printed Library Materials: ANSI Z39.48-1992.

Typeset in Adobe Garamond

Composition by Circle Graphics
Columbia, Maryland

Printed by R. R. Donnelley
Harrisonburg, Virginia

Contents

Acknowledgments

This volume is the product of a conference hosted by the Yale Center for the Study of Globalization in October 2005 to debate global climate policy after 2012.

The conference convened experts from various fields, countries, and professional backgrounds to discuss climate change with the objective of providing an interdisciplinary forum to identify the best policies for advancing international efforts to address the challenges it poses. At the time of the conference, first experiences with the European carbon dioxide emissions trading system had taken place, and new information on climate science was available from meetings of the working groups of the Intergovernmental Panel on Climate Change held the previous April.

This volume contains individual authors' efforts to address constructively various aspects of the climate change debate with the goal of proposing improvements in climate policy. The scholars and practitioners who accepted our invitation to participate and who followed up their presentations by producing the chapters that follow are some of the most thoughtful, skillful, and effective voices commenting today on climate change. We wish to express our gratitude to all of them for the time and effort they have contributed to this volume.

The William and Flora Hewlett Foundation provided major funding for the conference, and for that we extend our most sincere appreciation. The Center owes special thanks also to Whitney and Betty MacMillan and to a number of loyal Yale alumni and friends for their support.

We are indebted to Ulrich Wagner, who began his work with us while a Ph.D. student in the Economics Department and followed through even after leaving Yale for a postdoctoral fellowship. His command of the subject was a useful input for organizing the conference.

We wish to thank Strobe Talbott, president of the Brookings Institution, who continues to support and facilitate the work of the Yale Center for the Study of Globalization whenever he can, and Diane Hammond and Elizabeth Forsyth, who have worked with Janet Walker at the Brookings Institution Press and have been understanding and patient editors. Holly Hodder provided initial editorial assistance. Finally, the book benefited immensely from the oversight provided by the Center's associate director, Haynie Wheeler, who not only looked after every organizational detail of the October 2005 conference but also applied her many skills to pull this volume together.

Introduction

ERNESTO ZEDILLO

The pace and face of globalization in the twentieth-first century will be critically influenced by whether or not some specific issues that call for collective action by countries are properly addressed. The evolution of globalization and its capacity to facilitate convergence of standards of living among all countries will not be independent of how well the provision of some key global public goods is organized by the international community. Peace and security, financial stability, open markets, and prevention of pandemics are obvious examples of public goods that cannot possibly be delivered without international coordination and whose persistent shortage would impair global integration and prosperity. Assuming that the scientific consensus on climate change is ultimately confirmed, then mitigation of global warming and, to some extent, adaptation to it constitute another global public good whose provision will influence how the global economy and geopolitics look in the future.

Since political borders cannot, of course, enclose climate variability, there should be no question that mitigation of climate change is a global public good. Mitigation manifestly poses the problems typically encountered in the provision of global public goods, such as issues of sovereignty, the temptation of free riding, differing preferences and priorities across societies, and the summation problem.[1] Collective action is a requisite to address this set of problems. On the other hand, given that the purported direct consequences of global warming would be felt locally, one could posit that adaptation to this phenomenon does not really constitute a global public good. This is true to some extent—but not to the full extent. The local consequences of global warming, as argued by various authors in this volume, would in turn lead to economic and social effects that irremediably would spill across borders. If the decision were taken to prevent or contain those effects, then international cooperation would also be required. Consequently, the two generally acknowledged public policy challenges stemming from the risk of climate change, mitigation, and adaptation cannot be properly undertaken without international collective action.

Leaving aside the continuing debate on whether mitigation of climate change is more urgent than providing other global public goods, it is clear that the phenomenon and its implications must be subjected to serious analysis with the goal of providing a sound basis for coherent policies. In fact this is what the international community has intermittently tried to do for almost two decades. The Intergovernmental Panel on Climate Change (IPCC)—charged with scientifically assessing the pertinent information—was established in 1988, and in 1992 most countries, including the United States, adopted the United Nations Framework Convention on Climate Change (UNFCCC), with the objective of stabilizing greenhouse concentrations in the atmosphere at a safe level. Subsequently, as a measure for implementing the UNFCCC, the Kyoto Protocol—by which the developed countries that are part of it committed to specific reductions of greenhouse gas emissions—was adopted in 1995 and came into force in 2005.

Nevertheless, the issue is far from settled. For one thing, the science of climate change is still evolving, a fact that in and of itself helps to explain why the policy decisions so far adopted must necessarily be seen as partial or trial steps. This is clearly the case with the Kyoto Protocol. It stipulates only short-term emissions targets, limited to the so-called first budget period, 2008–12; however its goal is to address a long-term challenge. Furthermore, the treaty excludes the largest emitters: by withdrawal, in the case of the United States, and by exemption at the protocol's negotiation, in the case of large developing countries like China. On all fronts—scientific, economic, and geopolitical—building international cooperation to deal with climate change is a work in progress.

In this process, what comes after Kyoto's first budget period constitutes the most important challenge for both analysts and policymakers. The Yale Center for the Study of Globalization has adopted the discussion of the global climate change challenge as one of its core topics. As part of this endeavor, in October 2005 the center convened a group of leading experts and policymakers from various parts of the world to debate global climate policy after 2012. Following up on the presentations, a significant number of the participants formalized their papers, utilizing their notes and the transcriptions we provided, and were kind enough to submit the documents that are now included in this volume.

True, since we held the conference, many events on the subject have taken place, some with significant intellectual content and others rendering meaningful policy decisions. For example, the *Stern Review on the Economics of Climate Change* was published, the reports of the three working groups of the IPCC Fourth Assessment Report were released, the European Union pledged unilaterally to reduce carbon emissions by 20 percent by 2020 as measured against 1990 levels, and the United States government began to engage again more actively in the international discussion on climate change.[2] In fact, thanks to the generosity of Sir Nicholas Stern and other authors, the Yale Center for the Study of Globalization had the opportunity of hosting a stimulating symposium on the *Stern Review* in February 2007.[3] Notwithstanding the latest analyses, the contributions stemming from our fall 2005 Yale conference retain a significant degree of pertinence that makes it worth publishing them as a volume. Although the authors were not required to update their chapters in light of recent evidence, some of the chapters do take it into account. In particular, in this introduction I have taken the liberty of making reference to some of the presentations that were made at our symposium on the *Stern Review.*

Recent events have scaled up the discussion of the issues tackled at the 2005 Yale conference. The debate on the science of climate change, reflected in the contributions by R. K. Pachauri, Richard Lindzen, Stefan Rahmstorf, and Stephen Schneider, has acquired a higher profile with the publication of the IPCC's Fourth Assessment Report.[4] Pachauri's contribution to this volume underlines the report's conclusion that the warming of the climate is unequivocal and that most of the observed warming over the last fifty years is *very likely* (rather than *likely,* as submitted in the IPCC's previous report) due to the observed increase in anthropogenic greenhouse concentrations.[5]

Lindzen does not dispute that there is global warming, although he considers it to have been relatively small over the past century; furthermore, he is skeptical of the evidence provided to impute the concentration of greenhouse gases as the cause of that warming. Essentially, he argues that the present climate alarmism is not warranted by the scientific evidence and he claims that the alarm has been unduly created by predictions based on models that exaggerate climate sensitivity to added greenhouse gases. He maintains that there are climatic processes, not yet properly represented in the prediction models, that will mitigate the impact of increasing atmospheric concentrations of greenhouse gases.

Rahmstorf, who differs strongly with Lindzen's argumentation, believes that the available evidence, which he reviews in his chapter, indeed proves that human activities already have altered the global climate, and in the absence of effective climate policies those activities will lead to significant global warming, which is highly likely to come with major risks and extreme events. Rahmstorf, in other words, endorses the consensus idea that the world is already in a trend of dangerous climate change.

Precisely this scrutiny of the notion of key vulnerabilities of climate change (meaning severe or dangerous impacts) is the subject of Schneider's contribution.

This author examines in detail why it is not possible to provide an unambiguous definition of dangerous climate change. Since individuals across regions and countries have different stakes in aspects such as productive capacity, biodiversity, and cultural traditions that could be affected by climate change, the concept of dangerous human interference with the climate system cannot be free of value judgments. Schneider points out that scientific knowledge can only inform the political processes by which conflicting judgments of what is valuable are settled and, furthermore, that knowledge by itself is not unequivocal, since it is based on limited information and projections generated by models that are semiempirical constructs. The assessment of climate vulnerability, observes Schneider, requires risk analysis, which in turn calls for probability distributions over outcomes instead of single-value expectations.

The fact that the impacts of climate change will not be uniform across countries is also highlighted in Robert Mendelsohn's chapter. This author estimates that, under either moderate or severe climate change scenarios, most of the damages will fall most heavily on the poorest countries, while the richest countries would actually benefit under both scenarios. This asymmetry, in his view, calls for "a compensation package" for poor countries, aimed at helping them grow faster so that their economies can move away more easily from climate-sensitive activities. Mendelsohn recommends, however, spending only limited resources on climate change mitigation in the near term. Relying on estimates of the net present value of future damages in various climate change scenarios, he concludes that it would be uneconomical for present generations to invest heavily in abatement.

The latter policy recommendation contrasts significantly with the chief conclusions of the *Stern Review*: climate change is a serious and urgent issue that warrants strong and urgent action to reduce greenhouse gas emissions around the world; the benefits of strong and early action far outweigh the economic costs of not acting; the overall costs of climate change will be equivalent to losing at least 5 percent, and as much as 20 percent, of global GDP each year; and the cost of mitigation can be limited to around 1 percent of GDP each year.

William Nordhaus, a pioneer and a most distinguished scholar in the field of climate change economics, who long ago submitted that unchecked warming may lead to enormous and costly long-run ecological and economic impacts, does not fully concur with Stern's policy recommendations. Shortly after the publication of the review and at the aforementioned Yale symposium, Nordhaus showed that Stern's economic case for strong and early action stems crucially from an intertemporal cost-benefit analysis that, by virtue of using a near-zero social discount rate, exaggerates manyfold today's valuation of damages that may occur in the very remote future.[6] This approach is what allows the *Stern Review* to validate the near-term cost of the mitigation effort that it recommends. Nordhaus suggests that, had the review used a more conventional real interest rate, it would have found it very hard to justify urgent and large investments for climate change mitigation. He believes that there are no new reasons to invalidate the prescription provided by mainstream environmental economic analysis, which recommends that our generation should certainly contribute to ameliorating the risk of global warming, but that the proportion of resources diverted to this should be stepped up only as subsequent generations become richer. From this viewpoint, it is better to invest now in solving growth and development problems, thereby bequeathing bigger economies to future generations, who subsequently will be better endowed to mitigate and adapt to climate change.

Stern has responded that the review's use of formal modeling with a low discount rate is just one part of its argument for stronger action now.[7] Moreover, Stern also suggests that his results stemming from the integrated assessment model used in the review differ from those provided in previous analyses: that model uses the latest climate change science, which reveals larger temperature changes than previously thought, as well as the latest probabilistic assessments of climate sensitivity. Furthermore, Stern has insisted on the validity of a low discount rate; he is of the opinion that discounting at a high rate is unethical, for it involves discrimination among individuals by date of birth.

In his comments on the *Stern Review*, Scott Barrett granted that ethics are important in discussing the impact of climate change on different groups of people but explained that there are several ethical dimensions to it, not just one.[8] The issue is not only about comparing the well-being of future generations relative to ours but also about comparing the well-being of richer and poorer societies, today and in the future. Barrett indicated that the review's purported equity concerns are not well served by proposing that today's relatively poorer generations should help richer generations in the future to live better. One could add that this proposition would be particularly hard to sell to the present citizens of poor developing countries who will have to sacrifice if the review's prescription of strong and early action across all countries is embraced by the international community.

Interestingly, it appears that the prescription can be rescued even if the issue of how to compare the well-being of different groups across countries and over time is not fully settled. In critiquing the *Stern Review*, Martin Weitzman has suggested that if investing in climate change mitigation were seen less as a problem of long-term cost-benefit analysis and more as a problem of deciding how much insurance to buy to offset the slight chance of a future catastrophe that could ruin the entire world, then perhaps it would be more efficient and fair for our generation to more seriously entertain harsher measures now than those it is presently willing to undertake.[9] Weitzman's analysis implies that the *Stern Review* may be right for the wrong reason. The chapter by Schneider in this volume also makes reference to the normative challenge when one is dealing with uncertainty and insists on the need to determine the thresholds at which the chance of catastrophic climate impacts will not be taken without some hedging strategies to mitigate them.

Irrespective of the ultimate choice made between early aggressive mitigation or ramped-up mitigation, internationally coordinated policy action is needed, an undertaking that from any perspective poses a huge and complex challenge, as suggested by various contributions in this volume. Thomas Heller is markedly pessimistic about the chances of building any time soon a regime congruent with the objectives established in the UNFCCC. In fact he predicts that current attempts to extend the framework enshrined in the Kyoto Protocol will meet a dead end. He does not see in that architecture the elements that would make a cooperative solution feasible. Not only is he skeptical that a Kyoto-based regime will succeed in attracting the effective participation of the leading emitters, who so far have been absent, but he also observes little enthusiasm among many of the previously engaged parties to deepen their commitments at the forthcoming negotiation of the second-period obligations.

In the context of their assessment of the European Emissions Trading Scheme, Gernot Klepper and Sonja Peterson provide a more positive vision than Heller's about the future value of the Kyoto Protocol. They credit the UNFCCC with significant achievements, such as providing the broad objectives of climate policy, introducing emissions reduction (albeit insufficient), and constructing complex institutional structures that are beginning to be success stories. They count among the latter both the tools to certify projects for the flexible mechanisms of the Kyoto Protocol as well as the European Emissions Trading Scheme, which in these authors' view shows that international emissions trading is feasible. Klepper and Peterson are confident that the Kyoto Protocol will prove more valuable than now predicted by Kyoto skeptics.

In the case of the so-called Annex I group, it is obvious that each country's attitude toward a Kyoto framework for the post-2012 period will depend to some extent on its experience in meeting the first budget period target. These experiences are heterogeneous, as shown in some of the contributions to this volume.

Canada's experience, analyzed by John Stone, is expected to be one of non-compliance with Kyoto. Although the Canadian government has announced a long-term emission abatement policy that includes targets by 2050 and even will include regulation of specific sectors, it has already admitted that Canada will not meet its Kyoto targets. In fact, as reported by Stone, rather than delivering a 6 percent reduction of greenhouse gas emissions, Canada's 2008–12 emissions levels might be 28 percent *above* the 1990 level.

In contrast, as a result of policies that started to be developed in the late 1980s, the United Kingdom is on track to comply with its Kyoto targets. The chapter by Howard Dalton provides an account of how the United Kingdom has played a leading role in supporting climate science by introducing targets, by trading greenhouse gas emissions, and also by promoting international negotiations on climate change.

Russia is another country that will meet its Kyoto targets. In fact it will have a surplus of emissions rights eligible to be placed on the international carbon market; but unlike the U.K. it has engaged rather cautiously in the Kyoto process. In his chapter, Alexander Golub relates how Russia, despite having a wide margin to comply with the previously agreed targets and despite being in the position to make an economic gain from joining Kyoto, not only delayed its ratification practically to the last moment but also is moving very slowly to put in place the infrastructure that it needs to participate in the treaty's flexible mechanisms. It is not audacious to anticipate a highly defensive, if not frankly oppositional, attitude on the part of the Russian government at the post-Kyoto negotiations.

Needless to say, strong defensive positions should also be expected from the developing countries, particularly the large emitters. In this respect, the contributions by Jyoti Parikh on India and Shen Longhai on China are quite suggestive. Both authors make clear that sustaining high growth and reducing poverty should be their respective countries' highest priority for a long time. They also consider that the burden of reducing carbon emissions within the next few decades should fall on the developed countries, given both their contribution to the world's accumulated greenhouse gases and also their much higher per capita emissions.

Parikh believes that India, with a low GDP per capita and a large proportion of its population without access to modern cooking and lighting energy sources, has a long way to go before it can accept binding commitments for carbon emissions reductions. Even more meaningful, this author rejects an idea that is gaining traction in places like the United States: that large emitters should be singled out among developing countries for future climate change policy decisions. She affirms that per capita emissions, rather than the sheer size of emissions, should be the defining criterion in whatever specific notion of differentiated responsibility is entertained in the future by the international community. Similarly, although Shen anticipates a sustained effort by China to improve its energy efficiency and also to reduce its dependency on coal (which will still provide 60 percent of its total energy consumption by 2020), he does not envision that his country will accept emissions targets anytime soon.

If Parikh's and Shen's opinions are representative of the way in which the large developing countries will go about negotiating a possible post-Kyoto regime, it is clear that achieving an agreement will be an enormously complex and difficult undertaking. Yet in his proposal for a post-2012 regime in this volume, Robert Stavins suggests that broad participation by key developing countries is essential to address the challenge of climate change, not only because of the absolute and mounting size of their emissions but also because, being relative latecomers to the energy markets, they have the greatest potential to adopt cost-effective, low-emissions technologies to satisfy their incremental energy demand.

Furthermore, if developing countries are not an effective part of a post-Kyoto agreement, Stavins indicates that the risk of an "emissions leakage" factor (distorting the international pattern of production and trade) would become significant—and inhibitory to industrialized countries' participation.

Stavins believes that engagement by developing countries is possible if, unlike in the present protocol, a truly long-term agreement is negotiated. He conceives of a regime with global emissions targets and trading but one whereby developing countries' commitments become binding only when their respective per capita gross domestic product reaches certain thresholds. This author essentially thinks that a suitable modified Kyoto architecture will provide the necessary and negotiable regime for the future.

In contrast, Nordhaus, in his contribution to this volume, opines that "life after Kyoto" should be different from Kyoto—or that at least alternative approaches should receive serious consideration from the pertinent stakeholders. He warns of, and explains, serious pitfalls in any climate change regime based on quantity targets, even if provided with trading and auction of permits. Nordhaus's preferred alternative would consist of internationally harmonized carbon taxes on emissions. His analysis implies that all in all the negotiation and administration of this option could prove less complicated than a quantity-based system. Taxing carbon emissions, by acting directly at the source of the problem, would be more effective and efficient than permits for coordinating policies and mitigating climate change. In Nordhaus's proposal the principle of common but differentiated responsibility would be instilled in a system in which developing countries commit to enact the agreed carbon taxes only as they achieve certain levels of per capita income; furthermore, poor countries would receive transfers of income to hasten their early participation.

What, then, after Kyoto?

The above summary makes clear that, even among people who take climate change seriously, views on the subject can be markedly dissimilar and even contrary. The mosaic of opinions in this volume is indicative of what lies ahead as the international community prepares to discuss what to do about climate change. Scott Barrett is probably right: climate change may not be the world's most pressing problem (as I am convinced it is not), but it still could prove to be the most complex challenge the world has ever faced.[10]

The problem is a multidimensional one, which eludes straightforward solutions. It is not only that governments and societies are facing the complications involved in the provision of a truly global public good but also that it entails unprecedented uncertainties about costs and benefits, and these benefits have a term for delivery much longer than in any previous international undertaking. Analyzing mitigation as a global public good is further complicated by the possibility of catastrophic climatic change with irreversible damages to the world's human, natural, and physical capital, damages that could prove immensely asymmetric to the cost of preventing such disasters (even if such prevention required front loading the necessary expenditures, which involves sacrifice by the present generation and its immediate successors). Yet to be justifiable, a much larger expenditure early on and stronger action would have to be seen more as a payment toward insurance on the human habitat than as an investment with a sufficiently attractive expected social and economic return.

To think of climate change mitigation as insurance against an uncertain catastrophe rather than as an investment in the future may provide analysts with a more reasonable rationale for stronger action sooner rather than later, but it does not make it easier to design, agree on, and implement emissions reduction policies. Governments and the populations they represent must still grapple with tough choices under practically any policy strategy intended to modify the present trend of global emissions and warming. It is not possible to escape the fact that somebody, somewhere soon, will need to start paying the price for such a policy.

It does not seem useful or fair to represent mitigation to citizens as good business for society at large. It can certainly be good business for some—but hardly for all. The real deal is that a sacrifice of some sort will have to be incurred by the present generation for the sake of people who will exist many years from now, in richer societies than ours, and most probably in countries that are not our own. Full transparency on this essential fact may not be good short-term politics, but it is indispensable if serious long-term policies are to be adopted.

It is important to recognize that previous exercises resulting in effective coordination among members of the international community were undertaken to address issues for which the near-term cost of failing to act was relatively obvious to the parties involved. Think of the creation of the United Nations at the end of the monstrous Second World War; of the General Agreement on Tariffs and Trade (GATT) after the regression into impoverishing protectionism during the 1930s; of the International Monetary Fund after many years of international monetary chaos; and of the successes in preventing pandemics, even eradicating diseases like smallpox, which were scourges upon humanity for centuries.

In each of these examples—and any other from humanity's past—experience or even downright evidence on the immediate cost of failing to act proved crucial to trigger international cooperation. The case for collective action to mitigate climate change, at least for the foreseeable future, cannot be built on the same kind of manifest basis. Whoever is willing and possessed of the authority to promote that action will have to rely on materially distinct arguments. It is an ineluctable fact that, if the world truly is contending with an unprecedented phenomenon, then organizing the indispensable international cooperation to deal with it poses an unprecedented challenge.

Were the challenge to be taken on resolutely, then the principles inscribed in the UNFCCC would certainly prove fitting, and the knowledge gathered by the IPCC in its various reports would continue to be invaluable; still, the question of whether other parts of the available international structure would serve to build further the system that is needed would remain a valid question. For one thing, the world does not have the right forum for leaders to discuss the issue in a way conducive to adopting policies to effectively reduce exposure to the catastrophic impacts of climate change potentially many years in the future. That forum will have to be convened not in lieu of the existing multilateral mechanisms but rather to catalyze decisions to enable those mechanisms to perform their intended function.

Moreover, the process of policy analysis, negotiation, implementation, and compliance will be well served by transparency and simplicity, two attributes not yet present in the ongoing deliberations to define a post-Kyoto Treaty regime. When one considers that to be effective this regime will have to overcome not only the challenges stemming from the sovereignty and free rider issues but also the challenges posed by the intercountry and intergenerational equity questions unique to climate change mitigation, then William Nordhaus's insistence on an international agreement focused on adopting harmonized carbon taxes rather than on emissions limits makes eminent sense.

Notes

1. These problems are discussed in International Task Force on Global Public Goods, *Meeting Global Challenges: International Cooperation in the National Interest,* Final Report (Stockholm, 2006). Hard copies of this report can be obtained from the Department for Development Policy, Ministry for Foreign Affairs, SE-103 39 (Stockholm). The full text is available at www.gpgtaskforce.org/bazment.aspx.
2. Nicholas Stern, *The Economics of Climate Change: The Stern Review* (Cambridge University Press, 2007).
3. The presentations and discussions of the symposium on the *Stern Review on the Economics of Climate Change* are available at www.ycsg.yale.edu/climate/stern.html.
4. The volumes of IPCC, *Climate Change 2007,* are *The Physical Science Basis,* Contribution of Working Group I to the Fourth Assessment Report (Bangkok, 2007); *Impacts, Adaptation. and Vulnerability,* Contribution of Working Group II to the Fourth Assessment Report (Bangkok, 2007); and *Mitigation of Climate Change,* Contribution of Working Group III to the Fourth Assessment Report (Bangkok, 2007).
5. Very likely > 90% probability of occurrence. Likely > 66% probability of occurrence.
6. See William D. Nordhaus, "A Review of the *Stern Review on the Economics of Climate Change,*" *Journal of Economic Literature* 45 (2007): 686–702; William D. Nordhaus, "Comments on the *Stern Review on the Economics of Climate Change,*" Symposium on the *Stern Review,* 2007, Yale Center for the Study of Globalization (www.ycsg.yale.edu/climate/stern.html).
7. Nicholas Stern, "Reaction to the Panelists," Symposium on the *Stern Review,* 2007, Yale Center for the Study of Globalization (www.ycsg.yale.edu/climate/stern.html).
8. Scott Barrett, "Comments on the *Stern Review on the Economics of Climate Change,*" Symposium on the *Stern Review,* 2007, Yale Center for the Study of Globalization (www.ycsg.yale.edu/climate/stern.html).
9. Martin Weitzman, "The *Stern Review on the Economics of Climate Change,*" *Journal of Economic Literature* 45 (2007): 703–24.
10. Barrett, "Comments on the *Stern Review.*"

PART ONE

Climate Change Detection and Scenarios: Reexamining the Evidence

1

The IPCC: Establishing the Evidence

R. K. PACHAURI

The Intergovernmental Panel on Climate Change (IPCC) was established in 1988 by the World Meteorological Organization and the United Nations Environment Program. Reexamination of the evidence on climate change is the basic purpose of the IPCC.[1] The thorough, consensual, and objective manner in which these assessments are carried out provides solid credibility for the findings.

One example: the IPCC nominated close to 2,000 experts to compile the Fourth Assessment Report.[2] From this group it appointed about 600. The first draft was prepared and reviewed by other experts. On the basis of this review, the authors prepared the second draft, which went the rounds of expert and government reviews. Following this second review, the authors prepared the final draft along with a synthesis of the report for policymakers.[3] These two sets of documents were approved by the working group that oversaw the preparation of the report and by the IPCC as a whole.

The IPCC has followed a similar elaborate process for every report. The Fourth Assessment Report, currently in hand, closes some gaps and provides fresh knowledge on the science of climate change. The three reports of working groups 1, 2, and 3, which form part of the Fourth Assessment Report, were completed and released in early in 2007 (February, April, and May, respectively). The synthesis report of the Fourth Assessment Report is due to be completed and released in November 2007. Although the first three assessment reports strengthened previous basic findings, the fourth provides even stronger scientific evidence and a stronger basis for actions necessary to move forward during the second commitment period of the Kyoto Protocol. It is in the context of this report that this chapter addresses not only the geophysical aspects of climate change but also the socioeconomic aspects, including equity implications.

It is also important to view immediate actions as part of a continuum, as they would telescope within the perspective of long-term developments. As such, we need to adopt a scenario-based, comprehensive approach for seeing what developments are likely to happen and to place their implications for mitigation and adaptation measures to tackle the threat of climate change within a larger socioeconomic framework. Any global agreement for action would involve negotiations through the process established for this purpose. But political strategies, which have to be determined by negotiators, must be driven by the science of climate change.

The Fourth Assessment Report finds that "warming of the climate system is unequivocal, as is now evident from observations of increases in global average air and ocean temperatures, widespread melting of snow and ice, and rising global mean sea level."[4] In addition, rainfall in the Northern Hemisphere has been increasing in the higher latitudes and decreasing in the lower latitudes. Further, the frequency and intensity of extreme precipitation have increased.

Some regions of the world are far more vulnerable to climate change than other regions. The most vulnerable are the Arctic, sub-Saharan Africa, small islands, and the Asian megadeltas. Mountain glaciers and snow cover have declined on average in both hemispheres. Widespread decreases in glaciers and ice caps have contributed to sea-level rise: the global average sea level rose at an average rate of 1.8 millimeters (0.07 inch) a year over the period 1961 to 2003 and about 3.1 millimeters (0.12 inch) a year during 1993 to 2003. It will be seen, therefore, that climate change has serious equity implications, since several of the poorest regions of the world (which have had hardly any role in the increase of greenhouse gases in the atmosphere) are likely to be the most affected. Equity dimensions are built into the United Nations Framework Convention on Climate Change (UNFCCC). Negotiations took place for almost three years before agreement was reached on the framework convention. A major factor in the negotiations and the agreement on the framework was the First Assessment Report, which provided a scientific foundation for consensus.

Climate change will affect sustainable development, just as climate change itself is the result of unsustainable development. The subject of sustainable development, in fact, is a cross-cutting theme and is included in the Fourth Assessment Report. Also included are other cross-cutting themes: stronger regional focus, key vulnerabilities, risk and uncertainty, climate change and water, and integrating adaptation and mitigation. It is hoped that these will get much more attention than they have received in the past.

By the time all volumes of the Fourth Assessment Report come out, the panel will have completed almost two decades of existence. In this period, not only has scientific expertise grown substantially, but the capacity for scientific research on various aspects of climate change has also grown in parts of the world where very limited work had been done in previous years. To that extent, the activities of the IPCC and its deliberate efforts to ensure geographic balance in tapping expertise and knowledge across the globe have indeed been a major factor in the development of scientific expertise on climate change across the world.

Some of the major findings of the Fourth Assessment Report will be an important basis for action in contemplating future possibilities for mitigating the emissions of greenhouse gases and adapting to climate change. One of these is that, if earth's atmosphere and related temperature increase are to be stabilized at one of the lower trajectories shown in the report, then emissions can be allowed to increase only up to the year 2015, beyond which they must decline. Even at this low stabilization level, the equilibrium temperature increase would be between 2.0°C and 2.4°C.

Eleven of the twelve-year span 1995–2006 rank among the warmest years in the instrumental record of global surface temperature. Further, the updated hundred-year linear trend (1906–2005) of 0.74°C is larger than the corresponding trend for 1901–2000, which is given in the Third Assessment Report as 0.6°C. The linear warming trend over the last fifty years is nearly twice that for the last one hundred years. During the twentieth century glaciers and ice caps have had massive losses, contributing to the rise in sea level (see figure 1-1).

Overall projections of temperature increase in the twenty-first century are shown in figure 4-1 (see chapter 4). The best estimates for a global average of surface air warming (shown in six emissions marker scenarios) range from 1.8°C as the best estimate for the low scenario to 4.0°C as the best estimate for the high scenario. This is consistent with the span reported in the Third Assessment Report of 1.4°C to 5.8°C, even though the two projections are not directly comparable. The Fourth Assessment Report provides best estimates and an assessed likelihood range for each of the marker scenarios, relying on a larger number of climate models of increasing complexity and realism as well as on new information regarding the nature of the carbon cycle and on observed constraints on climate response.

Needless to say, warming is not uniform across the globe and nor, therefore, are the related impacts. For instance, the Arctic region is already warming at twice the rate of the global average. More focused regional research and, therefore, more focused regional assessments are needed, but the IPCC functions on the basis of peer-reviewed literature and so is bound by what is available. In some cases this is not enough. Undoubtedly regional assessments will require substantial research—and soon—especially in the context of the next phase of the Kyoto Protocol.

Figure 1-1. *Cumulative Loss of Glacier Mass in Many Regions*

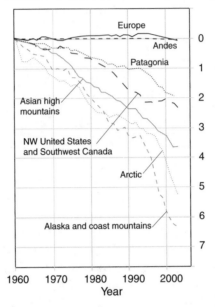

Cumulative total mass balance [mm SLE]

Source: IPCC, *Climate Change 2007: Synthesis Report* (Bangkok, 2007).

Some criticize the IPCC for using market exchange rates in its scenarios. In actual fact, scenarios assessed by the IPCC also use purchasing power parity. Again, in keeping with IPCC procedures, the assessment of these scenarios is based entirely on material available in peer-reviewed literature. Another criticism is that projections for developing regions are implausibly high, that in arriving at economic projections the IPCC did not use an adequate level of expertise in the field of statistics, and that it did not use the insights available in the economic ministries of the various governments.

These criticisms are addressed herein by authors associated with the IPCC. The emissions scenarios, as well as the methodologies adopted, are consistent with work carried out by organizations such as the World Bank, the International Energy Agency, and the United States Department of Energy. Material assessed is drawn from publications produced by a very active research community working in this area. Table 1-1 shows historical growth rates for the United Kingdom, the United States, Canada, and Japan: it can be seen that the data used in the IPCC scenarios are consistent with historically established rates achieved in the developed world.

It needs to be emphasized that climate change will have an extreme effect on developing countries and poor people in every part of the world. We have seen

Table 1-1. *Historical per Capita Growth Rates of Purchasing Power Parity for the Past 100 Years and for the Four Special Reports on Emissions Scenarios (SRES) World Regions*

| Country or area | 1980 U.S. $10 billions, purchasing power parity | | 1870–1985 | |
	1870	*1985*	*Factor*	*Annual percentage*
United Kingdom	59.0	510.9	8.7	1.9
United States	61.7	2,947.1	47.8	3.4
Canada	4.9	306.8	62.1	3.7
Japan	17.2	1,202.2	69.8	3.8
	SRES ranges[a] *1990–2100*			
Countries members of OECD in 1990	3.6–7.6		1.2–1.9	
Countries undertaking economic reform	6.2–13.2		1.7–2.4	
Asia	18.9–39.1		2.7–3.4	
Africa and Latin America	17.1–43.7		2.6–3.5	

Sources: A. Kausel. ed., *150 Years of Economic Growth in Austria and the Western World as Reflected in Statistics* (Vienna: Verlag der Österreichischen Staatsdruckerei, 1985, in German); IPCC, *Emissions Scenarios,* edited by Nebojsa Nakicenovic and Rob Swart, special report of the IPCC Working Group III (Cambridge University Press, 2000).

a. Projections for B2, B1, A1 scenarios are calculated using the MESSAGE model. For the detailed definition of SRES regions, please see www.grida.no/climate/ipcc/emission/149.htm.

this in the disaster that followed Hurricane Katrina in New Orleans: the poorest people suffered the most. This happens in the developing world on a very large scale, and to understand the problem it is reasonable to multiply several times over the comparable experience with such events in the developed world, given the large population concentration that characterizes parts of the developing world, with its extreme poverty and weak infrastructure.

It is also relevant to highlight the possibility of singular events as a consequence of climate change. For some of these, of course, the science is still evolving, but if these events do happen, they could overwhelm all response strategies. But if we exercise the precautionary principle, then it is important to take actions that obviate any reasonable chance of these events happening in the first place. Two possibilities that deserve mention are the weakening of the meridional overturning circulation, which could lead to a reduction of the heat transported into high latitudes of Europe and a weakening of the Greenland ice sheet, which is likely to lose mass substantially during the twenty-first century. This could contribute substantially to sea-level rise. In fact the contraction of the Greenland ice sheet is projected to continue to contribute to sea-level rise after the year 2100. Current models suggest that loss of ice mass increases with

Table 1-2. *Global Estimated Macroeconomic Costs for 2030, Least-Cost Trajectories, Three Long-Term Stabilization Levels*

Stabilization level (ppm CO$_2$ equivalent)	Median GDP reduction (percent)	Range of GDP reduction (percent)	Reduction of average annual GDP growth rates (percentage points)
590–710	0.2	−0.6 to 1.2	< 0.06
535–590	0.6	0.2 to 2.5	< 0.10
445–535	n.a.	< 3	< 0.12

n.a. = Not available.

temperature rises more rapidly than with precipitation and that the surface-mass balance becomes negative at a global average warming (relative to preindustrial values) in excess of 1.9°C to 4.6°C.

Quite apart from the danger of singular events and discontinuities, the duration, location, frequency, and intensity of extreme weather and climate events is very likely to change, and these will result in mostly adverse impacts on biophysical systems. For instance, the intensity of tropical cyclones is likely to increase. Further, inertia in the system will require us to act quickly to adapt to those impacts for long-term effects. This is particularly relevant regarding the rise in sea level, which could continue for centuries—certainly for decades—as a result of both the thermal expansion of the oceans and the melting of ice bodies.

Thus it is extremely important for vulnerable nations to put in place adaptation measures. In addition, there is a need for cooperation among nations, because any national response to climate change can be more effective if it is part of a combined effort. This is also important for mitigation measures for greenhouse gas emissions. Exchange of knowledge would provide a basis for coordinated actions using the best technology, the best policy instruments, and the best experience. The cost of reducing emissions has been assessed by the IPCC to be moderate in relation to economic output. So also are the costs of improving the efficiency of energy use, an important element of emissions reduction.

To really reduce greenhouse gas emissions, it would be necessary to reduce energy consumption in a range of economic activities in addition to more efficient energy use. There is an enormous disparity between developed and developing countries in their energy efficiency. Much of this disparity stems from variations in the spread of land areas, the extent of transportation required, and so on; and of course some climates require use of air conditioning or heating. Table 1-2 shows the estimated economic impacts of mitigation in the year 2030. The models used establish that to stabilize concentration at 445–535 parts per million of CO$_2$, a reduction of less than 3 percent of GDP in the year 2030 may take place. This means that the level of prosperity that would have been attained in 2030 may be delayed by at most a few months.

Yoichi Kaya, the distinguished Japanese academic, has come up with what is now known as the Kaya Identity, an equation that describes the variables that determine the human impact on climate in the form of emissions of greenhouse gases.[5]

Global CO_2 emissions = GDP × energy intensity × carbon intensity.

A reduction in energy intensity would reduce end-use demand and increase efficiency. A reduction in net carbon intensity would shift toward low-carbon options such as renewables, hydrogen and fuel cells biomass energy, and carbon sequestration. The historic record of improving energy efficiency provides adequate confidence in the ability of the world to attain major improvements in energy efficiency. However, to bring about a commensurate reduction in the carbon intensity of energy use, a major deviation, and major improvement over historical rates, would be required. In other words, technology development using low carbon energy inputs would be essential for achieving low carbon intensity in the world energy system.

Investment in, and worldwide deployment of, technologies with low greenhouse gas emissions are essential for achieving stabilization targets as well as for adequately reducing costs. Such technologies would require public and private research, development and demonstration, and investment in new technologies during the next few decades. There are several barriers to the development and dissemination of low-carbon technologies, and appropriate incentives are required to address these barriers to the development, acquisition, deployment, and diffusion of such technologies. Perhaps the most important policy requirement for the mitigation of greenhouse gas emissions is to ensure that a proper price is paid for carbon dioxide emissions. An effective price signal could realize significant mitigation potential in all sectors. Modeling studies show these prices rising to U.S.\$20–\$80 per ton of CO_2 equivalent by 2030 and U.S.\$30–\$155 per ton by 2050. These numbers are consistent with stabilization at around 550 parts per million CO_2 equivalent by 2100. Most top-down, as well as some 2050 bottom-up, assessments suggest that real or implicit carbon prices of U.S.\$20–\$50 per ton of CO_2 equivalent, sustained or increased over decades, could lead to a power generation sector with low greenhouses gas emissions by 2050 and make many mitigation options in the end-use sectors economically attractive.

Another important element of mitigation is changes in lifestyle and behavior patterns. Lifestyle and behavior changes can reduce greenhouse gas emissions by changing consumption patterns, thus helping conserve resources. The equity dimensions of climate change make it imperative that lifestyle changes take place in a manner that does not continue the skewed utilization of natural resources. At the global level allocation of resources would need to ensure the most effective resource utilization for mitigation and the most equitable resource allocation for risk reduction targeting the most vulnerable regions of the world.

Notes

1. IPCC published the following volumes of *Climate Change 1990: Scientific Assessment of Climate Change,* Report of Working Group I, edited by J. T. Houghton, G. J. Jenkins, and J. J. Ephraums (Cambridge University Press, 1991); *Impacts Assessment of Climate Change,* Report of Working Group II, edited by W. J. M. Tegard, G. W. Sheldon, and D. C. Griffiths (Canberra: Australian Government Publishing Service, 1991); *The IPCC Response Strategies,* Report of Working Group III (Covelo, Calif.: Island Press, 1991).
2. IPCC published the following volumes of *Climate Change 2007: The Physical Science Basis,* Contribution of Working Group I to the Fourth Assessment Report; *Impacts, Adaptation, and Vulnerability,* Contribution of Working Group II to the Fourth Assessment Report; *Mitigation of Climate Change,* Contribution of Working Group III to the Fourth Assessment Report (Bangkok, 2007).
3. IPCC, *Climate Change 2007: Synthesis Report* (Bangkok, 2007).
4. Ibid., p. x.
5. Yoichi Kaya and Keiichi Yokobori, *Environment, Energy, and Economy: Strategies for Sustainability* (United Nations University Press, 1997).

2

Is the Global Warming Alarm Founded on Fact?

RICHARD S. LINDZEN

For the sensitive reader or listener, the language used in connection with the issue of "global warming" must frequently sound strange. Weather and climate catastrophes of all sorts are claimed to be the inevitable result of global warming, and global warming is uniquely associated with man's activities. The reality of the threat of global warming is frequently attested to by reference to a scientific consensus. According to Tony Blair, "The overwhelming view of experts is that climate change, to a greater or lesser extent, is man-made and, without action, will get worse."[1] Elizabeth Kolbert, in *The New Yorker,* says, "All that the theory of global warming says is that if you increase the concentration of greenhouse gases in the atmosphere, you will also increase the Earth's average temperature. It is indisputable that we have increased greenhouse gas concentrations in the air as a result of human activity, and it's also indisputable that over the last few decades average global temperatures have gone up."[2]

Given the alarm surrounding the issue, such statements seem peculiarly inconclusive and irrelevant to the catastrophes cited. To be sure, these references are one-sided. They fail to note that there are many sources of climate change and that profound climate change has occurred many times both before and after man appeared on the Earth; given the ubiquity of climate change, it is implausible that all change is for the worse. Moreover, the coincidence of increasing carbon dioxide (CO_2) and the small warming over the past century hardly establishes causality. For the most part, I do not disagree with the consensus, but

I am disturbed by the absence of quantitative considerations. Indeed, I know of no serious split and suspect that the claim that there is opposition to this consensus amounts to no more than setting up a straw man to scoff at. However, I believe that people are being led astray by the suggestion that this agreement constitutes support for alarm.

Let me review the components that constitute this consensus a little more precisely, while recognizing that there is, indeed, some legitimate controversy connected with specific aspects of even these items.

1. The global mean surface temperature is always changing. Over the past sixty years, it has both decreased and increased. For the past century, it has probably increased by about $0.6° \pm 0.15°C$ (centigrade). That is to say, we have had some global mean warming.

2. CO_2 is a greenhouse gas, and its increase contributes to warming. It is, in fact, increasing, and a doubling would increase the greenhouse effect (mainly due to water vapor and clouds) by about 2 percent.

3. There is good evidence that man is responsible for the recent increase in CO_2, although climate itself (as well as other natural phenomena) can also cause changes in CO_2.

In some respects, these three pillars of consensus are relatively trivial. Remaining completely open is the question of whether there is any reason to consider these facts as particularly alarming. Is there any objective basis for considering the approximate $0.6°C$ increase in global mean surface temperature to be large or small regardless of its cause? The answer to both questions depends on whether $0.6°C$ is larger or smaller than what we might expect on the basis of models that have led to the present concern. These models are generally called general circulation models (GCMs). We may, therefore, seek to determine how the current level of man-made climate forcing compares with what we would have were CO_2 to be doubled (a common reference level for GCM calculations).

In terms of climate forcing, greenhouse gases added to the atmosphere through man's activities since the late nineteenth century have already produced three-quarters of the radiative forcing that we expect from a doubling of CO_2.[3] There are two main reasons for this. First, CO_2 is not the only anthropogenic greenhouse gas. Others like methane also contribute. Second, the impact of CO_2 is nonlinear in the sense that each added unit contributes less than its predecessor. For example, if doubling CO_2 from its value in the late nineteenth century—from about 290 parts per million by volume (ppmv) to 580 ppmv—causes a 2 percent increase in radiative forcing,[4] then to obtain another 2 percent increase in radiative forcing we must increase CO_2 by an additional 580 ppmv rather than by another 290 ppmv. At present, the concentration of CO_2 is about 380 ppmv. The easiest way to understand this is to consider adding thin layers of paint to a pane of glass. The first layer cuts out much of the light, the next layer cuts out more, but subsequent layers do less and less because the painted pane is already essentially opaque.

It should be stressed that we are interested in climate forcing and not simply levels of CO_2; the two most certainly not linearly proportional.

Essential to alarm is the fact that most current climate models predict a response to a doubling of CO_2 of about 4°C (which is much larger than what one expects the simple doubling of CO_2 to produce: that is, about 1°C). The reason for this is that, in these models, the most important greenhouse substances—water vapor and clouds—act in such a way as to amplify the response to anthropogenic greenhouse gases alone (that is, they act as what are called large positive feedbacks). However, as all assessments of the Intergovernmental Panel on Climate Change (IPCC) have stated (at least in the main text, although not in the various summaries for policymakers), the models simply fail to get clouds right. We know this because in official comparisons all models fail miserably to replicate observed distributions of cloud cover. Thus the model predictions are critically dependent on features that we know must be wrong. As shown in figure 2-1, the treatment of clouds involves errors an order of magnitude greater than the forcing from a doubling of CO_2.[5] While the IPCC allows for the possibility that the models get water vapor right, the intimate relation between water vapor and clouds makes such a conclusion implausible.

Let me summarize the main points thus far:

—It is *not* the level of CO_2 that is important, but rather the impact of man-made greenhouse gases on climate.

Figure 2-1. *Observed and Modeled Percentage Cloud Cover Averaged by Latitude*[a]

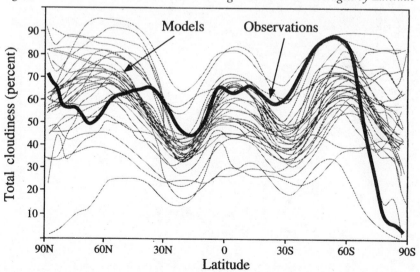

a. Each thin gray line shows an individual model's hindcast of percentage cloud cover averaged by latitude. The black line shows the observed cloud cover.

—Although we are far from the benchmark of doubled CO_2, climate forcing is already about three-fourths of what we expect from such a doubling.

—Even if we attribute all warming over the past century to man-made greenhouse gases (which we have no basis for doing), the observed warming is only about a third to a sixth of what models project.

This raises two possibilities: either the models are greatly overestimating the sensitivity of climate to man-made greenhouse gases, or the models are correct, but some unknown process has canceled most of the warming. Calling the unknown process "aerosols" does not change this statement, since aerosols and their impact are unknown to a factor of ten or more; indeed, even the sign is in doubt.

In arguing for climate alarmism, we are choosing the second possibility. Moreover, we are assuming that the unknown cancellation will soon cease. What supports the second possibility, given that it involves so many more assumptions than the first possibility?

The IPCC Third Assessment Report made use of a peculiar exercise in curve fitting using results from the Hadley Centre for Climate Change. It consists of three plots, which are reproduced in figure 2-2. The first panel shows an observed temperature record (without error bars) and the outputs of four model

Figure 2-2. *Simulations of Global Mean Temperature with Various Combinations of "Forcing"*

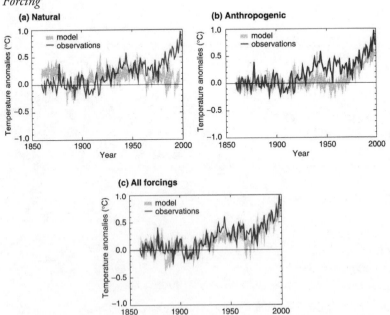

runs (using the coupled ocean-atmosphere model) with so-called natural forcing for the period 1860–2000. There is a small spread in the model runs (which presumably displays model uncertainty; it most assuredly does not represent natural internal variability). In any event, the models look roughly like the observations until the last thirty years. A second diagram reproduces the observed curve, and the four models are run with anthropogenic forcing. Here there is rough agreement over the last thirty years and less agreement in the earlier period. Finally, the observations and the model runs with both natural and anthropogenic forcing are presented, showing rough agreement over the whole record. The models used have relatively low sensitivity to a doubling of CO_2 of about 2.5°C.

In order to know what to make of this exercise, one must know exactly what was done. The natural forcing consisted of volcanoes and solar variability. Prior to the Pinatubo eruption in 1991, the radiative impact of volcanoes was not well measured, and estimates vary by about a factor of three. Solar forcing is essentially unknown. Thus natural forcing is, in essence, adjustable. Anthropogenic forcing includes not only anthropogenic greenhouse gases, but also aerosols that act to cancel warming (in the Hadley Centre outputs, aerosols and other factors canceled two-thirds of the greenhouse forcing). Unfortunately, the properties of aerosols are largely unknown. In the present instance, therefore, aerosols constitute simply another adjustable parameter (indeed, both the magnitude and the time history are adjustable, and even the sign is in question). This is remarked upon in a recent paper in *Science*,[6] which notes that the uncertainty is so great that estimating aerosol properties by tuning them to optimize agreement between models and observations (referred to as an inverse method) is probably as good as any other method, but that the use of such estimates to test the models constitutes a circular procedure. This is as strong a criticism of model procedures as is likely to be found in *Science*. The authors are all prominent in aerosol work. The first author is the most junior, and when it was pointed out that the article reflects negatively on model outputs, he vehemently denied any such intent. In the present example, the choice of models with relatively low sensitivity allows adjustments that are not so extreme.

New uncertainties are always entering the aerosol picture. Some are quite bizarre. A recent article in *Science* proposed that airborne dandruff has a significant role.[7] Other articles suggest that the primary impact of aerosols is actually warming.[8] Of course, this is the beauty of the global warming issue for many scientists. The issue deals with such small climate forcing and small temperature changes that it permits scientists to argue that everything and anything is important for climate.

In brief, the defense of the models starts by assuming that the model is correct. Then differences between the model behavior in the absence of external forcing and observed changes in "global mean temperature" are attributed to external forcing. Next "natural" forcing is introduced, and a "best fit" to the observations is obtained. If, finally, it is possible to remove any remaining discrepancies by introducing "anthropogenic" forcing, part of the observed change must be attributable to the greenhouse component of "anthropogenic" forcing.

Of course, the internal variability of the model is not correct, and "anthropogenic" forcing includes not only CO_2 but also aerosols, which are unknown to a factor of ten to twenty (and perhaps even the sign is unknown). Finally, there is little quantitative knowledge of "natural" forcing, so this too is adjustable. Recall that the Hadley Centre acknowledges that the "aerosols" have canceled most of the forcing from CO_2.

The argument just presented is the basis for all popular and scientific claims that man is responsible for much of the observed warming. It would appear that the current role of the scientist in the global warming issue is simply to defend the possibility of ominous predictions so as to justify his belief.

To be fair, the authors of chapter 12 of the *Scientific Assessment of Climate Change,* a volume of the IPCC Third Assessment Report, provided the following for the draft statement of the Summary for Policymakers:

> From the body of evidence since IPCC (1996), we conclude that there has been a discernible human influence on global climate. Studies are beginning to separate the contributions to observed climate change attributable to individual external influences, both anthropogenic and natural. This work suggests that anthropogenic greenhouse gases are a substantial contributor to the observed warming, especially over the past thirty years. However, the accuracy of these estimates continues to be limited by uncertainties in estimates of internal variability, natural and anthropogenic forcing, and the climate response to external forcing.

This statement is not too bad, especially the last sentence. To be sure, it does not emphasize the dependence of the results on the model, but the statement is vastly more honest than what the Summary for Policymakers in the IPCC's Third Assessment Report ultimately presented:

> In the light of new evidence and taking into account the remaining uncertainties, most of the observed warming over the last fifty years is likely to have been due to the increase in greenhouse gas concentrations.

In point of fact, the impact of man remains indiscernible simply because the signal is too small compared to the natural noise. Claims that the current temperatures are "record breaking" or "unprecedented," however questionable or misleading, obscure the fact that the observed warming is too small compared to what models suggest. Even the fact that the oceans' heat uptake capacity leads to a delay in the response of the surface does not alter this conclusion (especially since the Hadley Centre results are obtained with a coupled model).

Moreover, the fact that we already have three-quarters of the climate forcing expected from a doubling of CO_2 means that if one truly believes the models, then we have long since passed the point where mitigation is a viable strategy. What remains is to maximize our ability to adapt. However, the promotion of alarm does not follow from the science, as is clearly illustrated by the following example.

According to any textbook on dynamic meteorology, one may reasonably conclude that in a warmer world, extratropical storminess and weather variability will decrease. The reasoning is as follows. Judging by historical climate change, changes are greater in high latitudes than in the tropics. Thus in a warmer world, we would expect the temperature difference between high and low latitudes to diminish. However, it is precisely this difference that gives rise to extratropical large-scale weather disturbances. Moreover, when a winter day in Boston is unusually warm, the wind is blowing from the south. Similarly, when the day is unusually cold, the wind is generally blowing from the north. The possible extent of these extremes is determined by how warm low latitudes are and how cold high latitudes are. Given that we expect high latitudes to warm much more than low latitudes in a warmer climate, the difference is expected to diminish, leading to less variance.

Nevertheless, advocates and the media tell us that exactly the opposite is the case: that the models predict this (which, to their credit, they do not) and that the basic agreement discussed earlier signifies scientific agreement on this matter as well. Clearly more storms and greater extremes are regarded as more alarming than not. Thus the opposite of our current understanding is invoked in order to promote public concern. The crucial point here is that once the principle of consensus is accepted, agreement on anything is taken to infer agreement on everything.

The example given focuses on extratropical storms. However, given the relatively heavy hurricane season we have had recently, the emphasis has been on tropical storms. Political activists have seized on recent papers suggesting that, in a warmer world, such storms may become more powerful.[9] Needless to say, the articles seized upon have been extremely controversial, but more to the point, no such relation was uncovered for storms reaching land—only for those over water.

At this point, it is doubtful that we are even dealing with a serious problem. If this is correct, then no policy addressing this non-problem would be cost-effective. Even if we believe the problem to be serious, we have already reached the levels of climate forcing that have been claimed to be serious. However, when it comes to the Kyoto Protocol, the situation is even worse. Here, there is widespread and even rigorous scientific agreement that complete adherence to the Kyoto Protocol would have no discernible impact on climate.

What about the first possibility—namely, that the models are much too sensitive? Not only is this the possibility that scientists would normally prefer on the basis of Occam's famous razor, but it is also a possibility for which there is substantial support.[10] I focus here on one line of this evidence: tropical warming in the 1990s was associated with much greater outgoing long-wave radiation than models produce. This discrepancy suggests that current models lack a strong negative feedback.

The discrepancy has been confirmed by at least four independent groups: the National Aeronautics and Space Administration's (NASA's) Goddard Institute for Space Studies; NASA Langley; State University of New York, Stony Brook; and the University of Miami.[11]

This discrepancy would normally suggest exaggerated model sensitivity. However, the papers attribute it either to circulation changes or to "unknown" cloud properties, except for the paper by Clement and Soden. Using four separate models, they show that changes in dynamics could not produce changes averaged over the tropics. Chou and Lindzen show the discrepancy theoretically, while Clement and Soden show that the discrepancy could be resolved by allowing convective precipitation efficiency to increase with surface temperature.[12] Such dependence is at the heart of the iris effect, which was first found by Lindzen, Chou, and Hou and was theoretically predicted by Sun and Lindzen.[13] In the first paper, we attempt to examine how tropical clouds respond to changing surface temperature and find that existing satellite data are only marginally capable of dealing with this issue. The results, however, suggest that there are strong negative feedbacks, counter to what models suggest, and that the models in no way replicate the cloud behavior that is observed.

It may turn out that precipitation can be measured rigorously using ground-based radar. Ground-based radar allows the almost continuous measurement of precipitation and the separation of convective precipitation from stratiform precipitation (albeit with remaining questions of accuracy). In the tropics, both types of precipitation originate in condensation within cumulus towers. However, condensation that does not form precipitation is carried aloft as ice, which is detrained to form cirrus from which the condensate eventually falls as stratiform precipitation. Precipitation efficiency is given by the following relation: $e =$ (convective precipitation) / (convective precipitation + stratiform precipitation). Using data from Kwajalein Atoll in the western Pacific, we have studied how e varies with sea surface temperature. In addition, the Kwajalein radar makes it possible to look explicitly at the area of stratiform rain per unit of convective mass flux.

Figure 2-3 shows that e increases about 7.1 percent per degree centigrade increase in sea surface temperature (compared with 7.5 percent estimated by Sun and Lindzen in 1993) and that this increase is associated with a decrease in normalized stratiform area of about 25 percent per degree centigrade (which is a bit

Figure 2-3. *Precipitation Efficiency and Cirrus Area per Unit of Convective Activity versus Sea Surface Temperature*

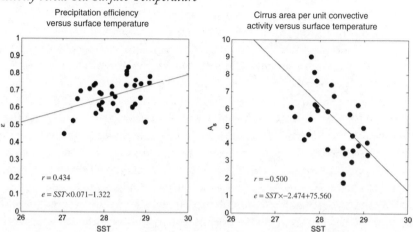

larger than what was estimated from space observations by Lindzen, Chou, and Hou in 2001).[14] If correct, this confirms the iris effect and the fact that models have greatly exaggerated climate sensitivity because, in contrast to models, nature itself acts to limit rather than exaggerate the influence of added greenhouse gases.

What do these simple results imply? The primary implication is that for more than twenty-five years we have based not only our worst-case scenarios but even our best-case scenarios on model exaggeration. This was suggested by previous results, but the present result has the virtue of specifically identifying a basic and crucially relevant error. Under the circumstances, the main question we will be confronting is how long the momentum generated by this issue will prevent us from seeing that it has been an illusion based on model error.

The public discourse on global warming has little in common with the standards of scientific discourse. Rather, it is part of political discourse, where comments are made to secure the political base and frighten the opposition, not illuminate issues. In political discourse, information is to be "spun" to reinforce preexisting beliefs and to discourage opposition. The chief example of the latter is the claim of universal scientific agreement. This claim was part of the media treatment of global cooling (in the 1970s) and has been part of the treatment of global warming since 1988 (well before most climate change institutes were created). The consensus preceded the research.

The fact that media discourse on climate change is political rather than scientific should come as no surprise. However, even scientific literature and institutions have become politicized. Some scientists issue meaningless remarks in what I believe to be the full expectation that the media and the environmental movement will provide the "spin." Since the societal response to alarm has, so far, been to generate scientific funding, there has been little reason for scientists to complain. Should scientists feel any guilt, it is assuaged by two irresistible factors: the advocates define public virtue, and administrators are delighted with the growing grant overhead. The situation has been recognized since time immemorial. In Federalist Paper no. 79, Alexander Hamilton brooded about abuses that might arise from legislative tampering with judges' salaries. "In the general course of human nature," he wrote, "a power over a man's subsistence amounts to a power over his will." An indication of such an attitude occurred when, in 2003, the draft of the U.S. National Climate Plan urged giving high priority to improving our knowledge of climate sensitivity (that is, in finding the answer). A National Research Council review panel instead urged giving broader support for numerous groups to study the impacts of warming. The panel apparently was more interested in spreading the wealth than in finding an answer.

A second aspect of politicization of discourse specifically involves the scientific literature. Articles challenging the urgent need to address anthropogenic greenhouse gases are met with unusually quick rebuttals. These rebuttals are usually published as independent papers rather than as correspondence concerning the original articles, the latter being the usual practice. When the usual practice is followed, then the response of the original author(s) is published side by side with the critique. However, in the present situation, such responses are delayed by as much as a year. In my experience, criticisms do not reflect a good understanding of the original work. When the original authors' responses finally appear, they are accompanied by another rebuttal that generally ignores the responses but repeats the criticism. This process clearly is not conducive to scientific progress, but it is not clear that progress is what is desired. Rather, the mere existence of criticism entitles the environmental press to refer to the original result as "discredited," while the long delay of the response by the original authors permits these responses to be totally ignored.

A final aspect of politicization is the explicit intimidation of scientists. Intimidation has mostly, but not exclusively, been used against those questioning alarmism. Victims of such intimidation generally remain silent. Congressional hearings have been used to pressure scientists who question the "consensus." These scientists are pitted against carefully selected opponents. The clear intent is to discredit the "skeptical" scientist from whom a "recantation" is sought.

Advocates frequently attempt to use the news media as an instrument for this intimidation. A notable example in the early 1990s was when Ted Koppel announced on *Nightline* that Vice President Al Gore had asked him to find connections between unsavory interests and scientists questioning global warming alarm. After editorializing on the inappropriateness of the request, Koppel proceeded to present a balanced exposure of the debate. Newspaper and magazine articles routinely proclaim that scientists who differ with the consensus view are stooges of the fossil fuel industry. All of this would be bad enough, but the real source of intimidation is the fact that neither the American Meteorological Society nor the American Geophysical Society sees fit to object to any of this.

These are not isolated examples. Before 1991, some of Europe's most prominent climate experts were voicing significant doubts about climate alarm. The issue has always concerned the basis for alarm rather than the presence of warming (however small). Only the most cynical propagandist could have anticipated that sentient human beings could be driven into panic by the mere existence of some warming. In any event, among these questioners were such distinguished individuals as Sir John Mason, former head of the U.K. Meteorological Office and secretary of the Royal Society; Professor Hubert Lamb, Europe's foremost climatologist and founder of the Climate Research Unit at East Anglia University; Dr. Henk Tennekes, director of research at the Royal Dutch Meteorological Institute; and Dr. Aksel Wiin-Nielsen, professor at the University of Copenhagen, former director of the European Centre for Medium Range Weather Forecasting, and former secretary general of the World Meteorological Organization. All of these figures except Tennekes have disappeared from the public discourse. Lamb is now dead. Tennekes was dismissed from his position, and Wiin-Nielsen was tarred by Bert Bolin (the first head of the IPCC) as a tool of the coal industry. In Russia a number of internationally recognized pioneers of climate science like Kiril Kondratyev (who died in 2006) and Yuri Izrael continue to oppose climate alarm, but Russian scientists eager for connections with the rest of Europe are much more reluctant to express such views.

Not all such situations have ended badly. When a senior Energy Department official, William Happer, was dismissed in 1993 after questioning the scientific basis for global warming, the physics community was generally supportive and sympathetic.[15] In another more bizarre case, an attempt was made to remove the name of Roger Revelle from a paper he had coauthored with S. Fred Singer and Chauncy Starr in which they discouraged hasty action on ill-understood warming. Those pursuing the action claimed that Singer had cajoled an allegedly senile Roger Revelle into permitting himself to be so used. It should be noted that Revelle was the professor whom Al Gore frequently cites as having introduced him to the horrors of global warming. In any event, Singer took the issue to court and won. His description of the case makes interesting reading.[16]

More recent is a controversy over a thousand-year reconstruction of mean temperature purporting to show that the half degree (centigrade) rise of the past century was unprecedented.[17] Because of the extensive use of this work in the politics of global warming, Representative Joe Barton demanded the analytical detail since the research was supported by U.S. funds. Both the American Meteorological Society and the American Geophysical Union protested Barton's request. One need not go into the merits of this controversy to see that the response of professional organizations sends a chilling message. Only the defenders of orthodoxy will be defended against intimidation.

The *basic agreement* frequently described as representing a global warming "consensus" is entirely consistent with there being virtually no problem. Actual observations suggest that the sensitivity of the real climate is much less than that found in computer models whose sensitivity depends on processes that are clearly misrepresented. Attempts to assess climate sensitivity by direct observation of cloud processes, and other means, point to a conclusion that doubling of CO_2 would lead to about 0.5°C warming or less.

Unfortunately, a significant part of the scientific community appears committed to the notion that alarm *may* be warranted. Alarm is felt to be essential to the maintenance of funding. The argument is no longer over whether the models are correct (they are not), but rather *whether their results are at all possible.* It is impossible to prove that something is impossible. The global warming issue parts company with normative science at an early stage. A good indicator of this disconnect is widespread and rigorous scientific agreement that the Kyoto Protocol would have no discernible impact on climate. This clearly is of no importance to the thousands of negotiators, diplomats, regulators, general-purpose bureaucrats, and advocates whose livelihood is tied to climate alarmism.

A rarely asked, but important, question is whether promoting alarmism is good for science. The situation may not be so remote from the impact of Lysenkoism on Soviet genetics. However, I believe that the future will view the response of contemporary society to "global warming" as simply another example of the appropriateness of the fable of the "Emperor's New Clothes." For the sake of science, I hope that future arrives soon. In the meantime, we can continue to play our parts in this modern version of the fable. Our descendants will be amused for generations to come.

Notes

1. *Economist*, December 24, 2004.
2. Elizabeth Kolbert, "The Climate of Man: I." *New Yorker,* April 25, 2005, p. 56.
3. Gunnar Myhre and others, "New Estimates of Radiative Forcing due to Well-Mixed Greenhouse Gases," *Geophysical Research Letters* 25, no. 14 (1998): 2715–18; James Hansen and Makiko Sato, "Greenhouse Gas Growth Rates," *Proceedings of the National Academy of Sciences* 101, no. 46 (2004): 16109–14.
4. The term "forcing" refers to the imbalance in radiative energy flux that would be produced by the addition of greenhouse gases. Such forcing is generally described either as a percentage increase in the greenhouse effect or as a flux with units of watts per square meter. Such a flux acts to warm the Earth.
5. W. Lawrence Gates and others, "An Overview of the Atmospheric Model Intercomparison Project (AMIP I)," *Bulletin of the American Meteorological Society* 80, no. 1 (1999): 29–55.
6. Theodore L. Anderson and others, "Climate Forcing by Aerosols: A Hazy Picture," *Science* 300, no. 5622 (2003): 1103–04.
7. Ruprecht Jaenicke, "Abundance of Cellular Material and Proteins in the Atmosphere," *Science* 308, no. 5718 (2005): 73.

8. Mark Z. Jacobson, "Strong Radiative Heating due to the Mixing State of Black Carbon in Atmospheric Aerosols," *Nature* 409, no. 6821 (February 8, 2001): 695–97. Yang Chen and Joyce E. Penner, "Uncertainty Analysis for Estimates of the First Indirect Aerosol Effect," *Atmospheric Chemistry and Physics* 5, no. 11 (2005): 2935–48.

9. Kerry Emanuel, "Increasing Destructiveness of Tropical Cyclones over the Past Thirty Years," *Nature* 436, no. 7051 (2005): 686–88; Peter J. Webster and others, "Changes in Tropical Cyclone Number, Duration, and Intensity in a Warming Environment," *Science* 309, no. 5742 (2005): 1844–46.

10. One line of inquiry involves looking at the temporal response to identifiable perturbations like volcanoes or so-called regime changes. Rapid responses correspond to low sensitivity, while slow responses imply higher sensitivity. Such inquiries invariably show rapid responses. Some examples are Richard S. Lindzen and Constantine Giannitsis, "On the Climatic Implications of Volcanic Cooling," *Journal of Geophysical Research* 103, no. D6 (1998): 5929–41; Richard S. Lindzen and Constantine Giannitsis, "Reconciling Observations of Global Temperature Change," *Geophysical Research Letters* 29, no. 12 (2002): doi:10.1029/2001GL014074; David H. Douglass and Robert S. Knox, "Climate Forcing by the Volcanic Eruption of Mount Pinatubo," *Geophysical Research Letters* 32, no. 20 (2005): doi:L05710 10.1029/2005GL023829.

11. Junye Chen, Barbara E. Carlson, and Anthony D. Del Genio, "Evidence for Strengthening of the Tropical General Circulation in the 1990s," *Science* 295, no. 295 (2002): 838–41. Anthony D. Del Genio and William Kovari, "Climatic Properties of Tropical Precipitating Convection under Varying Environmental Conditions," *Journal of Climate* 15, no. 18 (2002): 2597–615. Bruce A. Wielicki and others, "Evidence for Large Decadal Variability in the Tropical Mean Radiative Energy Budget," *Science* 295, no. 5556 (2002): 841–44; Bing Lin and others, "Examination of the Decadal Tropical Mean ERBS Nonscanner Radiation Data for the Iris Hypothesis," *Journal of Climate* 17, no. 6 (2004): 1239–46. Robert D. Cess and Petra M. Udelhofen, "Climate Change during 1985–1999: Cloud Interactions Determined from Satellite Measurements," *Geophysical Research Letters* 30, no. 1 (2003): 1019. Amy C. Clement and Brian J. Soden, "The Sensitivity of the Tropical-Mean Radiation Budget," *Journal of Climate* 18, no. 6 (2005): 3189–203.

12. Ming-Dah Chou and Richard S. Lindzen, "Comments on 'Examination of the Decadal Tropical Mean ERBS Nonscanner Radiation Data for the Iris Hypothesis,'" *Journal of Climate* 18, no. 12 (2004): 2123–27. Clement and Soden, "Sensitivity of the Tropical-Mean Radiation Budget."

13. Richard S. Lindzen, Ming-Dah Chou, and Arthur Y. Hou, "Does the Earth Have an Adaptive Infrared Iris?" *Bulletin of the American Meteorological Society* 82, no. 3 (2001): 417–32. De-Zheng Sun and Richard S. Lindzen, "Distribution of Tropical Tropospheric Water Vapor," *Journal of Atmospheric Sciences* 50, no. 12 (1993): 1643–60.

14. Sun and Lindzen, "Distribution of Tropical Tropospheric Water Vapor"; Lindzen, Chou, and Hou, "Does the Earth Have an Adaptive Infrared Iris?"

15. This situation is described in William Happer, "Harmful Politicization of Science," in *Politicizing Science: The Alchemy of Policymaking,* edited by Michael Gough (Hoover Institution Press, 2003).

16. S. Fred Singer, "The Revelle-Gore Story: Attempted Political Suppression of Science," in Gough, ed., *Politicizing Science.*

17. Michael E. Mann, Raymond S. Bradley, and Malcolm K. Hughes, "Northern Hemisphere Temperatures during the Past Millennium: Inferences, Uncertainties, and Limitations," *Geophysical Research Letters* 26, no. 6 (1999): 759–62.

3

Anthropogenic Climate Change: Revisiting the Facts

STEFAN RAHMSTORF

The idea that humans *can* change and *are* in fact changing the climate of our planet has developed gradually over more than a hundred years. A fringe idea in the nineteenth and early twentieth centuries,[1] it is close to a well-established scientific consensus at the turn of the twenty-first century.[2] The history of this development is grippingly told in a small book, *The Discovery of Global Warming,* by science historian Spencer Weart.[3] During the course of this history, the initially outlandish concept of human-caused global warming has won over practically every skeptical climatologist who has cared to look dispassionately at the evidence. But with new developments in the field almost every year—for example, the growing understanding of abrupt climate changes, the record-breaking hurricane season of 2005, or the renewed concerns about the stability of the ice sheets—the "basics" are seldom discussed any more. Few people besides climatologists themselves, even in the climate policy community, could easily recount the main cornerstones of scientific evidence on which the case for anthropogenic warming rests. The goal of this paper is to do just that: to revisit the basic evidence for anthropogenic global warming.

The Meaning of "Anthropogenic Climate Change"

To start, we need to clarify what we mean by "anthropogenic climate change." It is useful to distinguish two different meanings of the term, since they are often confounded. The first one, let us call it statement A, can be summed up as follows: *anthropogenic emissions of greenhouse gases will lead to significant global warming.* This is a statement about the future. It is reflected, for example, in the well-known range of future scenarios of the 2001 Intergovernmental Panel on Climate Change (IPCC) report, which concluded that, in the absence of effective climate policies, we must expect a warming of between 1.4 and 5.8°C (centigrade) between the years 1990 and 2100.[4]

The second meaning, let us call it statement B, can be phrased thus: *human activities already have noticeably changed global climate.* This is a statement about the past and about what we can observe now. It is reflected in the famous IPCC statement of 1996: "The balance of evidence suggests that there is a discernible human influence on global climate."[5] It is reinforced considerably in the light of new evidence in the 2001 report: "There is new and stronger evidence that most of the warming observed over the last fifty years is attributable to human activities."[6]

Only statement A is relevant to policy, because no current or planned policy can affect the past. Such policies are shaped by our expectations for the future. It is important to realize that statement A is not conditional on statement B. Thus, even if too much natural variability was masking any anthropogenic trend or if the quality of the data that we have simply was not good enough to detect any human influence on climate so far, we could (and would) still come to conclusion A. Nevertheless, both statement A and statement B are supported very strongly by the available evidence.

Discussions about climate change in the popular media suggest that many people are misled by fallacious logic, for example, "If the Middle Ages were warmer than temperatures today, then recent warming is perfectly natural (this questions statement B), and we do not need to worry about the effect of our emissions (this questions statement A)." Both these conclusions are, of course, non sequiturs, quite apart from the fact that their premise (warmer Middle Ages) is not supported by the data.

The Carbon Dioxide Effect on Climate

What evidence do we have for statement A—that anthropogenic emissions will lead to significant global warming? I break this into three parts. First, *the carbon dioxide (CO_2) concentration is rising.* This is proven by direct measurement in the atmosphere since the 1950s, set forth as the famous Keeling curve, and it is undisputed.[7] Current CO_2 data from the Global CO_2 Monitoring Network are made available by the Cooperative Air Sampling Network.[8] Ice core data, which provide a reliable and accurate record of CO_2 concentration going back hundreds of thousands of years, show further that this rise is, in fact, very unusual.[9]

Figure 3-1. *Climate History of the Past 350,000 Years*[a]

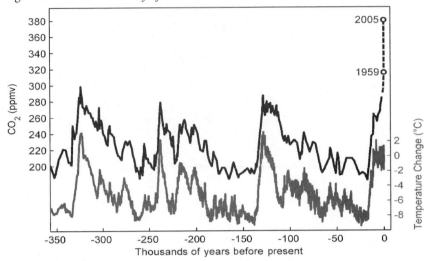

Source: J. R. Petit and others, "Climate and Atmospheric History of the Past 420,000 Years from the Vostok Ice Core, Antarctica," *Nature* 399 (June 1999): 429–36.

a. Based on Vostok ice core in Antarctica. These ice core data end before the onset of anthropogenic changes. Anthropogenic emissions have now increased the CO_2 concentration to 380 ppm (as of 2005).

For at least 650,000 years and probably ever since humans walked the Earth, the carbon dioxide concentration in the atmosphere was never even close to as high as it is at present, as shown in figure 3-1. Current CO_2 concentration has risen above 380 parts per million (ppm), while the preindustrial level back throughout the Holocene (the past 10,000 years) was close to 280 ppm. Similar values apply for previous interglacial periods.

We now come to the second part: *the recent rise in CO_2 is entirely anthropogenic.* This is also undisputed. We have tracked and we know how much fossil fuel has been burned and therefore how much CO_2 we have injected directly into the atmosphere. The observed increase in CO_2 concentration over the past decades is equal to 57 percent of our cumulative emissions. Other parts of the climate system—the ocean and the land biosphere—have absorbed the remaining 43 percent of emissions from the atmosphere. For the ocean, this is documented by around 10,000 oceanographic measurements, which show that the ocean has taken up about 2 gigatons (Gt) of carbon per year, or 30 percent of anthropogenic emissions (see figure 3-2).[10] This CO_2 uptake of the ocean makes the sea water more acidic and threatens marine life, which in itself is sufficient reason to reduce our carbon dioxide emissions significantly, even in the absence of climate change.[11]

Many other pieces of evidence corroborate the fact that the rise in CO_2 is anthropogenic: the isotope composition, the corresponding decline in

Figure 3-2. *Column Inventory of Anthropogenic CO_2 in the Ocean*

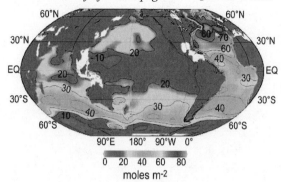

Source: Christopher L. Sabine, "Oceanic Sink for Anthropogenic CO_2," *Science* 305, no. 5682 (2004): 367–71. Ocean measurements are from Hans E. Suess, "Radiocarbon Concentration in Modern Wood," *Science* 122, no. 3166 (1955): 415–17.

atmospheric oxygen as carbon is burned, or the hemispheric gradient in CO_2 concentration.[12]

The third part is the following: *carbon dioxide is a greenhouse gas; doubling its concentration will warm global climate in equilibrium by $3°C \pm 1.5°C$.* That carbon dioxide acts as a greenhouse gas is hardly a new insight. It is by now well-established nineteenth-century physics. The crucial question is, just how strong is the effect of an increase in CO_2 on climate? This is the only component of statement A about which there can still be legitimate scientific debate, as all the other parts are proven beyond reasonable doubt. So let us spend some time on it.

Swedish Nobel Prize winner Svante Arrhenius made the first estimate in 1896, when he determined a 4–6°C warming for a doubling of atmospheric CO_2.[13] This number is called "climate sensitivity." It is defined simply as the global mean warming that is reached in equilibrium (that is, after a long time) after doubling the CO_2 concentration in the atmosphere. Strictly speaking, this refers to a doubling from its preindustrial value of 280 ppm to 560 ppm. This is seldom mentioned because the radiative forcing increases with the logarithm of CO_2 concentration due to the near-saturation of the CO_2 absorption bands. This means that a doubling of CO_2 from a different value (say, from the present value or from 560 ppm) gives the same forcing as a doubling from 280 ppm. But the response of the climate system, of course, could differ somewhat for different initial states, which is why "doubling from 280 ppm" should be included in any exact definition.

This climate sensitivity cannot be related directly to the actual warming at a particular time, because the climate system has the capacity to store heat and therefore lags in its response. The warming at a particular time therefore depends on the time history of past CO_2 (and other forcing) changes, not just on the CO_2 concentration at that point in time. But the climate sensitivity is nevertheless a simple and very useful measure of the strength of the CO_2 effect on climate, because it is a property that characterizes a model (or the real climate system) alone, independent of any particular scenario. Today, there are various independent ways of estimating climate sensitivity, and a great deal of effort is spent on this issue.

One method consists of using radiative forcing (that is, the change in radiation budget in watts per square meter, W/m^2), combined with information on the strength of physical feedbacks, to compute the expected temperature change. That is what Arrhenius did with pencil and paper; today, detailed calculations employing computer models are used in order to account for all the feedbacks. Without any feedbacks, a doubling of CO_2 (which amounts to a forcing of 3.7 W/m^2) would result in 1°C global warming, which is easy to calculate and is undisputed.[14]

The remaining uncertainty is due entirely to feedbacks in the system, namely, the water vapor feedback, the ice-albedo feedback, the cloud feedback, and the lapse rate feedback.[15] The water vapor feedback, for example, amplifies climate warming, because in a warmer climate the atmosphere contains more water vapor, which then acts as a greenhouse gas. While these feedbacks are understood in principle, there is still uncertainty about their exact magnitude, particularly that of the cloud feedback. However, we possess good information about the operation of these feedbacks, gathered from observations of natural variability, including the daily weather variations and the seasonal cycle. These variations are used to measure, for example, how vapor concentration, lapse rate, or cloud properties change with temperature. In many regions of our planet these variations cover a much larger range than is expected for the amplitude of future climate change (in some places, the seasonal cycle exceeds 40°C in amplitude). Getting the seasonal cycle right is therefore a crucial validation test for any climate model, and special observational programs are under way to measure cloud properties in different climatic regions of the world in order to narrow down uncertainties in cloud behavior.

The very first climate model calculations in the 1970s showed climate sensitivities of 2°C and 4°C. When the National Academy of Sciences in 1979 issued its first warning of an approaching global warming as a result of increased CO_2 emissions, it cited an uncertainty range of 1.5 to 4.5°C for climate sensitivity based on those early model results.[16] At that time, this range was on very shaky ground. Since then, many vastly improved models have been developed by a number of climate research centers around the world. Current state-of-the-art climate models span a range of 2.6–4.1°C, most clustering around 3°C. (The claim by Lindzen, in this volume, that "most current climate models predict a response to a doubling of CO_2 of about 4°C" is incorrect.)

Another way to estimate climate sensitivity is by looking at data from past variations of CO_2 and climate. How strongly climate was affected by CO_2 variations of the past can be estimated from data using correlation analysis. This has been done for the Vostok ice core data for variations over an ice age cycle. Of course, CO_2 is not the primary cause of an ice age, but it provides a feedback in this case. One needs to be very careful to account for all factors, including the presence of large continental ice sheets, methane variations, and atmospheric dust variations. Those data can be obtained from the ice core. The French scientists of the Vostok team that drilled the core performed such a correlation analysis and arrived at 3–4°C for climate sensitivity.[17] That is an estimate made solely on the basis of data.

A third, relatively new approach to estimating climate sensitivity, made possible by the growing power of computing technology, is to study the systematic variation of uncertain parameters in models. This includes, for example, parameters in the equations used to calculate cloud behavior. In this way, many different versions of a climate model are produced, typically up to a thousand versions, in which clouds or other components respond in different ways, to cover the range of current uncertainty in our knowledge. All these models are then checked against observational data, which are used to separate the wheat from the chaff. It is possible to create models with widely differing climate sensitivities—even as high as 11°C—but which of all these versions can stand up to a good reality check? Most of these model versions already fail to reproduce properly the present-day climate and its seasonal cycle. But an even tougher data constraint is one that tests for the response to large CO_2 changes. The two major CO_2 changes in recent climate history are the anthropogenic increase from 280 to 380 ppm since the preindustrial era and the increase from 180 to 280 ppm between the last Ice Age and the Holocene. Both of these have been used to constrain model ensembles to derive climate sensitivity.

The first such studies used twentieth-century data.[18] These provided a good constraint on the lower limit of climate sensitivity, consistent with the original 1.5°C estimate of the National Academy of Sciences. But they also revealed a problem with the constraint of the upper limit of sensitivity. It could not be ruled out on the basis of these data that climate sensitivity could be much higher than 4.5°C. The prime reason for this is the uncertainty in the magnitude of the cooling effect of anthropogenic aerosols (smog particles that reflect sunlight) over the twentieth century. If this cooling effect is large and has canceled a substantial part of the CO_2 warming, then even a very high sensitivity to CO_2 would still be compatible with the observed global temperature rise.

At this point, a comment is put forth in response to a directly related claim made by Richard Lindzen (in chapter 2 of this volume). In his contribution to the Yale Climate Change conference, in his testimony for the British House of Lords, and in media appearances,[19] Lindzen has claimed that the observed global warming is far less than what one would expect from the scientific consensus due to the effect of greenhouse gases. This consensus holds that a doubling of CO_2

causes a radiative forcing of 3.7 W/m², which in equilibrium would cause 3°C ± 1.5°C of global warming.[20] Lindzen argues that the current radiative forcing due to anthropogenic greenhouse gases (2.6 W/m²) is already three-fourths of what we would expect from CO_2 doubling and that, "if we attribute all warming over the past century to man-made greenhouse gases, . . . the observed warming is only about one-third to one-sixth of what models project." He concludes that the "consensus view" must be wrong and claims that climatologists have introduced aerosol cooling as an ad hoc trick to make their numbers match.

This argument is incorrect because it ignores a critical factor: ocean heat uptake. Ocean heat uptake ("thermal inertia") leads to a time lag of the actual warming behind equilibrium warming. Ocean heat uptake is not just a theoretical or modeled phenomenon, but a measured fact. Data from about 1 million ocean temperature profiles show that the ocean has been taking up heat at a rate of 0.6 W/m² (averaged over the full surface of the Earth) for the period 1993–2003.[21] This rate must be subtracted from the greenhouse gas forcing of 2.6 W/m², as actual warming must reflect the *net* change in heat balance, including the heat flow into the ocean. With an observed temperature increase since the late nineteenth century of 0.8°C (see figure 3-3), and (as Lindzen posits, for the sake of argument) assuming this to be caused by greenhouse gases alone, we would infer a climate sensitivity of 0.8°C · (3.7 W/m²) / (2.0 W/m²) = 1.5°C. This is at the lower end of, but consistent with, the IPCC range.

Of course, we know that anthropogenic aerosols also affect climate; their radiative effect can be estimated, for example, from satellite data.[22] It is comparatively uncertain and spatially heterogeneous, but if 1.0 W/m² is used as a rough

Figure 3-3. *Global Surface Air Temperature, Over Land and Ocean Combined, since 1900*[a]

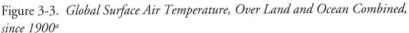
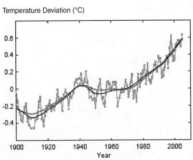

Source: NASA (data.giss.nasa.gov/gistemp/tabledata/GLB.Ts.txt [May 2007]); British Meteorological Service (hadobs.metoffice.com/hadcrut3/diagnostics/global/nh+sh/annual [May 2007]).
a. The data sets differ in their spatial coverage, interpolation, and quality control techniques. Thin lines and dots show the annual values; the heavy lines show the trend smoothed over eleven years. Deviations are given relative to the 1951–80 average; add 14°C to obtain approximate absolute temperature.

best estimate for the global mean effect (to be subtracted from the denominator), the preceding calculation becomes $0.8°C \cdot (3.7 \text{ W/m}^2) / (1.0 \text{ W/m}^2) = 3.0°C$. For larger aerosol cooling, the denominator gets smaller, and climate sensitivity quickly gets very large. That is why, as just mentioned, the uncertainty in aerosol forcing questions the upper limit of the IPCC range, not the lower limit.

Finally, solar radiation has also increased in the twentieth century, with a best estimate of 0.3 W/m^2 (although recent work argues that this estimate could be much too high).[23] Adding that to the denominator, we obtain $0.8°C \cdot (3.7 \text{ W/m}^2)/ (1.3 \text{ W/m}^2) = 2.3°C$. Thus whether we consider greenhouse gases alone, greenhouse gases plus aerosols, or these plus solar forcing, a simple back-of-the-envelope estimate shows that, in each case, observed warming is entirely consistent with the IPCC climate sensitivity range, as long as ocean heat uptake is not ignored. The reverse is also true: climate sensitivity smaller than the IPCC range, as proposed by Lindzen, is in all three cases inconsistent with the observed twentieth-century warming. Thus Lindzen's own argument, if carried out correctly by accounting for ocean heat uptake, disproves the very point he attempts to make.[24]

Let us come back to ensemble estimates. A recent study conducted by my group has applied this method with data constraints from the last glacial maximum (LGM).[25] The LGM climate was simulated with 1,000 versions of the CLIMBER-2 climate model (the first coupled model to realistically simulate Ice Age climate), with key parameters varied within their uncertainty range.[26] It turns out that only those model versions with sensitivities between 1.2 and 4.3°C are consistent with the data from the LGM, regardless of whether one uses tropical sea surface temperatures or Antarctic ice core–derived temperatures. The LGM data thus provide the hitherto missing constraint on the upper end of the climate sensitivity range. An important reason for this success is that aerosol cooling and CO_2 cooling work in the same direction for the LGM, so that the large aerosol uncertainty here weakens the constraint on the *lower*, not the upper, climate sensitivity limit. If aerosol cooling had been very large, then the CO_2 effect must have been small: otherwise, the simulated glacial climate would be too cold to be consistent with the data.

Despite allowing for large aerosol uncertainty, even this study suggests a minimum value of 1.2°C for climate sensitivity. I am not aware of any consistency check with observed past climate variations that would be consistent with Lindzen's unsubstantiated claim that "doubling of CO_2 would lead to about 0.5°C warming or less." The fact that the planet cooled strongly in the last glacial maximum, with the tropics cooling by 2–3°C, is unfortunately very good evidence against a strong negative feedback in the tropics (Lindzen's hypothetical "iris effect") that would prevent this kind of temperature change. Going back further in climate history, naturally elevated CO_2 levels associated with substantially warmer climates have been documented.[27] During the Middle

Pliocene about 3 million years ago, temperatures were 2–3°C warmer than at present, and sea level (due to smaller ice sheets) was 25–35 meters higher.[28] Even further back in time, about 35 million years ago in the late Eocene, temperatures were even 3–5°C warmer, and the planet was virtually free of ice for the last time (that is, sea level was about 70 meters higher than now).[29] Apparently, no negative feedback prevented these very large climate changes. Another piece of evidence against a strong negative feedback in the tropics is that tropical glaciers are melting away and the tropics are warming.[30]

Finally, in the ensemble studies, by far most of the climate model versions have climate sensitivity near 3°C, and only a small number of models have sensitivities below 2°C or above 4°C. I have argued here for the "consensus" range of past IPCC reports of 3°C ± 1.5°C, as the goal of this paper is to revisit the basics. But taking all ensemble studies and other constraints together, my personal assessment (and that of a growing number of other researchers) is that the uncertainty range can now be described more realistically as 3°C ± 1°C.[31]

The Observed Climatic Warming

It is time to turn to statement B: human activities are altering the climate. This can be broken into two parts. The first is as follows: *global climate is warming.* This is by now a generally undisputed point (except by novelist Michael Crichton), so we deal with it only briefly.[32] The two leading compilations of data measured with thermometers are shown in figure 3-3, that of the National Aeronautics and Space Administration (NASA) and that of the British Hadley Centre for Climate Change. Although they differ in the details, due to the inclusion of different data sets and use of different spatial averaging and quality control procedures, they both show a consistent picture, with a global mean warming of 0.8°C since the late nineteenth century.

Temperatures over the past ten years clearly were the warmest since measured records have been available. The year 1998 sticks out well above the long-term trend due to the occurrence of a major El Niño event that year (the last El Niño so far and one of the strongest on record). These events are examples of the largest natural climate variations on multiyear time scales and, by releasing heat from the ocean, generally cause positive anomalies in global mean temperature. It is remarkable that the year 2005 rivaled the heat of 1998 even though no El Niño event occurred that year. (A bizarre curiosity, perhaps worth mentioning, is that several prominent "climate skeptics" recently used the extreme year 1998 to claim in the media that global warming had ended. In Lindzen's words, "Indeed, the absence of any record breakers during the past seven years is statistical evidence that temperatures are not increasing.")[33]

In addition to the surface measurements, the more recent portion of the global warming trend (since 1979) is also documented by satellite data. It is not straightforward to derive a reliable surface temperature trend from satellites, as they measure radiation coming from throughout the atmosphere (not just near the surface), including the stratosphere, which has strongly cooled,[34] and the records are not homogeneous due to the short life span of individual satellites, the problem of orbital decay, observations at different times of day, and drifts in instrument calibration. Current analyses of these satellite data show trends that are fully consistent with surface measurements and model simulations.[35]

If no reliable temperature measurements existed, could we be sure that the climate is warming? The "canaries in the coal mine" of climate change (as glaciologist Lonnie Thompson puts it) are mountain glaciers. We know, both from old photographs and from the position of the terminal moraines heaped up by the flowing ice, that mountain glaciers have been in retreat all over the world during the past century. There are precious few exceptions, and they are associated with a strong increase in precipitation or local cooling.[36] I have inspected examples of shrinking glaciers myself in field trips to Switzerland, Norway, and New Zealand. As glaciers respond sensitively to temperature changes, data on the extent of glaciers have been used to reconstruct a history of Northern Hemisphere temperature over the past four centuries (see figure 3-4).[37] Cores drilled in tropical glaciers show signs of recent melting that is unprecedented at least throughout the Holocene—the past 10,000 years.[38] Another powerful sign of

Figure 3-4. *Temperature of the Northern Hemisphere during the Past Millennium*[a]

Temperature deviation °C

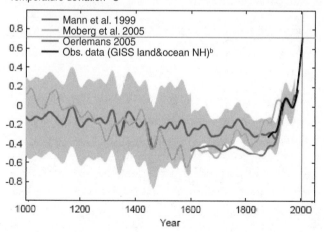

Source: Reconstructed from proxy data. Mann, Bradley, and Hughes, "Northern Hemisphere Temperatures during the Past Millennium," as shown in IPCC, *Climate Change 2001*; Moberg and others, "Highly Variable Northern Hemisphere Temperatures"; and Oerlemans, "Extracting a Climate Signal." For full references, see notes 37, 39, and 47. Instrumental data are from NASA up to 2005.

a. All curves are smoothed over twenty years, and values are given relative to the mean 1951–80.

b. Goddard Institute for Space Studies (GISS) data for land and ocean, Northern Hemisphere.

Figure 3-5. *Arctic Sea Ice Cover in September (the Summer Minimum Extent) in 1979 and in 2005*[a]

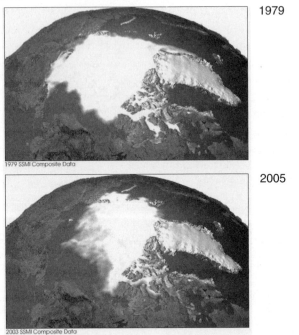

1979

2005

Source: NASA (www.nasa.gov/centers/goddard/news/topstory/2005/arcticice_decline.html [May 2007]).
a. The first year of satellite observation was 1979.

warming, visible clearly from satellites, is the shrinking Arctic sea ice cover (figure 3-5), which has declined 20 percent since satellite observations began in 1979.

While climate clearly became warmer in the twentieth century, much discussion particularly in the popular media has focused on the question of how "unusual" this warming is in a longer-term context. While this is an interesting question, it has often been mixed incorrectly with the question of causation. Scientifically, how unusual recent warming is—say, compared to the past millennium—in itself contains little information about its cause. Even a highly unusual warming could have a natural cause (for example, an exceptional increase in solar activity). And even a warming within the bounds of past natural variations could have a predominantly anthropogenic cause. I come to the question of causation shortly, after briefly visiting the evidence for past natural climate variations.

Records from the time before systematic temperature measurements were collected are based on "proxy data," coming from tree rings, ice cores, corals, and other sources. These proxy data are generally linked to local temperatures in some way, but they may be influenced by other parameters as well (for example, precipitation), they may have a seasonal bias (for example, the growth season for tree rings), and high-quality long records are difficult to obtain and therefore few in number and geographic coverage. Therefore, there is still substantial uncertainty in the evolution of past global or hemispheric temperatures. (Comparing only local or regional temperature, as in Europe, is of limited value for our purposes, as regional variations can be much larger than global ones and can have many regional causes, unrelated to global-scale forcing and climate change.)

The first quantitative reconstruction for the Northern Hemisphere temperature of the past millennium, including an error estimation, was presented by Mann, Bradley, and Hughes and rightly highlighted in the 2001 IPCC report as one of the major new findings since its 1995 report; it is shown in figure 3-6.[39] The analysis suggests that, despite the large error bars, twentieth-century warming is indeed highly unusual and probably was unprecedented during the past millennium. This result, presumably because of its symbolic power, has attracted much criticism, to some extent in scientific journals, but even more so in the popular media. The hockey stick–shaped curve became a symbol for the IPCC, and criticizing this particular data analysis became an avenue for some to question the credibility of the IPCC.

Figure 3-6. *Global Temperature Projections for the Twenty-First Century*[a]

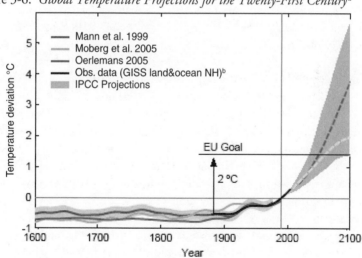

Source: Data from IPCC, *Climate Change 2001*.

a. The past evolution is shown as in figure 3-5, except that the global (not hemispheric) mean instrumental data are shown, and the temperature origin (0°C anomaly) is placed at the 1990 value of the smoothed instrumental data, since the IPCC projections start in 1990. Two example scenarios (A2, B1) are shown together with the full range (shaded). B1 is a relatively low- and A2 is a relatively high-emissions scenario. The observed temperature rise since 1990 runs along the upper edge of the scenarios.

Three important things have been overlooked in much of the media coverage. First, even if the scientific critics had been right, this would not have called into question the very cautious conclusion drawn by the IPCC from the reconstruction by Mann, Bradley, and Hughes: "New analyses of proxy data for the Northern Hemisphere indicate that the increase in temperature in the twentieth century is likely to have been the largest of any century during the past 1,000 years." This conclusion has since been supported further by every single one of close to a dozen new reconstructions (two of which are shown in figure 3-6).

Second, by far the most serious scientific criticism raised against Mann, Hughes, and Bradley was simply based on a mistake.[40] The prominent paper of von Storch and others, which claimed (based on a model test) that the method of Mann, Bradley, and Hughes systematically underestimated variability, "was [itself] based on incorrect implementation of the reconstruction procedure."[41] With correct implementation, climate field reconstruction procedures such as the one used by Mann, Bradley, and Hughes have been shown to perform well in similar model tests.[42] Third, whether their reconstruction is accurate or not has no bearing on policy. If their analysis underestimated past natural climate variability, this would certainly not argue for a smaller climate sensitivity and thus a lesser concern about the consequences of our emissions. Some have argued that, in contrast, it would point to a larger climate sensitivity.[43] While this is a valid point in principle, it does not apply in practice to the climate sensitivity estimates discussed herein or to the range given by IPCC, since these did not use the reconstruction of Mann, Hughes, and Bradley or any other proxy records of the past millennium. Media claims that "a pillar of the Kyoto Protocol" had been called into question were therefore misinformed. As an aside, the protocol was agreed in 1997, before the reconstruction in question even existed.

The overheated public debate on this topic has, at least, helped to attract more researchers and funding to this area of paleoclimatology; its methodology has advanced significantly, and a number of new reconstructions have been presented in recent years. While the science has moved forward, the first seminal reconstruction by Mann, Hughes, and Bradley has held up remarkably well, with its main features reproduced by more recent work. Further progress probably will require substantial amounts of new proxy data, rather than further refinement of the statistical techniques pioneered by Mann, Hughes, and Bradley. Developing these data sets will require time and substantial effort.

It is time to address the final statement: *most of the observed warming over the past fifty years is anthropogenic.* A large number of studies exist that have taken different approaches to analyze this issue, which is generally called the "attribution problem." I do not discuss the exact share of the anthropogenic contribution (although this is an interesting question). By "most" I simply mean "more than 50 percent."

The first and crucial piece of evidence is, of course, that the magnitude of the warming is what is expected from the anthropogenic perturbation of the radiation balance, so anthropogenic forcing is able to explain *all* of the temperature rise. As discussed here, the rise in greenhouse gases alone corresponds to 2.6 W/m² of forcing. This by itself, after subtraction of the observed 0.6 W/m² of ocean heat uptake, would cause 1.6°C of warming since preindustrial times for medium climate sensitivity (3°C). With a current "best guess" aerosol forcing of 1 W/m², the expected warming is 0.8°C. The point here is not that it is possible to obtain the exact observed number—this is fortuitous because the amount of aerosol forcing is still very uncertain—but that the expected magnitude is roughly right. There can be little doubt that the anthropogenic forcing is large enough to explain most of the warming. Depending on aerosol forcing and climate sensitivity, it could explain a large fraction of the warming, or all of it, or even more warming than has been observed (leaving room for natural processes to counteract some of the warming).

The second important piece of evidence is clear: *there is no viable alternative explanation.* In the scientific literature, no serious alternative hypothesis has been proposed to explain the observed global warming. Other possible causes, such as solar activity, volcanic activity, cosmic rays, or orbital cycles, are well observed, but they do not show trends capable of explaining the observed warming. Since 1978, solar irradiance has been measured directly from satellites and shows the well-known eleven-year solar cycle, but no trend.[44] There are various estimates of solar variability before this time, based on sunspot numbers, solar cycle length, the geomagnetic AA index, neutron monitor data, and carbon-14 data. These indicate that solar activity probably increased somewhat up to 1940. While there is disagreement about the variation in previous centuries, different authors agree that solar activity did not significantly increase during the last sixty-five years.[45] Therefore, this cannot explain the warming, and neither can any of the other factors mentioned. Models driven by natural factors only, leaving the anthropogenic forcing aside, show a *cooling* in the second half of the twentieth century (for an example, see figure 2-2, panel a, in chapter 2 of this volume). The trend in the sum of natural forcings is downward.[46]

The only way out would be either some as yet undiscovered unknown forcing or a warming trend that arises *by chance* from an unforced internal variability in the climate system. The latter cannot be completely ruled out, but has to be considered highly unlikely. No evidence in the observed record, proxy data, or current models suggests that such internal variability could cause a sustained trend of global warming of the observed magnitude. As discussed, twentieth-century warming is unprecedented over the past 1,000 years (or even 2,000 years, as the few longer reconstructions available now suggest), which does not support the idea of large internal fluctuations.[47] Also, those past variations correlate well with past forcing (solar variability, volcanic activity) and thus appear to be largely forced rather than due to unforced internal variability.[48] And indeed, it would be difficult for a large and sustained unforced variability to satisfy the fundamental physical law of energy conservation. Natural internal variability generally shifts heat around different parts of the climate system—for example, the large El Niño event of 1998, which warmed the atmosphere by releasing heat stored in the ocean. This mechanism implies that the ocean heat content drops as the atmosphere warms. For past decades, as discussed, we observed the atmosphere warming *and* the ocean heat content increasing, which rules out heat release from the ocean as a cause of surface warming. The heat content of the whole climate system is increasing, and there is no plausible source of this heat other than the heat trapped by greenhouse gases.

A completely different approach to attribution is to analyze the spatial patterns of climate change. This is done in so-called fingerprint studies, which associate particular patterns or "fingerprints" with different forcings. It is plausible that the pattern of a solar-forced climate change differs from the pattern of a change caused by greenhouse gases. For example, a characteristic of greenhouse gases is that heat is trapped closer to the Earth's surface and that, unlike solar variability, greenhouse gases tend to warm more in winter and at night. Such studies have used different data sets and have been performed by different groups of researchers with different statistical methods. They consistently conclude that the observed spatial pattern of warming can only be explained by greenhouse gases.[49] Overall, it has to be considered highly likely that the observed warming is indeed predominantly due to the human-caused increase in greenhouse gases.

Discussion and Consequences

This paper discussed the evidence for the anthropogenic increase in atmospheric CO_2 concentration and the effect of CO_2 on climate, finding that this anthropogenic increase is proven beyond reasonable doubt and that a mass of evidence points to a CO_2 effect on climate of 3°C ± 1.5°C global warming for a doubling of concentration. (This is the classic IPCC range; my personal assessment is that, in the light of new studies since the IPCC Third Assessment Report, the uncertainty range can now be narrowed somewhat to 3°C ± 1°C.) This is based on consistent results from theory, models, and data analysis, and, even in the absence of any computer models, the same result would still hold based on physics and on data from climate history alone. Considering the plethora of consistent evidence, the chance that these conclusions are wrong has to be considered minute.

If the preceding is accepted, then it follows logically and incontrovertibly that a further increase in CO_2 concentration will lead to further warming. The magnitude of our emissions depends on human behavior, but the climatic response to various emissions scenarios can be computed from the information presented here. The result is the famous range of future global temperature scenarios shown in figure 3-6.[50]

Two additional steps are involved in these computations: the consideration of anthropogenic forcings other than CO_2 (for example, other greenhouse gases and aerosols) and the computation of concentrations from the emissions. Other gases are not discussed here, although they are important to get quantitatively accurate results. CO_2 is the largest and most important forcing. Concerning concentrations, the scenarios shown basically assume that ocean and biosphere take up a similar share of our emitted CO_2 as in the past. This could turn out to be an optimistic assumption; some models indicate the possibility of a positive feedback, with the biosphere turning into a carbon source rather than a sink under growing climatic stress.[51] It is clear that even in the more optimistic of the shown (non-mitigation) scenarios, global temperature would rise by 2–3°C above its preindustrial level by the end of this century. Even for a paleoclimatologist like myself, this is an extraordinarily high temperature, which is very likely unprecedented in at least the past 100,000 years. As far as the data show, we would have to go back about 3 million years, to the Pliocene, for comparable temperatures. The rate of this warming (which is important for the ability of ecosystems to cope) is also highly unusual and unprecedented probably for an even longer time. The last major global warming trend occurred when the last great Ice Age ended between 15,000 and 10,000 years ago: this was a warming of about 5°C over 5,000 years, that is, a rate of only 0.1°C per century.[52]

The expected magnitude and rate of planetary warming is highly likely to come with major risks and impacts in terms of sea level rise (Pliocene sea level was 25–35 meters higher than now due to smaller Greenland and Antarctic ice sheets), extreme events (for example, hurricane activity is expected to increase in a warmer climate), and ecosystem loss.[53]

The second part of this paper examined the evidence for the current warming of the planet and discussed what is known about its causes. This part showed that global warming is already a measured and well-established fact, not a theory. Many different lines of evidence consistently show that most of the observed warming of the past fifty years was caused by human activity. Above all, this warming is exactly what would be expected given the anthropogenic rise in greenhouse gases, and no viable alternative explanation for this warming has been proposed in the scientific literature.

Taken together, the very strong evidence, accumulated from thousands of independent studies, has over the past decades convinced virtually every climatologist around the world (many of whom were initially quite skeptical, including myself) that anthropogenic global warming is a reality with which we need to deal.

Personal Postscript

When I was confronted with the polemic presented by Lindzen (in this volume), my first reaction was a sense of disbelief. Does Lindzen really think that current models overestimate the observed global warming sixfold? Can he really believe that climate sensitivity is below 0.5°C, despite all the studies on climate sensitivity concluding the opposite, and that a barely correlating cloud of data from one station, as he presents in figure 2-3, somehow proves his view? Does he honestly think that global warming stopped in 1998? Can Lindzen seriously believe that a vast conspiracy of thousands of climatologists worldwide is misleading the public for personal gain? All this seems completely out of touch with the world of climate science as I know it and, to be frank, simply ludicrous.

As a young physicist working on aspects of general relativity theory,[54] I was confronted with a professor from a neighboring university who claimed in newspaper articles that relativity theory was complete nonsense and that a conspiracy of physicists was hiding this truth from the public to avoid embarrassment and cuts in their funding. (He referred to the "Emperor's New Clothes," as does Lindzen.) The "climate skeptics" often remind me of this "relativity skeptic," and perhaps the existence of people with rather eccentric ideas is not surprising, given the wonderful variety of people. What I find much harder to understand is the disproportionate attention and space that are afforded to such views in the political world and the media.

Notes

1. Svante Arrhenius, "On the Influence of Carbonic Acid in the Air upon the Temperature of the Ground," *London, Edinburgh, and Dublin Philosophical Magazine and Journal of Science* 5 (1896): 237–76. Guy S. Callendar, "The Artificial Production of Carbon Dioxide and Its Influence on Climate," *Quarterly Journal of the Royal Meteorological Society* 64 (1938): 223–40.
2. IPCC (Intergovernmental Panel on Climate Change), *Climate Change 2001: Synthesis Report,* Contribution of Working Groups I, II and III to the Third Assessment Report, edited by R. J. Watson and the Core Writing Team (Geneva, 2001). Naomi Oreskes, "Beyond the Ivory Tower: The Scientific Consensus on Climate Change," *Science* 306, no. 5702 (December 2004): 1686.
3. Spencer R. Weart, *The Discovery of Global Warming* (Harvard University Press, 2003).
4. IPCC, *Climate Change 2001: Synthesis Report.*
5. IPCC, *Climate Change 1995: The Science of Climate Change,* Contribution of Working Group I to the Second Assessment Report (Cambridge University Press, 1996).
6. IPCC, *Climate Change 2001: Synthesis Report.*
7. Charles D. Keeling, "The Concentration and Isotopic Abundances of Carbon Dioxide in the Atmosphere," *Tellus* 12 (1960): 200–03.
8. Cooperative Air Sampling Network (http://www.esrl.noaa.gov/gmd/ccgg/flask.html [June 2007]).
9. EPICA (European Project for Ice Coring in Antarctica) Community Members, "Eight Glacial Cycles from an Antarctic Ice Core," *Nature* 429, no. 6992 (2004): 623–28.

10. Christopher L. Sabine and others, "The Oceanic Sink for Anthropogenic CO_2," *Science* 305, no. 5682 (2004): 367–71.

11. James C. Orr and others, "Anthropogenic Ocean Acidification over the Twenty-First Century and Its Impact on Calcifying Organisms," *Nature* 437, no. 7059 (2005): 681–86.

12. For the isotope composition, see Hans E. Suess, "Radiocarbon Concentration in Modern Wood," *Science* 122, no. 3166 (1955): 415–17. For the decline in atmospheric oxygen, see Ralph Keeling, Stephen Piper, and Martin Heimann, "Global and Hemispheric CO_2 Sinks Deduced from Changes in Atmospheric O_2 Concentration," *Nature* 381, no. 6579 (1992): 218–21. For the hemispheric gradient, see A. Scott Denning, Inez Fung, and David Randall, "Latitudinal Gradient of Atmospheric CO_2 due to Seasonal Exchange with Land Biota," *Nature* 376, no. 6537 (2002): 240–43.

13. Arrhenius, "On the Influence of Carbonic Acid."

14. IPCC, *Climate Change 2001: Synthesis Report.*

15. Robert Colman, "A Comparison of Climate Feedbacks in General Circulation Models," *Climate Dynamics* 20, no. 7–8 (2003): 865–73.

16. For more on this history, see Weart, *Discovery of Global Warming.*

17. Claude Lorius and others, "The Ice Core Record: Climate Sensitivity and Future Greenhouse Warming," *Nature* 347, no. 6289 (1990): 139–45.

18. Chris E. Forest and others, "Quantifying Uncertainties in Climate System Properties with the Use of Recent Climate Observations," *Science* 295, no. 5552 (2002): 113–17. Reto Knutti and others, "Constraints on Radiative Forcing and Future Climate Change from Observations and Climate Model Ensembles," *Nature* 416, no. 6882 (2002): 719–23.

19. See www.publications.parliament.uk/pa/ld200506/ldselect/ldeconaf/12/5012501.htm [May 2007]. National Public Radio, February 16, 2006 (www.kqed.org/epArchive/R602160900 [May 2007]).

20. IPCC, *Climate Change 2001: Synthesis Report.*

21. Josh K. Willis, Dean Roemmich, and Bruce Cornuelle, "Interannual Variability in Upper Ocean Heat Content, Temperature, and Thermosteric Expansion on Global Scales," *Journal of Geophysical Research* 109, no. C12036 (2004): doi:10.1029/2003JC002260.

22. Nicolas Bellouin and others, "Global Estimate of Aerosol Direct Radiative Forcing from Satellite Measurements," *Nature* 438, no. 7071 (2005): 1138–41. IPCC, *Climate Change 2001: Synthesis Report.*

23. IPCC, *Climate Change 2001: Synthesis Report.* Peter Foukal, Gerald North, and Tom Wigley, "A Stellar View on Solar Variations and Climate," *Science* 306, no. 5693 (2004): 68–69.

24. This raises the question why Lindzen has left such a basic climate property as ocean heat uptake out of his argument, as including it reverses his conclusions. He clearly is aware of ocean heat uptake, citing it in a different context to make an (equally fallacious) argument in favor of a small climate sensitivity. Richard S. Lindzen, "Understanding Common Climate Claims," in *Proceedings of the 34th International Seminar on Nuclear War and Planetary Emergencies,* edited by R. Raigaini (Singapore: World Scientific Publishing Co., 2005), pp. 189–210.

25. Thomas Schneider von Deimling and others, "Climate Sensitivity Estimated from Ensemble Simulations of Glacial Climate," *Climate Dynamics* 27, no. 2–3 (2006): 149–63.

26. Andrey Ganopolski and others, "Simulation of Modern and Glacial Climates with a Coupled Global Model of Intermediate Complexity," *Nature* 391 (January 1998): 351–56.

27. On geologic time scales (millions of years), variations in atmospheric CO_2 concentration are controlled by tectonic processes; see climatology or geology textbooks such as William F. Ruddiman, *Earth's Climate: Past and Future* (New York: Freeman, 2000).

28. H. J. Dowsett and others, "Joint Investigations of the Middle Pliocene Climate I: PRISM Paleoenvironmental Reconstructions," *Global and Planetary Change* 9, no. 3–4 (1994): 169–95.

29. Peter Barrett, "Palaeoclimatology: Cooling a Continent," *Nature* 421, no. 6920 (2003): 221–23. James Zachos and others, "Trends, Rhythms, and Aberrations in Global Climate 65 Ma to Present," *Science* 292, no. 274 (2001): 686–93.

30. Lonnie G. Thompson and others, "Kilimanjaro Ice Core Records: Evidence of Holocene Climate Change in Tropical Africa," *Science* 298, no. 5593 (2002): 589–93.

31. James Hansen and others, "Global Temperature Change," *Proceedings of the National Academy of Science* 103, no. 39 (2006): 14288–93.

32. In his novel *State of Fear,* Crichton argues that there is no warming by picking from the thousands of weather stations worldwide a few that show a cooling trend. Michael Crichton, *State of Fear* (HarperCollins, 2004).

33. Richard Lindzen, "Understanding Common Climate Claims," in *International Seminar on Nuclear War and Planetary Emergencies—34th Session,* edited by Richard Ragaini (Hackensack, N.J.: World Scientific Publishing, 2006). Lindzen made the same claim on National Public Radio, February 16, 2006 (www.kqed.org/epArchive/R602160900 [May 2007]).

34. Qiang Fu and others, "Contribution of Stratospheric Cooling to Satellite-Inferred Tropospheric Temperature Trends," *Nature* 429, no. 6987 (2004): 55–58.

35. Thomas R. Karl and others, *Temperature Trends in the Lower Atmosphere: Steps for Understanding and Reconciling Differences* (Washington: Climate Change Science Program and the Subcommittee on Global Change Research, 2006). Smaller trends claimed by one group and often cited by "climate skeptics" have turned out to be due to a sign error in a calibration correction. Carl A. Mears and Frank J. Wentz, "The Effect of Diurnal Correction on Satellite-Derived Lower Tropospheric Temperature," *Science* 309, no. 5740 (2005): 1548–51.

36. For a compilation, see IPCC, *Climate Change 2001: Synthesis Report.*

37. Johannes H. Oerlemans, "Extracting a Climate Signal from 169 Glacier Records," *Science* 308, no. 5722 (2005): 675–77.

38. Lonnie G. Thompson and others, "Tropical Glacier and Ice Core Evidence of Climate Change on Annual to Millennial Time Scales," *Climate Change* 59, no. 1–2 (2003): 137–55. Thompson and others, "Kilimanjaro Ice Core Records."

39. Michael E. Mann, Raymond S. Bradley, and Malcolm K. Hughes, "Northern Hemisphere Temperatures during the Past Millennium," *Geophysical Research Letters* 26, no. 6 (1999): 759–62. IPCC, *Climate Change 2001: Synthesis Report;* IPCC, *Climate Change 1995: The Science of Climate Change.*

40. For a discussion of this mistake and its consequences, see www.realclimate.org/index.php/archives/2006/04/a-correction-with-repercussions/ [May 2007].

41. Hans von Storch and others, "Reconstructing Past Climate from Noisy Data," *Science* 306, no. 5696 (2004): 679–82. Eugene R. Wahl, David M. Ritson, and Caspar M. Amman, "Comment on 'Reconstructing Past Climate from Noisy Data,' " *Science* 312, no. 5773 (2006): 529. Mann, Bradley, and Hughes, "Northern Hemisphere Temperatures during the Past Millennium."

42. Michael E. Mann and others, "Testing the Fidelity of Methods Used in Proxy-Based Reconstructions of Past Climate," *Journal of Climate* 18, no. 20 (2005): 4097–107. Michael E. Mann and others, "Robustness of Proxy-Based Climate Field Reconstruction Methods," *Journal of Geophysical Research* 112 (2007): doi:10.1029/2006JD008272.

43. Timothy J. Osborn and Keith R. Briffa, "The Real Color of Climate Change?" *Science* 306, no 679 (2004): 621–22.

44. Claus Fröhlich and Judith Lean, "Solar Radiative Output and Its Variability: Evidence and Mechanisms," *Astronomy and Astrophysics Review* 12, no. 4 (2004): 273–320.
45. Raymond Muscheler and others, "How Unusual Is Today's Solar Activity?" *Nature* 436, no. 7050 (2004): E3–E4.
46. This is the real significance of such modeling studies: they demonstrate that, without anthropogenic greenhouse gas forcing, the observed temperature record cannot be reproduced. This holds true regardless of the uncertainty about the amplitudes.
47. Anders Moberg and others, "Highly Variable Northern Hemisphere Temperatures Reconstructed from Low- and High-Resolution Proxy Data," *Nature* 433, no. 7026 (2005): 613–17.
48. Eva Bauer and others, "Assessing Climate Forcings of the Earth System for the Past Millennium," *Geophysical Research Letters* 30, no. 6 (2002): 1276.
49. IPCC, *Climate Change 2001: Synthesis Report.*
50. The fact that observed warming runs along the upper edge of the model scenarios illustrates the absurdity of Lindzen's claim that models overestimate warming by a factor of three to six.
51. Peter M. Cox and others, "Acceleration of Global Warming due to Carbon-Cycle Feedbacks in a Coupled Climate Model," *Nature* 408, no. 6813 (2000): 184–87.
52. There is good evidence for faster *regional* rates of change—for example, during the abrupt glacial climate changes—but not for faster changes in global mean temperature.
53. Dowsett and others, "Joint Investigations of the Middle Pliocene Climate I: PRISM Palesenvironmental Reconstructions," *Global and Planetary Changes* 9 (1994): 169–95, and Thomas R. Knutson and Robert E. Tuleya, "Impact of CO_2-Induced Warming on Simulated Hurricane Intensity and Precipitation," *Journal of Climate* 17, no. 1818 (2004): 3477–95.
54. Bernhard Rose, Stefan Rahmstorf, and Heinz Dehnen, "Propagation of Self-Gravitating Density Waves in the deDonder Gauge on a Gravitational Background Field," *General Relativity and Gravitation* 20, no. 11 (1988): 1193–201.

PART TWO

Measuring our Vulnerabilities to Climate Change

4

"Dangerous" Climate Change: Key Vulnerabilities

STEPHEN H. SCHNEIDER

Assessing key vulnerabilities and their relationship with "dangerous" climate change begins with a conceptual overview, followed by a discussion of the major components and the methods that scientists and other analysts use to address uncertainties in any attempt to define what constitutes "dangerous climate change." Moreover, policymakers need a more complete set of assessment metrics than goods and services traded in markets; decisionmakers need to supplement the assessment of market impacts with an evaluation of the vulnerability of various species, regions, or groups to climate changes. Such impacts typically fall very unequally on different groups, as do the costs of policies to reduce key vulnerabilities. These distributional consequences of climate change—or policies to deal with it—are critical to any evaluation of more equitable strategies to adapt to or mitigate climate change.

Vulnerability to climate change is the degree to which geophysical, biological, and socioeconomic systems are susceptible to, and unable to cope with, adverse impacts of climate change. The term "vulnerability" may therefore refer to the vulnerable system itself, for example, low-lying islands or coastal cities; the impact to this system, such as flooding of coastal cities and agricultural lands or forced migration; or the mechanism causing these impacts, such as disintegration of the West Antarctic ice sheet. The term "key vulnerability" is used here to denote potentially significant impacts of climate change.[1] These merit particular attention by policymakers because they endanger the lives or well-

being of people or other valued attributes (for example, biodiversity preservation) of climate-sensitive systems. Key vulnerabilities are found in many social,
economic, biological, and geophysical systems. The identification of such key
vulnerabilities is intended to provide guidance for assessing levels and rates of
climate change that the 1992 United Nations Framework Convention on Climate Change (UNFCCC), in its Article 2, calls "dangerous."[2] The definition of
"dangerous anthropogenic interference" (DAI) with the climate system must
incorporate value judgments of what are "acceptable" risks and what are not,
while simultaneously being informed about the evolving state of scientific
knowledge—which can help to place policymaking on a firmer empirical and
theoretical basis.

One of the goals of the Intergovernmental Panel on Climate Change (IPCC)
is to address DAI, defined by the UNFCCC as follows: "The ultimate objective
of this convention and any related legal instruments that the Conference of the
Parties may adopt is to achieve, in accordance with the relevant provisions of
the convention, stabilization of greenhouse gas concentrations in the atmosphere at a level that would prevent dangerous anthropogenic interference with
the climate system." In addition, the UNFCCC Article 2 states, "Such a level
should be achieved within a time frame sufficient to allow ecosystems to adapt
naturally to climate change, to ensure that food production is not threatened,
and to enable economic development to proceed in a sustainable manner."

On June 12, 1992, President George Herbert Walker Bush signed and soon
after the U.S. Senate ratified the UNFCCC, including Article 2. Today, it is the
law of the land in 191 countries, including the United States.

Given that Article 2 calls for stabilizing greenhouse gas concentrations at a
level that would prevent dangerous anthropogenic interference with the climate
system, the question arises, who should decide what constitutes "dangerous"?
Governments have asked the IPCC, as a body of scientists, to help define what
is dangerous, whereas the scientists typically respond that defining "dangerous"
is a value judgment about acceptable levels of risk and therefore is the job of
policymakers. For example, not everybody is negatively affected by some levels
of climate change. Certain groups might decide that particular outcomes are
acceptable (or even beneficial), while others might decide that they are not. In an
Arctic region where the ice is melting, one stakeholder, the shipping industry,
may say, "Less polar ice will result in shorter, cheaper routes," while another,
the indigenous people of the region, may respond, "Our culture and our livelihood depend on the ice being near the shoreline." How can we weigh two such
opposing views within a cost-benefit model based on monetized value? One is a
monetized resource; the other is an attribute of culture linked to climate-as-
usual. When comparative vulnerability is being evaluated, a debate will ensue
about the appropriate metrics and analytic techniques used. How can one or the
other viewpoint be measured? Shipping costs can be monetized, whereas cul-

tural traditions may not be. Monetized costs or benefits are usually discounted to reflect alternative investment opportunities, whereas no clear discount rate larger than zero seems appropriate for an attribute like the survival of a culture or a species or an ice sheet—those are ethical more than economic choices. If so, then cost-benefit analysis per se would be an inappropriate tool for evaluating these trade-offs, given the incommensurate metrics of cost and benefit involved. Another formidable problem confronting the use of cost-benefit frameworks applied to climate assessments are the deep uncertainties associated with nearly every step in the analytic chain: from projecting population size, to economic growth rates, choosing appropriate discount rates or functions, to technological systems that will be in place, to climate sensitivity, to impacts modeling, and, ultimately, as just noted, to uncertainties in the valuation of damages in non-market metrics.

There are many ways to define "dangerous." Measures of acceptable dangers are based on political judgments, although those can, as noted, be informed by scientific data and reasoned choices. The problem is that some populations are vulnerable to lower levels of warming and others only to higher levels. In addition, different populations have different stakes in actions that would lead to adaptation to or mitigation of the problem. They may thus have very different views about what constitutes "dangerous." Such varying perspectives have to be adjudicated either by multilateral or by very large-scale international agreements, which are, at best, problematic to negotiate and enforce.

The identification of key vulnerabilities is intended to provide guidance for establishing levels and rates of climate change that could be considered dangerous. However, considerable complexity is involved in addressing this process. In Working Group II's chapter 19 of the IPCC's Fourth Assessment Report, the focus dictated by more than 100 governments responsible for writing the outline of the materials to be covered in each chapter is on vulnerability, not benefits, since the position societies take is one of concern that climate impacts create damage, even though some regions and sectors may benefit from certain levels of climate change.[3] Governments have made the deliberate choice to focus on vulnerability in this chapter, although other chapters try to weigh the costs and benefits—an admitted political value judgment, not an analytically definitive assessment because of the problems of inherent uncertainty and incommensurate metrics, as already mentioned. Governments asked the scientists to address key vulnerabilities, without defining the term "key." Rather, it was left to the group to define which vulnerabilities are key after examining a vast array of literature. Since many sources of vulnerability are associated with climate change, selecting which vulnerabilities are key involves expert scientific judgments along with subjective components.

Three factors produce what chapter 19 has identified as key vulnerabilities. These include the *exposure* of systems and populations to climate change, the *sensitivity* of those systems and populations to such climatic influences, and the *capacity* of those systems and populations *to adapt* to climate change. "Populations" can refer to populations of humans or to populations of plants and animals. The degree of vulnerability is affected by human development, which can produce emissions, potentially increasing climate impacts and vulnerability, but which also can lead to a resource base that more easily allows adaptive capacity building, potentially reducing vulnerability to any given level of climate change. Assessing key vulnerabilities involves analysis of a complex, coupled, human and natural system (CHANS).[4]

The criteria used to determine key vulnerabilities are both objective and subjective. In fact, it is impossible to make these determinations without employing elements of subjectivity. There is no way to observe future conditions now, in the present. Therefore, our empiricism is based on models of our understanding of how the physical, biological, and social systems work, models that are semiempirical constructs from theory built from experience. We combine these models of individual sub-systems like the atmosphere, oceans, or economic systems to create coupled models that we then, in turn, use to project the future.

A main subjective aspect of these models has to do with the extent to which the assumptions used in constructing them are likely to remain valid in a highly disturbed future world, a world that will require making expert judgments on various components of CHANS, along with estimates of the confidence that might be ascribed to each major conclusion or component of the analysis. Assessment is not simply about consensus—although when a strong one exists it is enthusiastically reported. Rather, assessment is about ranges of consequences, their estimated likelihood, their distributional implications, and the amount of confidence that state-of-the-art scientific assessors judge to be appropriate for each component. Governments have asked the IPCC—or the National Research Council in the United States—to help them sort through the bewildering amount of recent literature—some of it conflicting—and offer expert judgments on what might happen (Working Group I), what if it happened (Working Group II), and, therefore, what might be done to deal with the situation (Working Group III). The mantra of IPCC assessments is to be policy responsive without being policy prescriptive—that is, to answer or at least explicate questions needed by policymakers in their deliberations but to leave the value judgments on which responses should be preferred, or who should pay for them or benefit from them, to the policymakers themselves. The extensive IPCC review process helps to ensure that policy responsiveness without policy prescription is the basis for the final reports accepted by the governments.

Let us return to chapter 19 and its directive to address key vulnerabilities. Criteria are identified in the literature to help to assess which vulnerabilities are key (see table 4-1). These include

—magnitude (how large the impact is),

—timing (whether it occurs now or far in the future),

—persistence and reversibility (whether it is irreversible on time scales of many human generations),

—likelihood and confidence (how likely it is and how confident we are in our assessment of that likelihood),

—distributional impacts (for example, a scenario in which high-latitude agriculture is relatively unaffected, or even enhanced, but low-latitude food production is harmed, which would constitute an inequitable distribution of impacts that many would label as a "key" impact),

—the potential for adaptation (which can reduce vulnerability to a given level of climate change), and

—the "importance" of the vulnerable system (the word "importance" has a normative value component and will differ among stakeholders, governments, and assessors).

As an example of the last item listed above, in many people's judgment, the loss of an ecosystem would be a very different kind of impact than a short-term impact, one that could correct itself over time. Also, the Antarctic ozone hole is a very different problem from a rapidly deglaciating Greenland ice sheet or an Atlantic thermohaline circulation collapse, because now that the source of the ozone depletion problem has been substantially mitigated—that is, now that the release of chlorofluorocarbons into the atmosphere has been curtailed—the ozone hole will "heal" itself in about fifty years, whereas the impacts of many climate problems, such as large ice sheet deglaciation, would likely persist for millennia. Such virtually irreversible impacts—on civilization time scales—might be judged by many as more "important" than economically significant impacts on systems that could make up those damages via economic growth in only a few years. Regardless of how an analyst or policymaker weighs the relative importance of any vulnerability or element of the analysis, it is essential that there be a "traceable account" of the embedded assumptions, value judgments, and any aggregations performed in the assessment.[5]

The general conclusions about key impacts and vulnerabilities found in the literature today can be summarized as follows:

—Global mean temperature changes associated with different key vulnerabilities that are global in scale typically range from 1.5 to 4°C (centigrade) above current temperatures. Some impacts of climate change that are already under way have been identified in some studies as key vulnerabilities. Among these are loss of glaciers, adverse impacts on biodiversity, increases in the severity of extreme events, and loss of cultural amenities.

—World regions that are already at high risk from current climate variability are more likely to be adversely affected by anthropogenic climate change in the near future.

Hundreds of articles have been written on various systems ranging from glaciers to agriculture to forests to heat waves to ecosystems. Some systems have very

(text continued on p. 68)

Table 4-1. *Examples of Potential Key Vulnerabilities*[a]

Systems, processes, or groups at risk [cross-references]	Prime criteria for "key vulnerability" (from seven criteria; [19.2]), short, descriptive words	Relationship between temperature and risks (source to text), temperature change by 2100 (above 1990–2000 levels)					
		0°C	1°C	2°C	3°C	4°C	5°C
Global social systems							
Food supply [19.3.2.2]	Distribution, magnitude		Crop yield potential starts to decline at low latitudes** [5.2] Crop yield potential starts to increase at middle to high latitude** Global production potential is likely to increase** [5.6]		Global production potential increases to around 3°C** [5.6]		Yields of grain crops decline at middle to high latitudes** [5.2] Global production potential is very likely to decrease above about 3°C** [5.6]
Infrastructure [19.3.2]	Distribution, magnitude, timing			Damages are likely to increase exponentially; sensitive to rate of climate change, change in extreme events, and adaptive capacity*** [3.5, 6.5.3, 7.5]			
Health [19.3.2]	Distribution, magnitude, timing, irreversibility		Current effects are small but discernible** [1.3.7, 8.4.1]	Although some risks are reduced, aggregate health impacts increase, particularly from malnutrition, diarrhea, infectious diseases, floods and droughts, extreme heat, and other sources of risk**/***; sensitive to status of public health system**** [8.ES, 8.3, 8.4, 8.6]			
Water resources [19.3.2]	Distribution, magnitude, timing		Water availability decreases and drought increases in some middle latitudes and semiarid low latitudes*** [3.4, 3.7]	Severity of floods, droughts, erosion, and water quality deterioration increases with increasing climate change**** Sea level rise extends areas of salinization of groundwater, decreasing the availability of freshwater in coastal areas**** [Ch 3 ES] Hundreds of millions of people face reduced water supplies*** [3.4.3]			
Migration and conflict	Distribution, magnitude			Stresses such as increased drought, water shortages, and riverine and coastal flooding affect many local and regional populations*** This leads in some cases to relocation within or between countries, exacerbating conflicts and imposing migration pressures** [19.2]			

Aggregate market impacts and distribution	Magnitude, distribution	Net benefits are uncertain, and lower benefits or higher damages are more likely than in the Third Assessment Report* Net market benefits are felt in many high-latitude areas; net market losses are felt in many low-latitude areas** [20.6] Most people are negatively affected*/**	Net global negative market impacts increase with higher temperatures** [20.6] Most people are negatively affected**
Regional systems			
Africa [19.3.3]	Distribution, magnitude, timing, low adaptive capacity	Tens of millions of people are at risk of increased water stress; spread of malaria increases** [9.4.1, 9.4.4, 9.4.5]	Hundreds of millions of additional people are at risk of increased water stress; risk of malaria increases in high-lands; crop yields decline in many countries, and many ecosystems are harmed, such as succulent Karoo** [9.4.1, 9.4.4, 9.4.5]
Asia [19.3.3]	Distribution, magnitude, timing, low adaptive capacity		Over the temperature range, about 1 billion people face risks from reduced agricultural production potential, reduced water supplies, or increased frequency of extreme events** [10.4]
Latin America [19.3.3]	Magnitude, irreversibility, distribution, and timing, low adaptive capacity	Tens of millions of people are at risk of water shortages* [13.ES, 13.4.3] Many endemic species are at risk from land use and climate change*** (−1°C) [13.4.1, 13.4.2]	More than 100 million people are at risk of water short-ages** [13.ES, 13.4.3] Low-lying coastal areas, many of which are heavily populated, are at risk from sea level rise and more intense coastal storms** (about 2–3°C) [13.4.4]. Loss of biodiversity is widespread, particularly in the Amazon** [13.2, 13.4.1, 13.4.2]
Polar regions [19.3.3]	Timing, magnitude, irreversibility, distribution, low adaptive capacity	Climate change is already having substantial impacts on societal and ecological systems*** [15.ES]	Continued warming is likely to lead to further loss of ice cover and permafrost*** [15.3] Arctic ecosystems are further threatened,*** although net ecosystem productivity is estimated to increase*** [15.2.2, 15.4.2] While some economic opportunities open up (for example, shipping), traditional ways of life are disrupted*** [15.4]

(continued)

Table 4-1. *Examples of Potential Key Vulnerabilities*ᵃ (continued)

Systems, processes, or groups at risk [cross-references]	Prime criteria for "key vulnerability" (from seven criteria; [19.2]), short, descriptive words	Relationship between temperature and risks (source to text), temperature change by 2100 (above 1990–2000 levels)					
		0°C	1°C	2°C	3°C	4°C	5°C
Small island states [19.3.3]	Irreversibility, magnitude, distribution, low adaptive capacity	Many islands are already experiencing some negative effects*** [16.2]			Coastal inundation and damage to infrastructure occur due to sea level rise*** [16.4]		
Indigenous, poor, or isolated communities [19.3.3]	Irreversibility, distribution, timing, low adaptive capacity	Many of these communities are already stressed*** [11.4, 14.2.3, 15.4.6]		Climate change and sea level rise add to other stresses*** Communities in low-lying coastal and arid areas are especially threatened*** [6.4, 3.4]			
Drying in Mediterranean, western North America, southern Africa, southeastern Australia, and northeastern Brazil [19.3.3]	Distribution, magnitude, timing	Climate models generally project decreased precipitation in these regions [3.4.2, 3.5.1, 11.3.1] Reduced runoff exacerbates tight water supplies, decreases water quality, harms ecosystems, and results in lower crop yields*** [3.4.2; 11.3.2]					
Intertropical mountain glaciers and impacts on high-mountain communities [19.3.3]	Magnitude, timing, persistence, low adaptive capacity, distribution	Intertropical glaciers are melting and causing flooding in some areas; shifts in ecosystems are likely to cause water security problems due to decreased storage**/*** [10.ES, 10.2, 10.4.4, 13.ES, 13.2.4, 19.3, box 1.1]			The reduction of intertropical mountain glaciers accelerates; some of these systems disappear in the next few decades** [9.2.1, 10.ES, 10.2.4, 10.4.2, 13.ES, 13.2.4.1, box 1.1, box 9.1]		

(continued)

Global biological systems

System	Criteria			
Terrestrial ecosystems and biodiversity [19.3.4]	Irreversibility, magnitude, low adaptive capacity, persistence, rate of change, confidence	Many ecosystems are already affected**** [1.3]	About 20–30 percent of species are at increased high risk of commitment to extinction** [4.4] Terrestrial biosphere tends toward a net carbon source** [4.4]	Major extinctions occur around the globe (> 4°C)*** [4.4]
Marine ecosystems and biodiversity [19.3.4]	Irreversibility, magnitude, low adaptive capacity, persistence, rate of change, confidence	Coral bleaching increases*** [4.4]	Most coral reefs are bleached*** [4.4]	Coral mortality is widespread*** [4.4]
Freshwater ecosystems [19.3.2.2]	Irreversibility, magnitude, persistence, low adaptive capacity	Some lakes are already showing decreased fisheries output; poleward migration of aquatic species is evident*** [1.3.4, 4.4.9]	Hydrological cycles intensify, droughts and floods become more severe**** [3.4.3]	Many freshwater species become extinct*** Major changes occur in limnology of lakes*** Inland lakes become more saline***

Geophysical systems

System	Criteria	
Biogeochemical cycles [4.4.9, 19.3.5.1; WGI 7.3.3.2.2, 7.3.3.2.3, 7.3.5, 7.4.1.2, 10.4.1, 10.4.2]	Magnitude, persistence, confidence, low adaptive capacity, rate of change	Ocean acidification is already occurring, increasing as CO_2 concentration increases**** Ecological changes are potentially severe** [1.3.4, 4.4.9] Carbon cycle feedback increases projected CO_2 concentrations by 2100 by 20–220 ppm for SRES A2, with associated additional warming of 0.1–1.5°C*** Fourth Assessment Report temperature range (1.1–6.4°C) accounts for this feedback from all scenarios and models, but additional CO_2 and CH_4 releases are possible from permafrost, peat lands, wetlands, and large stores of marine hydrates at high latitudes** [4.4.6, 15.4.2] Permafrost is already melting, and above feedbacks generally increase with climate change, but rise in eustatic sea level is likely to increase the stability of hydrates**** [1.3.1]

Table 4-1. *Examples of Potential Key Vulnerabilities*[a] *(continued)*

Systems, processes, or groups at risk [cross-references]	Prime criteria for "key vulnerability" (from seven criteria; [19.2]), short, descriptive words	Relationship between temperature and risks (source to text), temperature change by 2100 (above 1990–2000 levels)					
		0°C	1°C	2°C	3°C	4°C	5°C
Greenland ice sheet [6.3, 19.3.5.2; WGI 4.7.4, 6.4.3.3, 10.7.4.3, 10.7.4.4]	Magnitude, irreversibility, low adaptive capacity, confidence		Localized deglaciation occurs (already observed due to local warming); extent increases with temperature**** [19.3.5]	Commitment is made to partial to near-total deglaciation** Sea level rises 2–7[b] meters over centuries to millennia [19.3.5]		Commitment is made to near-total deglaciation over centuries to millennia*** [19.3.5]	
West Antarctic ice sheet [6.3, 19.3.5.2; WGI 4.7.4, 6.4.3.3, 10.7.4.3, 10.7.4.4]	Magnitude, irreversibility, low adaptive capacity		Localized ice shelf loss and grounding line retreat are seen** (already observed, due to local warming) [1.3.1, 19.3.5]		Commitment to partial deglaciation is made Sea level rises 1.5–5 meters over centuries to millennia**/* [19.3.5]	Likelihood of near-total deglaciation increases with increases in temperature*** [19.3.5, 12.6]	
Meridional overturning circulation [19.3.5.3; WGI 8.7.2.1, 10.3.4]	Magnitude, persistence, distribution, timing, low adaptive capacity, confidence		Variations are seen, including regional weakening (already observed, but no trend is identified)		Considerable weakening occurs*** Commitment is made to large-scale and persistent change, including possible cooling in northern high-latitude areas near Greenland and northwestern Europe,* highly dependent on rate of climate change [19.3.5, 12.6]		
Extreme events							
Tropical cyclone intensity [6.5.2, 7.5, 8.7, 11.4.5, 16.2.2, 19.3.6; WGI table TS-4, observed 3.8.3, Q3.3, 9.5.3.6, projected Q10.1]	Magnitude, timing, distribution		Category 4–5 storms increase**/*** with impacts exacerbated by sea level rise		Tropical cyclone intensity increases further**/*** exceeding infrastructure design criteria with large economic costs*** and threatening many lives***		
Flooding, both large-scale and flash floods [14.4.1;	Timing, magnitude		Flash flooding increases in many regions due to		Flooding increases in many regions (for example, North America and Europe) due to greater increase		

66

WGI table TS-4, 10.3.6.1, Q10.1]		increased rainfall intensity*** Floods increase in large basins in middle and high latitudes***	in winter rainfall exacerbated by loss of winter snow storage*** The risk of dam bursts increases in glacial mountain lakes*** [10.2.4.2]
Extreme heat [14.4.5; WGI table TS-4, 10.3.6.2, Q10.1]	Timing, magnitude	Heat stress and heat waves increase, especially in continental areas****	Frequency of heat waves (according to current classification) increases rapidly, causing higher mortality, crop failures, forest die-back and fire, and damage to ecosystems****
Drought [WGI table TS-4, 10.3.6.1]	Magnitude, timing	Drought is already increasing** [1.3.3.2] Increasing frequency and intensity of drought are projected for middle-latitude continental areas*** [WGI 10.3.6.1]	Extreme drought increases from 1 percent of land area to 30 percent (A2 scenario) [WGI 10.3.6.1] Middle-latitude regions affected by poleward migration of Annular Modes are seriously affected*** [WGI 10.3.5.5]
Fire [1.3.6; WGI 7.3]	Timing, magnitude	Increased frequency and intensity of fires occur in many areas, particularly where drought increases*** [4.2.1, 14.2.2]	Frequency and intensity are likely to be greater, especially in boreal forests and dry peat lands after melting of permafrost*** [4.4.5, 11.3, 13.4.1, 14.4.2]

Source: Stephen H. Schneider and others, "Key Vulnerabilities and the Risk from Climate Change," in *Climate Change 2007: Impacts, Adaptation, and Vulnerability,* edited by Martin Parry and others (Cambridge University Press, in press). Sources in brackets are from chapters in the Fourth Assessment Report. Where no source is given, the entry represents conclusions of the authors of chapter 19.

*****Very high confidence.

****High confidence.

***Medium confidence.

**Low confidence.

a. This list is not ordered by priority but by category of systems, processes, or groups that either are affected by or that cause vulnerability. Information is presented where available on how impacts may change at larger increases in global mean temperature (GMT). All increases in GMT are relative to circa 1990. Entries are necessarily brief to limit the size of the table, so further details, caveats, and supporting evidence should be sought in the accompanying text, cross-references, and in the primary scientific studies referenced in this and other chapters of the Fourth Assessment Report. In many cases, climate change impacts are marginal or synergistic on top of other existing and changing stresses.

b. Range is based on a variety of methods, including models and analysis of paleo data [19.3.5.2].

low thresholds of danger or high vulnerability; others have much higher thresholds of danger. Relative to current temperatures, the typical thresholds of temperature increase found in the literature range from about 0.5 to 5°C above present temperatures. Still, many articles argue that the current 0.75°C warming above preindustrial temperatures has already created vulnerabilities in the Arctic, in high mountain ecosystems, in arid "Mediterranean" climates, and particularly in vulnerable coastal systems like mega-deltas, New Orleans being a recent example.

However, even though there are already key vulnerabilities associated with current temperature rises, the preponderance of these vulnerabilities are estimated to intensify somewhere between 0.8 and 3.3°C above current temperatures. Above 3.3°C warming, the bulk of the literature suggests significant vulnerability and diminished adaptive capacity.

The second point is that some impacts are already under way, including the loss of glaciers, adverse impacts on biodiversity, increased severity of extreme events, and loss of cultural amenities. We can see this today among indigenous peoples in the Arctic or in the high Andes, where their accustomed water supply from glaciers is rapidly waning.

Finally, there is a connection between climate variability and climate trends. There is a tendency for areas of the world that are already at high risk from current variability to be more likely to be affected adversely by future anthropogenic change—these are areas where adaptive capacity typically is lower and areas that are more sensitive and thus more vulnerable.

Let us return to the initial question, What does dangerous climate change mean? Key vulnerabilities for significantly affected people or systems may constitute dangerous climate change, which should be avoided. At an international climate conference in Argentina in 2004, Thomas Loster, senior executive and climate expert with Munich Re, said, "We need to stop this dangerous experiment humankind is conducting on the Earth's atmosphere."[6] He was referring to climate change, the use of the atmosphere as an unpriced sewer for our waste, and the increase in exceptional and extreme weather-related disasters and other concerns. However, like the majority of governments overseeing the IPCC, he did not define what constitutes dangerous, but was motivated by the well-known IPCC "reasons for concern" to advocate reducing vulnerabilities.[7]

An understanding has been reached between IPCC scientists and government decisionmakers in defining the aspects of dangerous climate change that scientists can address, as distinct from the aspects that decisionmakers at all scales— individuals, corporations, local governments, state governments, national governments, or international governments—have to define. One key task for scientists is to characterize the inherent uncertainty in the projections of future climate change, to try to bound the range of potential outcomes, and, if possible, to assign subjective confidence levels to various processes or outcomes.

The temperature thresholds (or temperature ranges) for various key vulnerabilities and the severity of the associated impacts have been discussed, and now estimates of how likely those thresholds are to be crossed should be considered. Because future greenhouse gas emissions depend partly on human behavior, future projections will differ depending on the human response to global warming and the trajectory of future greenhouse gas emissions.

In 2000 the IPCC released the Special Report on Emission Scenarios (SRES), which presented a suite of scenarios for greenhouse gas emissions based on different assumptions regarding economic growth, technological developments, and population growth, critical driving forces behind greenhouse gas emissions.[8] These scenarios, described in box 4-1, are explicitly intended to exclude climate policy controls on emissions, representing different possible "baselines" (often called "business-as-usual" scenarios) from which emissions could be reduced relative to the baselines through policy action. The IPCC, in both its 2001 Third Assessment Report and 2007 Fourth Assessment Report, used a suite of climate models to generate projections for future temperature change from each of these scenarios. While the SRES authors declined to assign relative likelihoods to the different SRES scenarios, some are more likely to represent "business as usual" than others. The SRES scenarios suggest that the atmospheric CO_2 concentrations are likely at least to double from their preindustrial value (that is, reach some 560 parts per million) sometime in the present century. Limiting concentrations below this projected doubling would require a major expansion of low-cost, low-carbon-emitting energy technologies or a major change in philosophy in the near future favoring environmental sustainability over traditional economic growth built on fossil fuel burning with little regard for the side effects.

One of the most interesting contrasts across the SRES scenarios is between the emission pathways of two variants of the A1 scenario family. The A1 family assumes relatively high economic growth, lower population growth, and considerable contraction in income differences across regions—a world that builds on current patterns of economic globalization and rapid income growth in the developing world. One variant, A1FI, is a fossil fuel–intensive scenario, in which the bulk of energy needed to fuel economic growth continues to be derived from burning fossil fuels, especially coal. Emissions grow from the current level of about 8 billion tons of carbon per year to nearly 30, resulting in a tripling of CO_2 (from current levels) in the atmosphere by 2100 and implying at least a quadrupling of CO_2 as the twenty-second century progresses. The contrasting variant is A1T—the technological innovation scenario—in which fossil fuel emissions increase from the present by about a factor of two until the mid-twenty-first century, but then, because of technological innovation and deployment of low-carbon-emitting technologies, global emissions drop to well below current levels by 2100. Even so, CO_2 levels roughly double by 2100. However,

Box 4-1. *The Emission Scenarios of the IPCC Special Report on Emission Scenarios (SRES)*

A1. The A1 storyline and scenario family describes a future world of very rapid economic growth, global population that peaks in mid-century and declines thereafter, and the rapid introduction of new and more efficient technologies. Major underlying themes are convergence among regions, capacity building, and increased cultural and social interactions, with a substantial reduction in regional differences in per capita income. The A1 scenario family develops into three groups that describe alternative directions of technological change in the energy system. The three A1 groups are distinguished by their technological emphasis: fossil intensive (A1FI), nonfossil energy sources (A1T), or a balance across all sources (A1B), where "balance" is defined as not relying too heavily on one particular energy source, on the assumption that similar improvement rates apply to all energy supply and end use technologies.

A2. The A2 storyline and scenario family describes a very heterogeneous world. The underlying theme is self-reliance and preservation of local identities. Fertility patterns across regions converge very slowly, which results in continuously increasing population. Economic development is primarily regionally oriented, and per capita economic growth and technological change are more fragmented and slower than in other storylines.

B1. The B1 storyline and scenario family describes a convergent world with the same global population, which peaks in mid-century and declines thereafter, as in the A1 storyline, but with rapid change in economic structures toward a service and information economy, with reductions in material intensity and the introduction of clean and resource-efficient technologies. The emphasis is on global solutions to economic, social, and environmental sustainability, including improved equity, but without additional climate initiatives.

B2. The B2 storyline and scenario family describes a world in which the emphasis is on local solutions to economic, social, and environmental sustainability. It is a world with continuously increasing global population, at a rate lower than A2, intermediate levels of economic development, and less rapid and more diverse technological change than in the B1 and A1 storylines. While the scenario is also oriented toward environmental protection and social equity, it focuses on local and regional levels.

An illustrative scenario was chosen for each of the six scenario groups: A1B, A1FI, A1T, A2, B1, and B2. All should be considered equally sound.

The SRES scenarios do not include additional climate initiatives, which means that no scenarios are included that explicitly assume implementation of the UNFCCC or the emissions targets of the Kyoto Protocol.

Source: IPCC, "Summary for Policymakers," in *Climate Change 2007: Mitigation of Climate Change—Contribution of Working Group III to the Fourth Assessment Report*, edited by Bert Metz and others (Cambridge University Press, in press).

Table 4-2. *Projected Global Average Surface Warming for Six Representative Emissions Scenarios at the End of the Twenty-First Century*

Case	Temperature change ($°C$ at 2090–99 relative to 1980–99)[a]	
	Best estimate	Likely range
Constant year 2000 concentrations[b]	0.6	0.3–0.9
B1 scenario	1.8	1.1–2.9
A1T scenario	2.4	1.4–3.8
B2 scenario	2.4	1.4–3.8
A1B scenario	2.8	1.7–4.4
A2 scenario	3.4	2.0–5.4
A1FI scenario	4.0	2.4–6.4

Source: Data from IPCC, "Summary for Policymakers," in *Climate Change 2007: The Physical Science Basis,* Contribution of Working Group I to the Fourth Assessment Report, edited by Susan D. Solomon and others (Cambridge University Press, forthcoming).

a. These estimates are assessed from a hierarchy of models that encompass a simple climate model, several Earth System Models of Intermediate Complexity, and a large number of Atmosphere-Ocean General Circulation Models (AOGCMs).

b. Year 2000 constant composition is derived from AOGCMs only.

they would not increase much more in the twenty-second century because emissions rapidly approach zero by 2100 (see table 4-2).

Figure 4-1 from the IPCC Fourth Assessment Report shows global mean temperature change (relative to 1980–99) from 1900 to the present as well as the range of temperature change projected through 2100 for three representative emissions scenarios. The range of future concentration projections primarily represents a fan of uncertainty derived from projecting human behavior, which depends on how many people there will be in the world, what the standards of living will be, and what technologies will be used to create and maintain such standards of living. The product of these factors determines emissions. How the natural physical and ecological systems dispose of human-injected emissions is an aspect not primarily dependent on assumptions of human behavior (though massive deforestation can slow the natural uptake of injected CO_2), but the bulk of the spread in the 2000–2100 trend curves in figure 4-1 is from estimates of alternative pathways of human development. The vertical spread, however, in the bars to the right of the trends is due primarily to uncertainties in the sensitivity of the biogeophysical climate system to the various emission scenarios. The full range of projections to 2100—1.1 to 6.4°C bracketing the "likely" range (that is, a 66 percent probability the actual climate sensitivity is in the likely range) for the SRES scenarios—involves the combined uncertainties of human behavior and climate system sensitivity.

In figure 4-1, the fossil fuel–intensive scenario (A1FI) projects a tripling of CO_2 by 2100. The lowest-emissions scenario (B1) represents a world of egalitar-

Figure 4-1. *Surface Warming, 1900, 2000, 2100*[a]

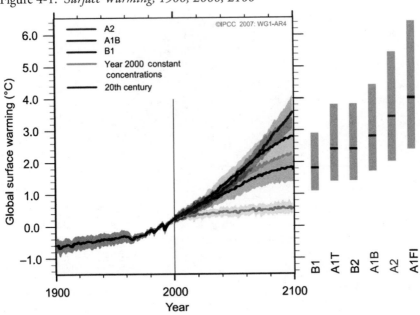

Source: Modified from IPCC, "Summary for Policymakers," in *Climate Change 2007*.

a. Multi-model global averages of surface warming (relative to 1980–99) for scenarios A2, A1B, and B1, shown as continuations of the twentieth-century simulations.

Shading denotes the ±1 standard deviation range of individual model annual averages. The lowest line from 2000 to 2100 is for the experiment where concentrations are held constant at year 2000 values. The line above it refers to the B1 scenario, the third line from the bottom refers to the A1B scenario, and the top line refers to the A2 scenario. The gray bars at right indicate the best estimate (solid line within each bar) and the likely range assessed for the six SRES marker scenarios. The assessment of the best estimate and likely ranges in the gray bars includes the AOGCMs in the left part of the figure as well as results from a hierarchy of independent models and observational constraints.

ian sharing of new technologies, resources, and information. The IPCC did not assess which scenario is more probable: business-as-usual globalization and lower costs to energy producers and consumers, which are more associated with scenario A1FI, or egalitarian sharing, which is more associated with scenario B1. It did not assign probabilities to any of the scenarios. When I ask audiences to give their subjective judgments on the likelihood of extrapolating business-as-usual activities to build wealth versus a world of egalitarian sharing, unhappily they overwhelmingly claim that business-as-usual is a much higher probability outcome than a shift to a more equitable, lower-emissions world. Although this is the outcome I obtained in several dozen informal elicitations of the opinions of my audiences, I hope a formal social scientific study on this will be performed in the near future, since providing probabilities for future scenarios plays an important role in risk management: risk, by definition, being probability times consequence; thus one cannot formally do risk management without probabilities.

Another very important factor is that the calculation of temperature change should not stop at 2100, as it does in figure 4-1, since emissions do not cease suddenly at that point; even if they miraculously did, it would take centuries for the large concentrations of greenhouse gases to relax back toward preindustrial levels. As the higher-emissions scenarios are still sloping upward, CO_2 concentration is not just tripling at 2100, as in the A1FI scenario, but is quadrupling, quintupling, or more, in the hundred years beyond 2100. Compare scenario A1FI to scenario A1T, a world in which an investment of roughly 1 percent of GDP is made to reduce emissions to almost zero by 2100 through the implementation of advanced technologies and in which, as a result, concentrations of greenhouse gases stabilize by 2100. Once concentrations stabilize and emissions are low, then the concentrations will continue to drop slowly over hundreds of years by natural removal processes (or that removal could be accelerated by controversial "geo-engineering" proposals to remove CO_2). Many think that we are likely to follow an increasing-emissions pathway for at least many more decades, enough eventually to triple or quadruple CO_2 in the atmosphere in the very long term. However, others think that by mid-century we will have deployed enough cost effective, low-emitting systems that we will be able to nearly uncouple our economies from carbon-emitting devices and reduce our emissions greatly. However, this "many decades" time delay in accomplishing such emissions reductions would allow future CO_2 concentrations to peak at well beyond what many would consider a "safe" long-term stabilization target (say, about 450 parts per million, ppm, as the European Union, EU, has supported). In this likely situation of exceeding 450PPM CO_2-equivalent and then over decades replacing high emitting production systems with lower-emitting ones, the world would experience an "overshoot scenario," in which the massive emissions of the unconstrained fossil fuel era lead to an overshoot of the final greenhouse gas stabilization level.

We have at least two fans of uncertainty in these analyses, as noted earlier. One involves social science and human behavior. The other involves natural science: the sensitivity of climate to emissions and the uncertainty in our understanding of the climate system. When these uncertainties are combined and the temperature increase is calculated, as shown in the bars on figure 4-1, the result is a range of temperatures in 2100 between 1.1 and 6.4°C above levels in 1990, as already pointed out. But we must also realize that this range is not inclusive of what might happen. There are non-zero probabilities of being above or below this range because other scenarios can be imagined, and these were not addressed by the IPCC as these were outside of the "likely" range mentioned earlier. For example, a collapse of the world economy that limits emissions or a breakthrough in the price of solar electric machines that lowers emissions dramatically, on the one hand, or the radical expansion of the use of tar sands or coal-to-liquids techniques without carbon capture and sequestration (CCS) to produce petroleum products with very high CO_2 emissions, on the other, are examples of how emissions and concentrations could even be outside the already broad ranges established by SRES authors. As noted, the vertical bars essentially represent the "likely" range of climate sensitivity, not the full range, which has some 15 percent chance of being more or a ~ 15 percent chance of being less than the 2.0–4.5°C "likely range" of global mean warming from a doubling of CO_2 as assessed by Working Group I (AR4).

Given these uncertainties, the bottom line is that climate policy is a *risk management* practice. Optimization is not a meaningful concept in setting targets for climate policy, because there are multiple uncertain parameters at every stage of analysis and because choosing explicit values for such parameters is at least a partially normative process. To use the concept of optimality at all, climate scientists and policy analysts have to pick multiple values of key parameters (climate sensitivity, climate damage functions, nonmarket valuation rules, discounting formulation), calculate an optimum for each of those choices, and then recalculate it multiple times with other choices, much like a Monte Carlo analysis, that would yield a distribution of "optimal" outcomes (as in a probability density function).[9] Based on this kind of probabilistic analysis, we would then have to decide what risks we will assume and how to trade off the myriad incommensurables. We have to assess risk as a function of policy choice.

Figure 4-2 shows plausible standard and overshoot emissions scenarios.[10] The bottom three curves at about 2150 show a slowly changing world stabilizing at 500 ppm in 2200, a more rapidly changing world stabilizing at 500 ppm CO_2-equivalent, and, in my opinion, a much more realistic world of overshooting and then returning to 500 ppm as we "invent our way out of the problem," assuming that the prices of alternative energy systems come down or more value is placed on the sustainability of the climate and people take decisive action. The upper three curves at 2150 represent the same pattern, but for stabilization of CO_2-equivalent concentrations at 600 ppm.

The significant likelihood of overshoot scenarios makes it important to incorporate how emissions, atmospheric concentrations, and temperatures change over time (transient changes). To study the impacts of climate change only in terms of equilibrium warming, rather than as a time-evolving transient, is really to miss a major component of dangerous anthropogenic interference assessment. We need to look at a range of these transients. Figure 4-3 shows the different transient implications of overshoot and non-overshoot scenarios for crossing one oft-cited threshold of DAI, although other potential DAI temperature thresholds can also be examined.

Figure 4-3 shows cumulative density functions (CDFs) of temperature increase (indicating the probability that temperature increase is equal to or below any given level) and the probability of exceeding the oft-cited EU threshold of 2°C above preindustrial levels (about 1.3°C above current temperatures)

Figure 4-2. *Stabilization Scenarios, 2000–50*[a]

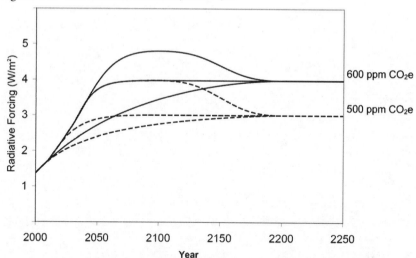

Source: Stabilization scenarios based on Brian C. O'Neill and Michael Oppenheimer, "Climate Change Impacts Are Sensitive to the Concentration Stabilization Path," *Proceedings of the National Academy of Sciences* 101, no. 47 (2004); presented by Michael D. Mastrandrea at the Conference on Avoiding Dangerous Climate Change, U.K. Department for Environment, Food, and Rural Affairs, Exeter, U.K., February 1–3, 2005.

a. Stabilizing at 500 ppm and 600 ppm CO_2 equivalent (CO_2e). Scenarios represent three different stabilization approach categories: slow approach, rapid approach, and overshoot.

for an overshoot and a non-overshoot scenario (although any DAI threshold between 0 and 4°C could be selected and read from the figure). The bottom curve represents the temperature distribution for a slowly rising, non-overshoot scenario in 2200. Under this scenario, there is about a 45 percent chance of exceeding this threshold by 2200. Probability density functions are used for climate sensitivity from the literature to construct these CDFs for each emissions scenario. Other sources of information could be used as well, and every single one of them is completely model dependent. The numbers should not be taken literally. Instead, the framework is what should be taken seriously.[9]

The middle curve is the CDF for an overshoot scenario stabilizing at 500 ppm in 2200. The likelihood of exceeding the EU threshold for the overshoot scenario in 2200 is only slightly increased (55 percent) over the likelihood of exceeding the EU DAI threshold for the non-overshoot scenario (45 percent) for a 500 ppm CO_2-equivalent stabilization target. That is because by 2200 the transient overshoot has almost played itself out. However, the peak of temperature increase with the overshoot scenario (the top curve) occurs prior to 2200, rather than at 2200 (the middle curve). This results in a dramatically increased chance of exceeding the EU DAI threshold (77 percent). Therefore, vulnerabil-

Figure 4-3. *Overshoot Scenario Analysis*[a]

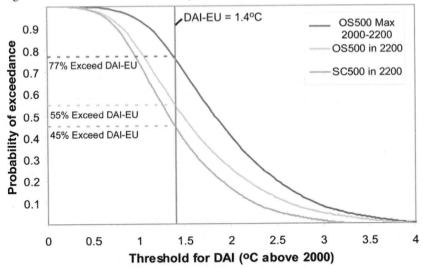

Source: Stephen H. Schneider and Michael D. Mastrandrea, "Probabilistic Assessment of 'Dangerous' Climate Change and Emissions Pathways," *Proceedings of the National Academy of Sciences* 102, no. 21 (2005).

a. The probability of exceedance of the EU DAI threshold for overshoot (OS500) and non-overshoot (SC500) concentration profiles stabilizing at 500 ppm CO_2e. The bottom two curves display probabilities of exceedance for transient temperature increase above 2000 in 2200, and the top curve displays probabilities of exceedance for the maximum temperature reached sometime between 2000 and 2200 for the overshoot (OS500) concentration profile. The spread in each curve is based on the literature for typically assessed climate sensitivities.

ity assessment and DAI analysis must be viewed as a transient problem. It is very difficult to analyze transients with high confidence, since they involve the coupling of models of physical, biological, and social subsystems, yet it is necessary to try, since that is the nature of the problem.

In figure 4-4, three metrics are presented for further evaluating the increase in the risk of exceeding a threshold for DAI associated with an overshoot profile. First, the maximum exceedance amplitude (MEA) above a given DAI threshold is defined as the maximum difference between the DAI threshold and a calculated temperature profile through a given time period. If a temperature profile never exceeds the DAI threshold, the MEA will be negative, representing the closest approach to the threshold during that period. The MEA metric provides information about the maximum temperature reached in a given time frame and the magnitude of exceedance (that is, by how much some specified DAI temperature threshold is exceeded). It does not provide information about the duration of exceedance. A prolonged period of temperatures above a threshold for DAI is likely to induce more severe impacts than a short exceedance of equal magnitude. Degree-days are a commonly used metric for measuring

Figure 4-4. *Emission Scenario Metrics*[a]

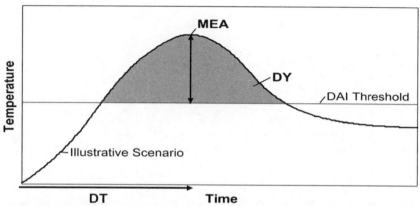

Source: Adapted from Schneider and Mastrandrea, "Probabilistic Assessment of 'Dangerous' Climate Change and Emissions Pathways."

a. The metrics are introduced to differentiate emissions pathways by the degree to which they exceed specified thresholds for DAI. For the illustrative temperature profile displayed here, MEA is measured as the maximum temperature increase reached above the indicated threshold for DAI (horizontal line), and degree-years (DY) is measured as the cumulative exceedance of that threshold by the profile (shading). Another metric is DT—the time between the present and when MEA occurs. The faster the transient occurs, the less likely it is that natural or human systems can successfully adapt, so the rate at which the temperature rises to maximum is also an important factor in vulnerability analysis.

cumulative departure from a given temperature level. For example, heating and cooling degree-days are used to measure energy demand, and growing degree-days are used in ecology, forestry, agriculture, and pest control. We adopt a similar metric—degree-years (DY)—as a measure of both the length and magnitude of exceedance for a given threshold of DAI. A third vulnerability metric is DT, the time between the present and when MEA occurs. The faster the temperature rises, the less likely it is that natural or human systems can fully adapt, so the rate at which the transient temperature rises to maximum is also an important factor in vulnerability analysis.

A discussion of risk, which, classically defined, is probability times consequence, is essential. But what are the metrics of harm? Typically, in policy analysis, the standard metric is commodities or services traded in markets. This could represent agricultural changes, losses associated with retreating coastlines, deaths from heat waves, and other adverse or beneficial impacts. However, when deaths from heat waves are considered, two methods of evaluation are possible: one is to value people at the monetary standard for saving a "statistical life"; the other is simply to compare lives lost without monetization. The value of a statistical life is a measure of how much a society is typically willing to spend to reduce the probability of a death by, for example, investing in better highway safety, more medical research, or reduced air pollution. Statistically speaking,

Table 4-3. *Five Numeraires for Judging the Significance of Climate Change Impacts*

Vulnerability to climate change	Numeraire
Market impact	U.S.$ per ton of carbon
Human lives lost	Persons per ton of carbon
Biodiversity loss	Species per ton of carbon
Distributional impacts	Income redistribution per ton of carbon
Quality of life	Loss of heritage sites, forced migration, disturbed cultural amenities, and so forth per ton of carbon

Source: Stephen H. Schneider, Kristin Kuntz-Duriseti, and Christian Azar, "Costing Nonlinearities, Surprises, and Irreversible Events," *Pacific and Asian Journal of Energy* 10, no. 1 (2000): 81–106.

such investments lower death rates overall and can thus be translated into a monetary value of statistical lives saved. If people are valued based on what the society is willing to pay, assigning, say, $10,000 per statistical life in Bangladesh and some $2 million per statistical life in Europe, many would take the position that a dollar aggregation of this type is an absolutely unethical metric. They would simply rather compare the number of lives lost without monetization.

Table 4-3 suggests "five numeraires" for judging the significance of climate change impacts.[12] These include market system costs in dollars per ton of carbon emitted; human lives lost in persons per ton of carbon emitted; species lost per ton of carbon emitted; distributional effects such as changes in income differentials between rich and poor per ton of carbon emitted; and quality of life changes, such as heritage sites lost per ton of carbon emitted or refugees created per ton of carbon emitted. One must consider all of these factors to arrive at a fair and accurate assessment of climate change damages.[13] However, as mentioned, it is difficult to assign a monetary value to non-market categories of damages (or benefits for that matter). Can we, for example, place a dollar value on a human life and the quality of that life? How do we value ecosystem goods and services, let alone the very existence of species threatened by human disturbances?[14]

A traditional cost-benefit analysis, as noted earlier, tends to consider a sole numeraire—market values—and is often viewed as unjust because nature and distributional aspects are rarely treated explicitly or are treated by very crude, controversial monetization metrics.[15] In a traditional cost-benefit analysis, the ethical principle is not even classical Benthamite utilitarianism—that is, the greatest good for the greatest number of *people*. Rather, it is an aggregated market power form of utilitarianism—that is, the greatest good for the greatest number of *dollars* in discounted benefit-cost ratios. It follows, then, that in the wake of equivalent, climate-induced physical damage, an industrial country with a large economy and more absolute monetary units should be rescued or rehabilitated before a developing nation with a less robust economy and fewer absolute monetary units at risk. Even more problematic would be the incidence of an industrial northern country benefiting from global warming due to longer growing seasons, while a less developed southern country suffers from excessive heating. Suppose the southern country loses the same dollar value to its economy as the northern country gains. This could hardly be viewed as a neutral outcome despite a net global monetary welfare change of zero, derived from summing the monetary gain in the North and the loss in the South. Very few would view a market valuation of impacts in which the rich get richer and the poor get poorer as ethically neutral, particularly since the bulk of increases in atmospheric concentrations to date have come from the greenhouse gas emissions of industrial countries. In international negotiations, members of the political South often challenge supporters of using aggregate market damages as the only numeraire for impacts analysis, which they view as being irrelevant at best and unethical at worst.

Under the framework of the five numeraires, the interests of natural systems, developing countries, and the less privileged within any of the affected nations would be given a greater weight on the basis of the threats to non-market entities such as biodiversity, human life, and cultural heritage sites. Take the example of Bangladesh. Assume that rising sea levels caused by climate change lead to the destruction of lives, property, and ecosystems equivalent to about 80 percent of the country's GDP. Although the losses would be indisputably catastrophic for Bangladesh, they would amount to 0.1 percent of global GDP,[16] causing a market-aggregation-only analysis to classify the damage as relatively insignificant. However, those considering multiple numeraires to assess key vulnerabilities would argue that this is clearly unfair: the loss of life, degraded quality of life, and potential loss of biodiversity are at least as important as the aggregate market impacts. All of these factors are dramatically important in international negotiations, yet they are very difficult to include quantitatively in analyses and models.

In the end, when we make a decision, we are making an implicit value judgment on how to evaluate and weigh all risk factors. I have long argued that the fairest approach to this treacherous valuation problem is to use transparency in every step of aggregation. Assessing dangerous anthropogenic interference with the climate system is analytically tractable for specified sets of assumptions, but what it means to different decisionmakers is subject to different interpretations by different regions and stakeholders with varying perspectives. Making those perspectives clear and recalculating all policy assessments to cover a broad range of such differing views provide the framework that is necessary to study this problem openly and honestly. Three-decimal-point precision and "optimal" policies are, by themselves, simply not appropriate analytic practices for a problem like climate policy, which is laced with deep uncertainties and many conflicting judgments on what is valuable. In my view, the analyst must be explicit as to what assumptions are made, what normative judgments are implicit, and what discounting process is used if any policy study is to be assessed fairly and broadly by the international community.

Expertise is required in every stage of the assessment of climate change and associated key vulnerabilities, which is why governments set up assessment bodies of scientists and policy analysts to help them sort out the bewildering set of often contradictory claims found in the public debate. But in the end these scientific judgments must be supplemented with value judgments of what is just, or how much should be invested in adaptation and mitigation activities, or who should pay for these policies now and over time, or even what questions are to be assessed.

Finally, rational policy is best accomplished when stakeholders, decision-makers, and the public are all well informed, which means an accurate media accounting that does not simply pit a few extreme opposite opinions against each other as if they were representative of a wholly divided expert community. Rather, the media should report the preponderance of evidence as assessed by peer-reviewed reports like those of the IPCC or those of the U.S. National Academy of Sciences, rather than the polarized, non-peer-reviewed press releases of myriad special interests that all too often dominate the media debate and do not reflect the best judgments of the relevant expert communities. Democracy thrives on credible information, particularly for complex topics like climate change science, impacts, and policy. To achieve that condition, assessments that both report the literature and assign confidence to the many available conclusions are essential. So too is an electorate informed by the findings of such assessments and not confused by angry and polarized debates of dueling special interests, which are hardly representative of the mainstream assessments of the scientific community set up by governments precisely to assist in the transfer of credible information in a risk-management framework.

Notes

1. Key vulnerabilities are assessed in chapter 19 of Working Group II of the Intergovernmental Panel on Climate Change (IPCC), in the Fourth Assessment Report: Stephen H. Schneider and others, "Key Vulnerabilities and the Risk from Climate Change," in *Climate Change 2007: Impacts, Adaptation, and Vulnerability, Contribution of Working Group II to the Fourth Assessment Report*, edited by Martin Parry and others (Cambridge University Press, in press).
2. United Nations Framework Convention on Climate Change (Bonn: UNFCCC, 1992). Available at http://unfccc.int/resource/docs/convkp/conveng.pdf.
3. Schneider and others, "Key Vulnerabilities and the Risk from Climate Change."
4. Liu and others, "Complexity of Coupled Human and Natural Systems," *Science* 317, no. 5844 (2007).
5. Richard H. Moss and Stephen H. Schneider, "Uncertainties in the IPCC TAR: Recommendations to Lead Authors for More Consistent Assessment and Reporting," in *Guidance Papers on the Cross Cutting Issues of the Third Assessment Report of the IPCC*, edited by R. T. Pachauri and others (World Meteorological Organization, 2000).

6. Quote by Thomas Loster, senior executive and climate expert with Munich Re, delivered at the tenth session of the Conference of Parties (COP-10), Buenos Aires, December 6–17, 2004, as reported by the United Nations Environment Programme, "Extreme Weather Losses Soar to Record High for Insurance Industry; Insurance Industry Facing $35 Billion Plus Bill for 2004," News Release 2004/52, December 15, 2004.

7. The five "reasons for concern" identified in the Third IPCC Assessment Report remain a viable framework to consider key vulnerabilities. These "reasons" are assessed to be stronger in the 2007 Synthesis Report, Section 5: Topic 5. Many risks are identified with higher confidence, and some risks are projected to be larger or to occur at lower increases in temperature. *IPCC Synthesis Report 2007—Contribution of Working Groups I, II, and III to the Fourth Assessment Report,* edited by the Core Writing Team (Cambridge University Press, 2007, in press). Available at www.ipcc.ch/.

8. Nebojsa Nakicenovic and others, *IPCC Special Report on Emissions Scenarios,* edited by Nebojsa Nakicenovic and Rob Swart, a special report of the IPCC Working Group III (Cambridge University Press, 2000).

9. Tim Roughgarden and Stephen H. Schneider, "Climate Change Policy: Quantifying Uncertainties for Damages and Optimal Carbon Taxes," *Energy Policy* 27, no. 7 (1999): 415–29; Michael D. Mastrandrea and Stephen H. Schneider, "Probabilistic Integrated Assessment of 'Dangerous' Climate Change," *Science* 304, no. 5670 (2004): 571–75.

10. Brian C. O'Neill and Michael Oppenheimer, "Climate Change Impacts Are Sensitive to the Concentration Stabilization Path," *Proceedings of the National Academy of Sciences* 101, no. 47 (2004): 16411–16.

11. Stephen H. Schneider and Michael D. Mastrandrea, "Probabilistic Assessment of 'Dangerous' Climate Change and Emissions Pathways," *Proceedings of the National Academy of Sciences* 102, no. 21 (2005): 15725–27.

12. Stephen H. Schneider, Kristin Kuntz-Duriseti, and Christian Azar, "Costing Nonlinearities, Surprises, and Irreversible Events," *Pacific and Asian Journal of Energy* 10, no. 1 (2000): 81–106.

13. Multiple metrics for the valuation of climatic impacts are suggested. Typically in economic cost-benefit calculations, only the first numeraire—market sector elements—is included. Different individuals, cultures, and governments might have very different weights on these five—or other—numeraires, and thus it is suggested that analysis of climatic impacts be first disaggregated into such dimensions and that any reaggregation provide a traceable account of the aggregation process so that decisionmakers can apply their own valuations to various components of analysis.

14. Gretchen C. Daily, *Nature's Services: Societal Dependence on Natural Ecosystems* (Washington: Island Press, 1997).

15. Glenn P. Jenkins, "Evaluation of Stakeholder Impacts in Cost-Benefit Analysis," *Impact Assessment and Project Appraisal* 17, no. 2 (Beech Tree Publishing, 1999).

16. IPCC, *Climate Change 2001: Impacts, Adaptation, and Vulnerability, Contribution of Working Group II to the Third Assessment Report of the Intergovernmental Panel on Climate Change,* edited by James J. McCarthy and others (Cambridge University Press, 2001).

5

The Policy Implications of Climate Change Impacts

ROBERT MENDELSOHN

R ecent research on the impacts of global warming has revealed that the net impacts of climate change are much smaller than first thought. Near-term damage will largely be offset by near-term benefits. Damages are expected to exceed benefits only in the second half of this century and only in scenarios with rapid climate change. The research also suggests that most of the damages will be felt in low-latitude countries, whereas the benefits will occur largely in the mid- to high-latitude countries. Because most of the poorest countries in the world are located in the low latitudes, most of the damages from climate change will happen to the world's poorest people. These impact results have important policy ramifications. First, the low net damages from current emissions imply that only limited resources should be devoted to near-term abatement. Second, mitigation is likely only to slow global warming. It is therefore important to plan an adaptation strategy to cope with global warming. Third, because the world's poorest people are the most affected by climate change, climate policy should also include a compensation package for poor countries.

The magnitude, timing, and distribution of the impacts of climate change have important ramifications for climate policies. As our understanding of these impacts progresses, it is important to update climate policies to take into account new findings. With a problem as long-standing as climate change, repeating the theme of learning and then acting should become standard policy practice.

This paper first reviews the history of the literature on the impact of climate change over the last twenty-five years. It concentrates on economic studies that have quantified the magnitude of impacts and highlights the major insights from this literature over time. The second section then draws the important policy implications suggested by the findings. The paper concludes with a final set of policy recommendations supported by the current literature.

Review of Impact Literature

The literature on the economic impacts of climate change has grown considerably over the last twenty-five years. The first comprehensive study of climate change impacts analyzed the United States.[1] Although this study did not arrive at a comprehensive estimate of the net damages from climate change, it introduced a number of methodologies that could be used to quantify climate impacts in various sectors. Subsequent authors relied heavily on these studies to produce quantitative estimates of net impacts.[2] The International Panel on Climate Change (IPCC) provided an authoritative review of this early literature in its Second Assessment Report.[3]

One significant finding in this initial literature is that most of the economy is not climate sensitive.[4] The market sectors that are judged to be climate sensitive include agriculture, coastal development, energy, forestry, and water (mostly irrigation). The climate-sensitive non-market sectors include ecosystems, biodiversity, and human health. Another important result is that the impacts were judged to be less than 2 percent of GDP, even including generous estimates of non-market effects.

Since this seminal work, impact research has focused on making a number of innovations. First, research has revealed that most sectors have a hill-shaped sensitivity to climate.[5] For each climate-sensitive sector, there is an optimal climate that is most productive. The farms or sectors cooler than this optimum are less productive, as are the farms or sectors warmer than this optimum. This implies that warming is likely to have different effects on countries depending on their initial climate with respect to the optimum. Countries that are cooler than the optimum will see benefits from warming at first. Countries that are near the optimal climate will see little change. Countries that are hotter than the optimum will see immediate damages from warming. The impacts of climate change will not be uniform; rather, they will vary across the planet. The results imply that warming will at first lead to damages in the low latitudes and benefits in the middle to high latitudes.[6] Only as warming becomes quite large will most of the planet be damaged, but even in this case, the low latitudes are expected to bear a larger share of the damages.[7]

Second, the impact literature has come to recognize the importance of adaptation.[8] The early literature sometimes included a few adaptive responses such as farmers' switching crops. However, the early impact literature generally underestimated adaptation. Adaptation both reduces damages and increases potential benefits. Including adaptation reduces the net damages from climate change. Comparisons of response functions with and without adaptation reveal that adaptation reduces the severity of changes in climate.[9]

Third, the early literature evaluated climate change given 1990 conditions and did not anticipate how conditions would change in the future. The impacts from climate change are only expected to become serious in the second half of this century and beyond.[10] It is therefore important to evaluate climate impacts to this future economy, not to the economy as it exists today. The new literature recognizes the importance of creating future baselines against which to test impacts. It is the economy in the future that must be studied, not the current economy. Because the economy is expected to grow, the magnitude of the impacts to climate-sensitive sectors will be larger. However, because the climate-sensitive sectors are expected to grow more slowly than the rest of the economy, the impacts as a fraction of GDP are expected to be smaller.

Finally, it is important for impact research to evaluate a broad set of climate scenarios. Climate science currently predicts that a broad range of climate scenarios is possible.[11] Warming may range from 1.5 to 5.8°C (centigrade) by 2100.[12] This full range must be studied since the impacts vary considerably across these possibilities. Climate scenarios near the low end of this range are likely to be beneficial (benefits exceed damages), whereas scenarios near the top end of the range will be quite harmful. For example, if experimental simulation response functions are used, a 2.5°C scenario, as predicted by the Parallel Climate Model, could lead to global benefits as high as $217 billion a year by 2100, whereas a 5.2°C scenario, as predicted by the Canadian Climate Centre climate model, could lead to global damages as large as $273 billion a year by 2100.[13]

Overall, the improvements in the literature have tended to reduce the predicted net impacts of climate change. Whereas the literature was previously estimating that impacts could be as high as 2 percent of GDP in 2100, the highest estimates in the current literature are closer to 0.2 percent of GDP. The estimated average impact is even lower, with the very real possibility that climate change will be beneficial this entire century.

Using the estimates of annual impacts from the early literature, the present value of future damages—the expected value of the damage from a ton of carbon—is about $5 per ton.[14] If one assumes that there is a large probability of a very bad consequence, the present value could be as high as $20 per ton.[15] With the much smaller damages in the new literature, the expected value per ton of carbon is closer to $0.5, and the uncertainty value is closer to $2 per ton.

Policy Implications

These impact results have important policy ramifications. For example, the impact research implies that the marginal damages from carbon emissions are quite low, in the neighborhood of a few dollars per ton. The marginal damages from emissions are the marginal benefits of abatement. If abatement delivers such low benefits, society should only be willing to spend a few dollars per ton on abatement. That is, because the marginal benefit of control is very low, the marginal cost of abatement should also be kept low. The low estimates for marginal damages imply that mitigation over the near term can only be justified if it costs less than $2 per ton. Given the very high cost of mitigating greenhouse gases, the low estimates for marginal benefits imply that little mitigation should be done. Control policies can be put in place, but the policies should begin with only modest targets.

The second important policy insight is that modest control policies will not stop greenhouse gases from accumulating, and so temperatures will warm. Mitigation may slow climate change, but not stop it. Governments and individuals must prepare to adapt to warmer climates. Adaptation will reduce the damages that would otherwise occur and increase the opportunities that warming will bring.

There is a substantial debate in the literature about whether adaptation should be proactive and anticipate climate change or be reactive and change only after the fact.[16] To the extent that people can predict how climate will change and can act on that knowledge in advance, they can pursue proactive adaptation. However, acting in advance is difficult. Adaptation is a local response. It depends on how climate changes in a particular location. Although climate scientists may be confident that the world will warm, they are less confident of local predictions. This is especially true about changes in precipitation. The different climate models make drastically different local predictions. They even make different predictions over time. It is not straightforward to anticipate local climate change. It also is not that easy to act on early warnings. If one adapts too soon, one may be out of step with the current climate. For example, farmers cannot plant new crops until the weather actually has changed enough to support the new crop. Long-term investments such as dams can benefit from anticipatory adaptation. However, if one builds a dam solely on the premise that the future climate will be more suitable, and if the climate change is delayed or wrong, the present value costs of the dam can quickly exceed the benefits.

Because of these problems, it is quite likely that most adaptation will be reactive, occurring after the fact. Reactive adaptation has the benefit of learning first and then acting. It is flexible and takes advantage of climate change as it unfolds rather than as it is predicted. Reactive adaptation does not require extensive monitoring networks and sophisticated modeling. Farmers, foresters, residents, and coastal dwellers just need to keep track of how climate is changing around them. These actors need to update their sense of what "normal" weather is, to weigh recent evidence more heavily than historical evidence. But they can quickly determine the new climate they live in through experience. Further, they can experiment with what works in this new climate. Since the climate will have arrived, they can use trial and error to see what new behavior works best. Even with more long-term investments, just updating the estimate of the current climate can improve the choice of alternatives for the next few decades.

Compensation is the final policy implication of the most recent research. Because most of the poorest countries in the world are in the low latitudes, the damages from climate change will fall most heavily on the poor. In a moderate-climate scenario, the world's poorest countries could suffer almost two-thirds of the global damages from climate change.[17] With a severe-climate scenario, the poorest 25 percent of the world's countries could suffer almost 50 percent of the damages from climate change.[18] In contrast, the richest 25 percent of countries would actually benefit as a group under both scenarios. The impacts of climate change are not uniform. Rather, they are distributed very unevenly.

These results imply that there is a third important policy implication of impact research. Policy must recognize the inequality of climate impacts across countries. Specifically, policy must address the share of damages that will fall on the poor as a result of climate change. Measures have been discussed to subsidize mitigation for poor countries. Most recently, policymakers are beginning to discuss adaptation measures that poor countries can take. These efforts will help. However, to address the inequity of climate change, policymakers should strongly consider helping the economies of developing countries to grow more rapidly.[19] With growth, developing countries can move away from climate-sensitive sectors such as agriculture. With growth, people can earn enough to take adaptive measures of their own, such as buying rather than growing food. With growth, low-latitude residents can be compensated for taking on the unwanted burden of climate change.

Conclusions

Climate impact research has found three important results. First, both benefits and damages are associated with climate change, and so the net effect of climate impacts is quite small. Second, adaptation will reduce the net impacts of climate change considerably. Third, the damages of climate change are likely to fall on poor, low-latitude countries, whereas the benefits will fall on relatively rich mid- to high-latitude countries.

These three results imply three important policy insights. First, because the marginal damages of greenhouse gases are expected to be low, the marginal cost of new regulations should also be low. Second, climate will warm, and as such, it is important to adapt. Policymakers should begin to prepare for adaptation measures across the world. Third, climate impacts will fall most heavily on low-latitude countries, which are home to the world's poorest residents. Policymakers should address the unfairness of this outcome and compensate these poor countries for damages they did not cause. Specifically, attempts to aid development in these countries would serve the dual goals of improving standards of living and moving these economies away from agriculture and toward less climate-sensitive activities.

Notes

1. Joel Smith and Dennis Tirpak, *The Potential Effects of Global Climate Change on the United States: Report to Congress,* EPA-230-05-89-050 (Washington: U.S. Environmental Protection Agency, 1989).
2. William Nordhaus, "To Slow or Not to Slow: The Economics of the Greenhouse Effect," *Economic Journal* 101, no. 407 (1991): 920–37; Richard Tol, "The Damage Costs of Climate Change toward More Comprehensive Calculations," *Environmental and Resource Economics* 5, no. 4 (1995): 353–74; Samuel Fankhauser, *Valuing Climate Change: The Economics of the Greenhouse* (London: Earthscan, 1995).
3. David Pearce and others, "The Social Cost of Climate Change: Greenhouse Damage and the Benefits of Control," in *Climate Change 1995: Economic and Social Dimensions of Climate Change,* Contribution of Working Group III to the Second Assessment, edited by J. P. Bruce, H. Lee, and E. F. Haites (Cambridge University Press, 1996).
4. Pearce and others, "Social Cost of Climate Change."
5. John Reilly and others, "Agriculture in a Changing Climate: Impacts and Adaptations," in IPCC, *Climate Change 1995: Impacts, Adaptations, and Mitigation of Climate Change; Scientific-Technical Analyses,* Contribution of Working Group II to the Second Assessment Report, edited by R. Watson and others (Cambridge University Press, 1996); Robert Mendelsohn and Michael Schlesinger, "Climate Response Functions," *Ambio* 28, no. 4 (1999): 362–66.
6. Richard Tol, "Estimates of the Damage Costs of Climate Change. Part 1: Benchmark Estimates," *Environmental and Resource Economics* 21, no. 1 (2002): 47–73; Robert Mendelsohn and others, "Country-Specific Market Impacts from Climate Change," *Climatic Change* 45, no. 3–4 (2000): 553–69.
7. Robert Mendelsohn and Larry Williams, "Comparing Forecasts of the Global Impacts of Climate Change," *Mitigation and Adaptation Strategies for Global Change* 9, no. 4 (2004): 315–33. Robert Mendelsohn, Ariel Dinar, and Larry Williams, "The Distributional Impact of Climate Change on Rich and Poor Countries," *Environment and Development Economics* 11, no. 2 (2006): 159–78.
8. Ian Burton, "Vulnerability and Adaptive Response in the Context of Climate and Climate Change," *Climatic Change* 36, no. 1–2 (1997): 185–96; Barry Smit, Ian Burton, and Richard J. T. Klein, "The Science of Adaptation: A Framework for Assessment," *Mitigation and Adaptation Strategies for Global Change* 4, no. 3–4 (1999): 199–213; Joel B. Smith and others, eds., *Adapting to Climate Change: An International Perspective* (New York: Springer, 1996).

9. Robert Mendelsohn, "The Role of Markets and Governments in Helping Society Adapt to a Changing Climate," *Climatic Change* 78, no. 1 (September 2006): 203–15.

10. IPCC, *Climate Change 2001: The Scientific Basis,* Contribution of Working Group I to the Third Assessment Report, edited by J. Houghton and others (Cambridge University Press, 2001).

11. IPCC, *Climate Change 1995: The State of the Science,* Contribution of Working Group I to the Second Assessment Report, edited by J. Houghton and others (Cambridge University Press, 1996); IPCC, *Climate Change 2001: The Scientific Basis.*

12. IPCC, *Climate Change 2001: The Scientific Basis.*

13. Mendelsohn and Williams, "Comparing Forecasts."

14. Pearce and others, "The Social Cost of Climate Change."

15. William Nordhaus and Joseph Boyer, *Warming the World: Economic Models of Global Warming* (MIT Press, 2000).

16. Burton, "Vulnerability and Adaptive Response"; Smit, Burton, and Klein, "The Science of Adaptation"; Smith and others, *Adapting to Climate Change;* Robert Mendelsohn and others, "Country-Specific Market Impacts from Climate Change."

17. Mendelsohn, Dinar, and Williams, "Distributional Impact of Climate Change on Rich and Poor Countries."

18. Ibid.

19. Thomas Schelling, "Some Economics of Global Warming," *American Economic Review* 82, no. 1 (1992): 1–14.

PART THREE

The Kyoto Protocol: Consequences and Opportunities for Transformation

6

Economic Analyses of the Kyoto Protocol: Is There Life after Kyoto?

WILLIAM D. NORDHAUS

This paper reviews different approaches to the political and economic control of global public goods like global warming. It compares quantity-oriented control mechanisms like the Kyoto Protocol with price-type control mechanisms such as internationally harmonized carbon taxes. The pros and cons of the two approaches are compared, focusing on such issues as performance under conditions of uncertainty, the volatility of induced carbon prices, the excess burden of taxation and regulation, accounting finagling, corruption, and implementation. Although virtually all policies involving economic global public goods rely on quantitative approaches, price-type approaches are likely to be more effective and more efficient.

After more than a decade of negotiations and planning under the United Nations Framework Convention on Climate Change (UNFCCC), the first binding international agreement to control the emissions of greenhouse gases has come into effect in the Kyoto Protocol. The first budget period of 2008–12 is at hand. Moreover, the scientific evidence on greenhouse warming strengthens steadily as observational evidence of warming accumulates. The institutional framework of the protocol has taken hold solidly in the European Union's Emissions Trading Scheme (ETS), which covers almost half of Europe's CO_2 emissions.

Notwithstanding this apparent success, the Kyoto Protocol is widely seen as somewhere between troubled and terminal. Early troubles came with the failure

Figure 6-1. *Fraction of World Emissions Covered by the Kyoto Protocol*

Percent

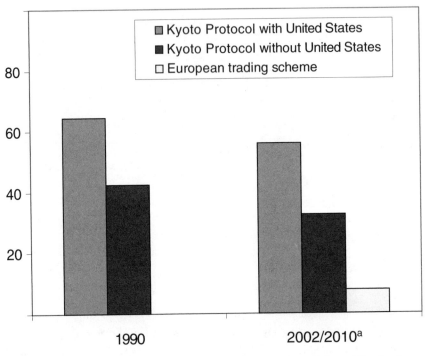

Source: The underlying model is described in William Nordhaus and Joseph Boyer, *Warming the World: Economic Models of Global Warming* (MIT Press, 2000), chap. 8. Input data are revised to reflect changes in trends since 1999.

a. The date 2002 includes coverage of the Kyoto Protocol; 2010 includes application of the Emissions Trading Scheme.

to include the major developing countries along with lack of an agreed-upon mechanism for including new countries and extending the agreement to new periods. The major blow came when the United States withdrew from the treaty in 2001. By 2002, the protocol covered only 30 percent of global emissions, while the hard enforcement mechanism in the ETS accounts for about 8 percent of global emissions (see figure 6-1).

Even if the current protocol is extended, models indicate that it will have little impact on global temperature change. Modeling estimates indicate that global emissions under the revised Kyoto Protocol will be very close to "business as usual." Global emissions in 2010 under the current protocol are estimated to be 1.5 percent lower than a no-controls scenario, if the new forestry offsets are ignored (see figure 6-2). Unless there is a dramatic breakthrough or a new design, the protocol threatens to be seen as a monument to institutional overreach.

Figure 6-2. *Estimated Emissions Reductions under Different Scenarios*[a]

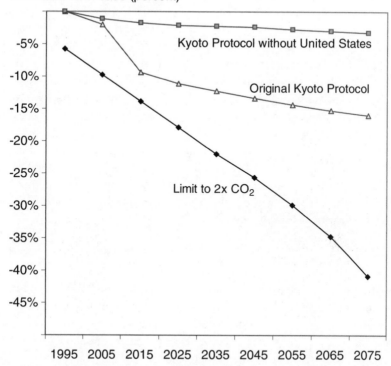

Difference from base (percent)

Source: The underlying model is described in Nordhaus and Boyer, *Warming the World*, chap. 8. Input data are revised to reflect changes in trends since 1999.

a. Numbers are for total global industrial CO_2 emissions and measure the percent reduction relative to a business-as-usual path of no emissions reductions (or zero carbon prices). "Original Kyoto Protocol" shows the impact of the protocol with U.S. participation. "Kyoto Protocol without U.S." shows the impact of the protocol without the United States. "Limit to $2xCO_2$," shows the emissions reductions that would minimize the costs of limiting CO_2 concentrations to double preindustrial concentrations (that is, to 550 parts per million). The estimates are for the decades centered on the listed year. Estimates do not include reductions in targets due to new provisions regarding sinks and other technicalities contained in the most recent version of the Kyoto Protocol.

Nations are beginning to consider the structure of climate change policies for the period after 2008–12. Some countries, states, cities, companies, and even universities are adopting their own climate change policies. Are there in fact alternatives to the scheme of tradable emissions permits embodied in the protocol? The fact is that alterative approaches have not received a serious hearing among natural scientists or among policymakers. What are some of the alternatives?[1]

For global public goods, there are three potential approaches: command-and-control regulation, quantity-oriented market approaches, and tax- or price-based regimes.[2] Of these, only the tradable-quantity and price-based regimes have any hope of being reasonably efficient.

Under a tradable-quantity approach, an agreement proceeds by setting limits on emissions by different countries. The limits are partially or wholly transferable among countries. This is the approach taken under the Kyoto Protocol. This approach has very limited international experience under existing protocols such as the chlorofluorocarbon mechanisms and somewhat broader experience under national trading regimes, such as the U.S. SO_2 (sulfur dioxide) regime.

A radically different approach is to use harmonized prices, fees, or taxes as a method of coordinating policies among countries. This approach has no international experience in the environmental area, although it has modest experience nationally in such areas as the U.S. tax on ozone-depleting chemicals. In contrast, the use of harmonized price-type measures has extensive international experience in fiscal and trade policies, such as harmonized taxes in the EU and harmonized tariffs in international trade.

Price-Type Approaches to Climate Change

Price-type approaches (or hybrids that combine price and quantity controls) have been discussed in a handful of papers in the economics literature, but much careful analysis remains to be done.[3] I highlight a few of the details here.

For concreteness, I discuss harmonized carbon taxes. Under harmonized carbon taxes, there are no international emissions limits; rather, countries agree to penalize carbon emissions domestically at an agreed-upon and harmonized "carbon tax." This is essentially a dynamic Pigovian pollution tax for a global public good (Pigovian taxes are designed to align the social costs and social benefits of pollution). The carbon tax is negotiated, but conceptually it is determined by weighing environmental and economic objectives. This might involve aiming to limit changes in greenhouse gas concentrations or global mean temperature below some level, or it might use some kind of cost-benefit approach. Unlike the quantitative approach under the Kyoto Protocol, there are no country emissions quotas, no emissions trading, and no base-period emissions levels. The efficient tax would be equalized across space and grow over time at approximately the "real carbon interest rate."

It would be critical to distribute the cost of emissions reductions fairly among nations. It would be reasonable to allow participation to depend on the level of economic development. For example, countries might be expected to participate fully when their incomes reach a given threshold (perhaps $10,000 per capita), and poor countries would receive transfers to encourage early participation. The issues of sanctions, the location of taxation, international trade treatment, and transfers to developing countries under harmonized carbon taxes are important details that are subject to discussion and refinement. If carbon prices are equalized across participating countries, there will be no need for tariffs or border tax adjustments among participants. While much work on the details would be required, this is familiar terrain because countries have been dealing with tariffs, subsidies, and differential tax treatment for many years. The issues are elementary compared to those of a quantity-based regime.

The literature on regulatory mechanisms entertains a much richer set of approaches than the polar quantity and price types that are examined here. Important combinations or hybrids include quantity controls with price caps and floors or harmonized taxes with quantity caps. This discussion focuses on the price-type mechanism because it is superior in so many respects.

Comparison of Price and Quantity Approaches

Policymakers, environmentalists, and economists are so accustomed to quantity constraints in environmental policy that the fundamental advantages of price-type approaches have been largely overlooked. The price-type approach is particularly advantageous for "stock global public goods" such as global warming. Some points are familiar to environmental economists, but others have particular force in an international regime.

The fundamental defect of the Kyoto Protocol lies in its objective of reducing emissions relative to a baseline of 1990 emissions for high-income countries. This policy lacks any connection to ultimate economic or environmental policy objectives. The approach of freezing emissions at a given historical level for a group of countries is not related to any identifiable goal for concentrations, temperature, costs, damages, or "dangerous interferences."[4] It is not inevitable that quantity-type arrangements are inefficient. The target might be set to ensure that the rise in global temperature does not exceed 2 or 3°C (centigrade) or to achieve some other well-defined and well-designed economic and environmental objectives. That would be a welcome alternative to the current structure.

A related issue concerns the baseline policy against which countries set their policies. Quantity limits are particularly troublesome in a world of growing economies, differential economic growth, and uncertain technological change. These problems have become evident under the Kyoto Protocol, which set its targets thirteen years before the control period and used baseline emissions from *twenty years* before the control period. Base-year emissions have become increasingly obsolete as the economic and political fortunes of different countries have changed. The 1990 base year penalizes efficient countries (such as Sweden) or rapidly growing countries (such as Korea and the United States). It also gives a premium to countries with slow growth or with historically high carbon-energy use (such as Britain, Russia, and Ukraine).

The baselines for future budget periods and for new participants are deep problems for the Kyoto Protocol. The natural baseline, were it feasible to calculate, is the zero-restraint level of emissions. That level is impossible to calculate or predict with accuracy. Problems would arise in the future as to how to adjust baselines for changing conditions and how to take into account the extent of past emissions reductions.

Under a price approach, the natural baseline is a zero-carbon-tax level of emissions, which is a straightforward calculation for old and new countries. Countries' efforts are then judged relative to that baseline. It is not necessary to construct a historical base year of emissions. Countries are not advantaged or disadvantaged by their past policies or the choice of arbitrary dates for the baseline. Moreover, there is no asymmetry between early joiners and late joiners.

One key difference between price and quantity instruments concerns the structure of the uncertainties, and uncertainty is clearly a central feature of climate change policy. As is well known, if the curvature of the benefit function is small relative to the curvature of the cost function, then price-type regulation is more efficient; the converse holds as well.

While this issue has received little attention in the design of climate change policies, the structure of the costs and damages in climate change gives a strong presumption to price-type approaches. The reason is that the benefits are related to the stock of greenhouse gases, while the costs are related to the flow of emissions. This implies that the marginal costs of emissions reductions are highly sensitive to the level of reductions, while the marginal benefits of emissions reductions are essentially invariant to the current level of emissions reductions. More generally, where the damages are caused by stock externalities (as is the case for climate change because damages are a complicated function of the stock of greenhouse gases), then the damage function is likely to be close to linear with respect to current emissions. Abatement costs, by contrast, are likely to be highly nonlinear as a function of emissions. This combination of relative nonlinearities means that emissions fees or taxes are likely to be much more efficient than quantitative standards or auctionable quotas when there is considerable uncertainty, as is clearly the case for climate change.

Closely related to the point about uncertainty is that quantity-type regulations are likely to show extremely volatile trading prices for carbon emissions. Carbon prices are likely to be extremely volatile because of the complete inelasticity of supply of permits in the quantity case along with the presumption of quite inelastic demand for permits in the short run.

Preliminary indications are that European trading prices for CO_2 are highly volatile, fluctuating in a band of $\pm$ 50 percent over the last year. More extensive evidence comes from the history of the U.S. sulfur-emissions trading program. SO_2 trading prices have varied from a low of $70 per ton in 1996 to $1,500 per ton in late 2005. SO_2 allowances had a monthly volatility of 10 percent and an

Figure 6-3. *Prices of Sulfur Emissions Permits, 1994–2005*

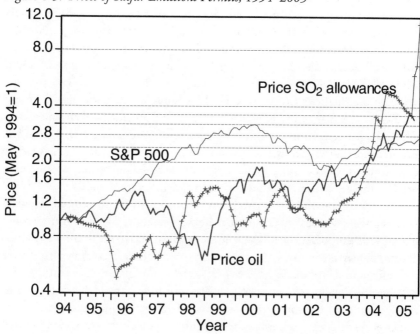

Source: Oil prices and consumer price index from Standard & Poor's DRI database. Price of SO_2 permits from Denny Ellerman, Environmental Protection Agency, and trade data.

annual volatility of 43 percent over the last decade. Figure 6-3 shows that sulfur prices are much more volatile than oil prices or stock market prices. This is analogous to a carbon-trading program because the supply is virtually fixed and the demand is inelastic because of the low substitutability of other inputs for sulfur in the short run. Both programs build in some banking features, which can, in principle, moderate price volatility.

Such rapid fluctuations would be extremely undesirable, particularly for an input (carbon) whose aggregate costs might be as great as those of petroleum in the coming decades. An analogous situation occurred in the United States during the "monetarist" period of 1979–82, when the Federal Reserve targeted quantities (monetary aggregates) rather than prices (interest rates). During that period, interest rates were extremely volatile. In part due to the increased volatility, the Fed changed back to a price-type approach after a short period of experimentation. This experience suggests that a regime of strict quantity limits might become extremely unpopular with market participants and economic policymakers, as price variability can cause significant changes in price levels and import and export values.

An important advantage of tax mechanisms is the strong fiscal policy preference for using revenue-raising measures rather than quantitative or regulatory
measures. When prices are raised and real incomes are reduced by regulations,
this increases the inefficiency (or "deadweight") losses from the overall tax system. This effect is the "double burden" of taxation (misnamed as the "double
dividend" from green taxes). If the carbon constraints are imposed through
taxes that are then rebated in taxes that have approximately the same marginal
deadweight loss as the carbon taxes, then the overall efficiency loss from taxation
will be unchanged. If, by contrast, the constraints under a quantity-based system are imposed by allocations that do not raise revenues, then the efficiency
losses from the price-raising elements should be added to the abatement costs.
Rough estimates indicate that the losses here are likely to be large.

While it is possible that emissions permits will be auctioned (thereby
retaining the revenues and removing the double burden of taxation), history
and current proposals suggest that most or all of the permits are likely to be
allocated at zero cost to "deserving" parties or will be distributed to reduce
political frictions. In the cases of SO_2 allowances and chlorofluorocarbon production allowances, *all* the permits were allocated to producers. The point
here is that using tax approaches rather than quantity approaches would promote a more efficient collection and recycling of the revenues from the carbon
constraints.

An additional question applies particularly to international environmental
agreements and concerns the administration of programs in a world where governments vary in terms of honesty, transparency, and effective administration.
One of the subtle and overlooked problems with quantity-type systems is that
they are much more susceptible to corruption than price-type regimes. An emissions trading system creates valuable tradable assets in the form of tradable emissions permits and allocates these to different countries. Limiting emissions
creates a scarcity where none previously existed—in essence, printing hard currency for those in control of the permits. Such wealth creation is potentially
dangerous because the country's leaders can use the value of the permits to pursue nonenvironmental goals rather than to reduce emissions. It would probably
become common practice for dictators and corrupt administrators to sell part of
their permits, pocket the proceeds, and enjoy wine, partners, and song along the
Riviera. Some analysts even believe that the presence of rents of this kind is
harmful to economic growth (the "resource curse").[5]

A few examples suffice to show the perils in the quantitative approach.
Simulations suggest that tens of billions of dollars of permits may be available
for export from Russia under the Kyoto Protocol. A Russian scientist recently
reported that people in Moscow were already considering how to profit from
"privatization" of the Russian carbon emissions permits. Alternatively, consider the case of Nigeria, which had emissions of around 90 million tons of

CO_2 in recent years. If Nigeria could sell its allowances for $20 per ton under the Clean Development Mechanism, this would raise around $2 billion each year of hard currency in a country whose non-oil exports in 2000 were around $600 million.

To prevent unacceptable diversions of funds, any broad-based emissions-trading plan would undoubtedly lead to a major monitoring system and might get bogged down in concerns about the diversion of funds to arms purchases, drugs, money laundering, and terrorism. It would be tempting to make participation and receipt of permits conditional on "good behavior" with respect to terrorism, human rights, environmental concerns, child and prison labor, and other worthy causes *du jour*. Reducing emissions permits would be a tempting target for sanctions for countries that violate international norms. Of course, the more burdensome are the "ethical" restrictions on the sale of permits, the less attractive participation becomes for countries. As the plan gets weighed down with ethical and process restrictions, it could easily founder.

A price approach gives less room for corruption because it does not create artificial scarcities, monopolies, or rents. No permits are transferred to countries or leaders of countries, so they cannot be sold abroad for wine or guns. Any revenues would need to be raised by taxation on domestic consumption of fuels. In fact, a carbon tax would add absolutely nothing to the instruments that countries have today. The only difference would be the international approval of carbon taxes, which probably adds little to their acceptability in corrupt or weakly governed countries. The dangers of quantity as compared to price approaches have been shown frequently when quotas are compared to tariffs in international trade interventions.

The coming years will undoubtedly witness intensive negotiations on global warming as concerns mount and the quantitative approach under the Kyoto Protocol is seen to make little difference. As policymakers search for more effective and efficient ways to slow the trends, they should consider the fact that harmonized environmental taxes on carbon are powerful tools for coordinating policies and slowing climate change.

Notes

1. There is a vast literature on the economics of climate change as well as on alternative institutional mechanisms. For a background paper with a more complete discussion and references, see the author's website at www.econ.yale.edu/~nordhaus/kyoto_long_2005.doc [May 2007].

2. This list is obviously drastically simplified. For a nuanced discussion of many alternatives, see Joseph Aldy, Scott Barrett, and Robert Stavins, "Thirteen Plus One: A Comparison of Global Climate Policy Architectures," *Climate Policy* 3, no. 4 (2003): 373–97, and the many references and proposals therein. These proposals include variants on the

two basic control mechanisms plus a portfolio of other policies such as enhanced research and development.

3. Some examples are Richard Cooper, "Toward a Real Treaty on Global Warming," *Foreign Affairs* 77, no. 2 (1998): 66–79; William A. Pizer, *Prices vs. Quantities Revisited: The Case of Climate Change,* Discussion Paper 98-02, revised (Resources for the Future, December 1998); David Victor, *The Collapse of the Kyoto Protocol and the Struggle to Slow Global Warming* (Princeton University Press, 2001). Also see the general comparison in Aldy, Barrett, and Stavins, "Thirteen Plus One."

4. The term is motivated by the UNFCCC, which states, "The ultimate objective of this convention . . . is to achieve . . . stabilization of greenhouse gas concentrations in the atmosphere at a level that would prevent dangerous anthropogenic interference with the climate system."

5. Ragnar Torvik, "Natural Resources, Rent Seeking, and Welfare," *Journal of Development Economics* 67, no. 2 (2002): 455–70.

7

The European Emissions Trading Regime and the Future of Kyoto

GERNOT KLEPPER AND SONJA PETERSON

When in the spring of 2005 the Kyoto Protocol finally entered into force, it established the first multilateral cap on emissions of greenhouse gases and coincided—more or less by accident due to a few delays—with the start of the European Emissions Trading Scheme (ETS) for carbon dioxide (CO_2), the first multinational scheme for trading emissions rights. Both are interrelated for many reasons. The ETS was established in the European Union (EU) in the hopes of providing an instrument for supporting efficient efforts to meet the Kyoto targets for the EU and the national burden-sharing requirements. It was constructed in such a way that it can be expanded beyond the borders of the European Union, and it has provisions to include the flexible mechanisms of the Kyoto Protocol—namely, the Clean Development Mechanism (CDM) and Joint Implementation (JI)—thus giving all nations access to the ETS.

It is evident that the Kyoto Protocol will not lead to a significant reduction in greenhouse gas emissions worldwide, but it did establish an institutional structure that has the potential to provide a forum for a stronger contribution of states to future emissions reduction efforts. The ETS demonstrates that international emissions trading on a large scale is politically and administratively feasible. Also the ETS is strongly interlinked with the flexible mechanisms of the

The authors would like to thank the participants at the conference for their comments and discussion, which we have tried to incorporate in this article.

Kyoto Protocol and its emissions caps. It thus seems worthwhile to look at the role that the ETS could play in the post-Kyoto era. In order to assess this role, the paper first describes the rules of the game of the ETS and its incentives for participating institutions—that is, firms as well as governments. Following that, it speculates about the impact of the changes that the ETS has brought to the global agenda for carbon management, in particular the attempts to integrate the non–Annex B countries into the Kyoto process.

A Short Primer on How the ETS Functions

The European Union has agreed to cap its greenhouse gas emissions at 8 percent below the levels of 1990. This overall cap is distributed among the original EU fifteen member states (EU15) in the so-called "burden sharing," such that country-specific caps range between a reduction of 21 percent relative to 1990 for Germany and Denmark and an increase of 27 percent for Portugal. The ten member countries that joined the European Union in May 2004 have their own individual Kyoto targets.

To achieve these objectives, the EU member states have implemented two types of policies. Except for energy-intensive installations, member states are responsible for their own emissions reduction policies, which they can design according to their national preferences. Energy-intensive installations, however, are subject to the ETS. The governments of the member states need to make three fundamental decisions. First, they must determine how much of the emissions reductions necessary to meet the Kyoto targets will be met within the country and how many emissions credits (JI and CDM) they plan to acquire through the flexible mechanisms of the Kyoto Protocol. Second, they need to determine the emissions targets for the energy-intensive installations. From this, the targets for the other sectors are then determined. Third, since the ETS predominantly grandfathers the emissions rights of the energy-intensive installations, these emissions rights need to be allocated to the roughly 12,000 installations. This is done independently by the national governments.

So far the ETS has been established for two trading periods. The first trading period encompasses 2005 to 2007, during which the trading system gets under way and the first constraints are placed on emissions with a view to achieving the 2012 targets. The second trading period encompasses 2008 to 2012, during which countries have to meet the emissions caps of the European Union's burden sharing. The linking directive of the European Union also establishes the possibility of converting CDM credits, the so-called CER (certified emissions reductions) and JI credits, and the so-called ERUs (emissions reduction units) into allowances within the ETS. The emissions allowances that are allocated to the installations participating in the ETS are defined in the national allocation plans (NAPs). The NAPs of the first trading period have been completed, and the EU Commission's suggestions for setting the NAPs for 2008 to 2012 were

Figure 7-1. *Current Climate Policy Plans of EU Member States for Reaching the Kyoto Targets under Different Schemes*[a]

Reductions relative to 2002

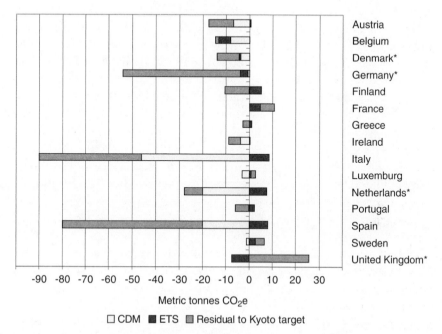

Metric tonnes CO_2e

□ CDM   ■ ETS   ▨ Residual to Kyoto target

Source: Gernot Klepper and Sonja Peterson, "Emissions Trading, CDM, JI, and More: The Climate Strategy of the EU," *Energy Journal* 27, no. 2 (2006).

a. Targets are for 2007, except for countries with an asterisk, which are for 2012.

published by the end of 2005.[1] CERs are valid in the first trading period, whereas ERUs can only be converted into ETS allowances in the second period. CERs can be banked, but not borrowed. This creates a special incentive to acquire CERs, since ETS allowances from the first trading period cannot be transferred to the second.

Figure 7-1 shows the current national plans for the EU15 countries with respect to the allocated emissions allowances in the ETS, the planned CERs to be acquired through the CDM project, as well as the difference that would exist if these targets were kept until 2012.[2] This difference will have to be met either through reductions outside the ETS sectors or through stricter ETS targets in the second trading period. The most important information in figure 7-1 is the indication that many governments have endowed the installations of the ETS with more emissions rights than actual 2002 emissions. This is most pronounced in Italy, the Netherlands, Finland, and France. The governments of some countries, such as Germany, have announced that they will not use CERs to meet the Kyoto targets, whereas others did not specify the CERs in their NAPs. In any case, energy-intensive installations can receive CERs through CDM projects without government involvement. Several countries are far from their Kyoto targets and will have difficulty meeting them by 2012. This problem is likely to be most serious for countries like Ireland, Denmark, Austria, Spain, and Italy, all of which need to reduce their emissions between 2002 and 2012 by more than 20 percent.

The ETS market has been growing over time, although—due to some administrative problems—even by the end of 2005, not all installations were yet able to trade. While annual trade in 2004 amounted to approximately 8 $MtCO_2$ (million tons of carbon dioxide), today around 1 $MtCO_2$ is traded per day. In 2005 prices varied around approximately €20 per ton of CO_2, which is substantially above all the previous estimates for this market.[3] A lack of understanding of the allowance market by companies, thin markets, uncertainty about the future of emissions trading, risk aversion, and price volatility, particularly regarding the volatility in the price of the low-carbon fuels, gas and oil, versus that of carbon-intensive coal, are mentioned as reasons for the high prices.

The Impact of the ETS for Meeting the Kyoto Targets in 2012

Whereas emissions trading is generally considered to be an efficient instrument for reducing emissions, this is not necessarily the case in a hybrid system like the ETS. The reason is quite simple. The ETS covers only about half of the greenhouse gas emissions of the member states of the European Union. Hence half of the emissions will need to be controlled by other instruments. Simulations of the NAPs and the other climate policy instruments based on the computable general equilibrium model of the Kiel Institute's DART show that the most serious problem is that national governments have endowed the ETS sectors with too many allowances, thus placing a high reduction load on the non-ETS sectors.[4] This is illustrated in figure 7-2, which calculates the implicit CO_2 taxes necessary for the non-ETS sectors to meet the Kyoto targets in 2012. This is a highly conservative estimate, since many instruments of climate policy will not be as efficient as an emissions tax and governments will rely on much more expensive abatement activities such as subsidies to biofuels, wind energy, or photovoltaics.

Figure 7-2 shows four scenarios that describe different climate policy options for the second trading period. In scenario NAPS1, the allocation of emissions rights for 2005 to 2007 is kept constant for 2008 to 2012; in scenario Gap, the distance to the Kyoto emissions cap is reduced within and outside the ETS according to the current share of emissions. Scenario Equ uses an allocation that equalizes abatement costs between the ETS and non-ETS sectors within a country. Finally, in scenario NoLim, emissions rights are allocated as in NAPS1, but governments can buy as many emissions rights through the flexible mechanisms of the Kyoto Protocol as they wish. In the other three scenarios, those same governments are constrained to purchase the amounts announced in the NAPs for the first trading period.

Figure 7-2. *Implicit CO$_2$ Taxes in the EU for Meeting the Kyoto Targets in 2012 under Different Scenarios*

2000 Euro per tonne CO$_2$

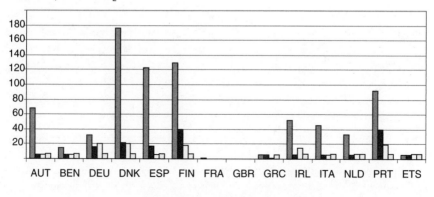

[NAPS1] [gap] [equ] [NoLim]

Source: Simulations of policy scenarios with the DART model.

The distortion becomes obvious when one compares the ETS price of about €8 per ton of carbon dioxide (on the far right of figure 7-2) with the implicit abatement costs in the non-ETS sectors, in which the energy-intensive industries receive the same endowments in the second commitment period as in the first one. Even under a scenario that reduces emissions proportionally (scenario Gap), some member states such as Finland, Portugal, and Spain still have substantial differences in abatement costs between the two sectors, whereas others get very close to an efficient distribution of emissions rights given the simple rule of allocating reductions proportional to current emissions. Even an equalization of national abatement costs would not equate ETS permit prices with the implicit taxes because of the impact of international trading. Only with an unrestricted use of the flexible mechanisms (scenario NoLim) can the non-ETS sectors achieve abatement costs comparable to the ETS prices.

Figure 7-3 reveals that the distortions imposed by the unequal treatment of emissions lead to sizable negative welfare effects for some countries, whereas in all scenarios except NAPS1, they remain far below 1 percent. Although the scenarios requiring a lower endowment for the ETS sectors produce small welfare effects on an economywide basis, a look at the sectoral effects reveals the difficulties in meeting such a target. Figure 7-4 shows the reductions necessary in the different scenarios. Several countries would have to reduce the allocation of emissions rights by about 30 percent, which, although economically feasible, would require substantial investment in new facilities with lower carbon intensities and be politically difficult, if not impossible.

Figure 7-3. *Welfare Effects of Alternative Permit Allocations in the ETS for 2012 under Different Scenarios*

Percent

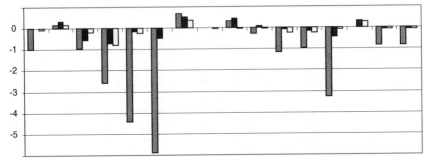

AUT BEN DEU DNK ESP FIN FRA GBR GRC IRL ITA NLD PRT SWE EU25 EU15

□ [NAPS1] ■ [equ] □ [NoLim]

Source: Simulations of policy scenarios with the DART model.

The first NAPs that have endowed the energy-intensive installations in many member states of the EU with a generous amount of allowances are apparently difficult to reverse in the second trading period. A continuation of the current NAPs would require high emissions reductions in the non-ETS sectors with high costs as indicated by high implicit taxes. A more efficient distribution of reduction activities between the ETS sectors and the rest of the economies

Figure 7-4. *Adjustments in the NAPs for the Second Trading Period under Different Scenarios*

Difference in percent

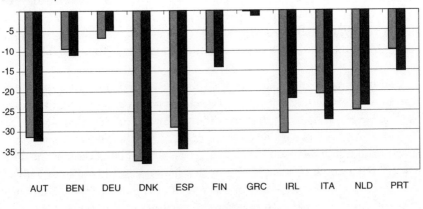

AUT   BEN   DEU   DNK   ESP   FIN   GRC   IRL   ITA   NLD   PRT

■ [gap] ■ [equ] □ [NoLim]

Source: Simulations of policy scenarios with the DART model.

Figure 7-5. *The Potential Market for CDM and JI Credits*

Metric tonnes CO_2

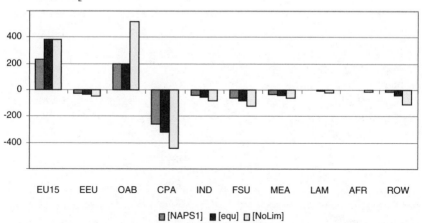

Source: Simulations of policy scenarios with the DART model.

would expose the ETS sectors to substantial reduction efforts compared to the previous endowment of allowances. Since both options are unlikely to be feasible politically, the role of the flexible mechanisms—that is, the CDM and JI projects—becomes even more important. The scenario NoLim in figure 7-5 indicates that the flexible mechanisms can resolve such problems, since no adjustment would be necessary at all.

The Role of the Flexible Mechanisms

In its linking directive, the EU has established a system by which the Kyoto targets can be met through project-based credits both inside and outside the ETS. Whereas firms in the ETS can acquire as many project credits as they wish and convert them into allowances, governments can use the flexible mechanisms to meet their Kyoto targets in 2012.

The global market for carbon credits from project-based mechanisms has been growing steadily in recent years. The latest World Bank report on the carbon market shows that, since 1996, sales have almost tripled from around 40 $MtCO_2e$ ($MtCO_2$-equivalent) to around 110 $MtCO_2e$ in 2004.[5] A study for the World Bank summarizes information on the market for CDM and JI credits.[6] Mainly based on modeling studies, the average annual demand from 2008 to 2012 for Kyoto units, excluding Australia and the United States, lies in the range of 600 to 1,150 $MtCO_2e$. This includes assigned amount unit (AAU) transfers as well as credits from CDM and JI. AAUs are the total amount of greenhouse gases that each Annex B country is allowed to emit during the first commitment period of the Kyoto Protocol. It also cites other studies that predict demand for CDM and JI credits from industry overall of 200 ± 100 MtCO$_2$e and demand from the European ETS of 110 ± 65 MtCO$_2$e. Yet only very few CDM projects have been approved, and large uncertainties surround the supply of CERs.

Concerning the demand for CDM and JI credits, announced plans for government purchases amount to 125 MtCO$_2$e per year in the EU25, 50 MtCO$_2$e (including AAUs) in Canada, 95 MtCO$_2$e in Japan, and 5–18 MtCO$_2$e in the European Free Trade Association (EFTA) countries.[7] But these numbers may rise substantially if the pressure for meeting the reduction requirements of the Kyoto Protocol rises and if the possibility of buying "hot air" at low prices offers an inexpensive way to fulfill the international commitments.

The project-based mechanisms will play an important role in the ETS and in the other climate policies of the EU and its member states. First of all, emissions reductions abroad are expected to be less costly than reductions within the EU. Second, the use of CERs and ERUs will help to reduce the inefficiencies of the current hybrid system, which combines emissions trading within the ETS with policies in the non-ETS sectors that are separated from the trading activities. In conjunction with the grandfathering of emissions rights in the ETS, energy-intensive industries have been generously endowed with allowances, thus placing a heavy burden on all other sources of emissions. In the case of unrestricted use, the project-based mechanisms act as a catalyst that connects the different policy instruments and provides a mechanism for equalizing abatement costs between ETS and non-ETS sectors. Finally, these mechanisms connect the allowance prices of the ETS to the international prices for CERs and ERUs.

Simulations with the DART model illustrate how the different scenarios influence the market for project-based emissions reductions. In the scenarios NAPS1 and Equ, the governmental demand for CDM and JI credits is limited to the announced expected purchases, whereas firms in the ETS can buy as many credits as they wish.[8] In scenario NoLim, governments from all countries can freely buy allowances, as can companies in the ETS sectors. In this case, there is an equalization of the prices for ETS allowances: CERS, ERUs, and the implicit tax in the non-ETS sectors. The simulations show the strong increase in demand by the ETS sectors when they are exposed to the tighter target of scenario Equ. The model also predicts that most of the supplies will come from China, which has the lowest abatement costs and a quantitatively large reduction potential. Currently such activities are only starting, but the Chinese authorities seem to be more inclined to use the flexible mechanisms than they have in the past.

The scenario NoLim relaxes all restrictions on trading project credits.[9] In 2012 it will result in a permit price of close to €7 per ton of CO$_2$. The European Union without the new member states (the EU15) will then buy close to

400 Mt of credits, whereas the other Annex B (OAB) countries will increase their purchases far beyond the restricted amounts that are imposed in the other scenarios. Overall, the flexible mechanisms will transfer yearly funds of roughly €6 billion per year to the developing countries.

Regardless of which policy solution with respect to the NAPs and the role of the flexible mechanisms eventually will materialize, these mechanisms clearly will play an important role in the strategies of those Annex B countries that make a serious effort to meet their Kyoto targets.

The Role of the ETS in the Post-Kyoto Process

The discussion about the options for international climate policy after 2012, the so-called post-Kyoto process, is strongly influenced by the negative experiences of the Kyoto process to date. The cap-and-trade approach has not been accepted by important countries like the United States. The reduction requirements for the Annex B countries are so weak that they cannot be used as an example for future negotiations if the objectives of Article 2 of the United Nations Framework Convention on Climate Change (UNFCCC)—namely, the avoidance of dangerous climate change—are to be met in the twenty-first century. The developing world is hardly included in the reduction efforts, although some countries like China and India are already large emitters of greenhouse gases and are doing so at an increasing rate. China will surpass the CO_2 emissions of the United States in the next few decades.

Since all these critical points constitute important obstacles to an effective climate policy, new approaches are being discussed that dispense with the idea of emissions caps and propose either setting intensity targets or reducing emissions directly through technology transfer and aid. For example, in chapter 6 of this volume, William Nordhaus proposes the introduction of a global CO_2 tax instead of using caps as quantitative targets. All of these proposals and discussions seem to move away from the idea of a market for emissions rights, which has been proposed by economists for many years. Although most of those who have argued in favor of permit trading will most likely still see the theoretical advantage, they will question the practicability of such an instrument.

The critical arguments against the Kyoto Protocol seem to focus too much on the problems and too little on the achievements of the UNFCCC process. In a short time, relative to international treaty standards, an agreement has been reached on the objectives of climate policy, and some first, although insufficient, steps have been introduced regarding emissions reductions. But most important, the Kyoto Protocol has resulted in an elaborate institutional structure, and the international institutions governing certification of the projects for the flexible mechanisms of the Kyoto Protocol are in place and have started working. Concerning the practicability of permit trading, the start of the European Emissions

Trading Scheme has shown that international emissions trading on a large scale is feasible, both politically and administratively. Even though the current hybrid system, which covers only part of the European greenhouse gas emissions, has both drawbacks and practical problems to be solved, the ETS is a success story. It demonstrates that emissions restrictions can be implemented at reasonable cost for society and industry. Extensions of the ETS—for example, not only to other sectors that are being discussed within the European Union but also to non-EU countries, like Norway and Switzerland, that are considering joining the system and its different trading mechanisms—are in the process of becoming linked. The inefficient allocation of emissions rights is due mainly to the grandfathering of these rights, a situation that the EU Commission is likely to attempt to resolve in the next trading periods.

Some experiences may have contributed to the success. One is that industry, including some of the international oil companies, has understood that there is no alternative to a mechanism that both limits emissions and simultaneously provides incentives for developing alternative energy sources and incentives for the efficient use of energy. These are all provided in a cap-and-trade scheme like the ETS. Another reason is the apparent willingness of developing countries to engage in CDM projects, thus constituting a first step toward integrating these countries with climate policy initiatives.

The institutional structure of the ETS, the markets that have developed around it, and the acceptance of carbon as a new tradable commodity within world business together constitute assets that should have high value in the design of the post-Kyoto process. It is likely that, by 2012, the carbon markets will have become more widespread than today and will be a standard tool in commercial decisions about carbon-emitting activities not only in Europe, but most likely in the developing world as well. Such markets can provide the basis for an agreement to continue with the flexible mechanisms. These activities need to be based on a continuation of caps for industrial countries, which could be accompanied by safety valves, because otherwise carbon cannot be a scarce commodity.

Developing countries will not accept, and in fact will not need, a binding cap in the beginning, if the criterion of the flexible mechanisms works sufficiently well. Already the fact that emissions reduction has a positive price attached will guide the economic agents in developing countries toward a more efficient use of fossil energy. Eventually, the developing countries will need to graduate and join the industrial world with binding caps. However, this process could build a contraction and convergence path that encompasses intensity targets instead of absolute caps. In this process, the project-based mechanisms involving substantial transaction costs could be reduced gradually.

The post-Kyoto process will be difficult to implement if the existing policies and institutions are dismantled simply because they have not resulted in efficient outcomes so far. Not only is there the danger that another well-intended design may turn out to be less efficient and effective than expected, but the negative judgment of the current Kyoto process is based mainly on current outcomes instead of the process as initiated so far. It is entirely possible that a new design without cap-and-trade features for post-Kyoto will emerge in the next few years and, at the same time, that the Kyoto process itself will be more successful in 2012 than expected. Overall, there is no reason to be overly pessimistic about the future of a carbon market. Businesses seem more and more willing to accept this restriction. It is the role of national governments to provide the legal background for such markets and to secure widespread participation in them according to the differentiated responsibilities as they are set forth in the UNFCCC.

Notes

1. Further guidance on allocation plans for the 2008–12 trading period of the EU emission trading scheme is available from the EU Commission, Brussels.
2. The emissions in all new member states except Slovenia are below their Kyoto targets.
3. For further information on traded volumes, prices, and other ETS news, see, for example, www.pointcarbon.com.
4. DART stands for dynamic applied regional trade model. For a short description, see Gernot Klepper and Sonja Peterson, "The EU Emissions Trading Scheme: Allowance Prices, Trade Flows, and Competitiveness Effects," *European Environment* 14, no. 4 (2004): 201–18, and Gernot Klepper and Sonja Peterson, "Emissions Trading, CDM, JI, and More: The Climate Strategy of the EU," *Energy Journal* 27, no. 2 (2006): 1–26.
5. Franck Lecocq, *State and Trends of the Market 2005* (Washington: International Emission Trading Association, 2005).
6. Erick Haites, "Estimating the Market Potential for the Clean Development Mechanism: Review of Models and Lessons Learned," PCFplus Report 19 (Washington: Word Bank Carbon Finance Business PCFplus Program, International Energy Agency, and International Emissions Trading Association, 2004).
7. For the EU25 figure, see Klepper and Peterson, "Emissions Trading, CDM, JI, and More: The Climate Strategy of the EU."
8. The purchases of the other annex B countries are restricted to 200 $MtCO_2$ since these markets are not modeled explicitly.
9. Hot air is not included in the simulations. An unrestricted supply of hot air would lower the permit prices toward almost zero, which would not be in the interest of the countries with hot air such as Russia and the Ukraine.

PART FOUR

Alternative Climate Policy Options

8

Climate Change: Designing an Effective Response

THOMAS HELLER

The future of the Kyoto Protocol is, at very best, problematic. The most realistic appraisal of negotiations that might extend and deepen a climate change regime built upon the architecture of the protocol is that they will meet a dead end. Put more diplomatically, there remains little chance that a regime so structured can be a credible foundation for sustained and effective movement toward the defined objective of the United Nations Framework Convention on Climate Change (UNFCCC), namely, "stabilization of greenhouse gas concentrations in the atmosphere at a level that would prevent dangerous anthropogenic interference with the climate system."[1]

At first glance, after the Eleventh Conference of the Parties (COP-11) to the UNFCCC in December 2005, such a conclusion will be seen by many as overly bleak or at any rate premature. After all, the nations party to the Kyoto Protocol decided in Montreal that there would be a second period of commitments after the 2012 expiration of the current arrangements and that they would negotiate the shape and scale of those commitments in the coming several years. And the still wider group of nations party to the UNFCCC itself was able to agree that a dialogue about how to go forward toward the ultimate goal of stabilization of greenhouse gas (GHG) concentrations would also be initiated. The problem with the second-period negotiation decision is that it is explicitly limited to those nations established as part of Annex I under the UNFCCC, nations that already agreed to first-period mitigation commitments. The negotiation therefore explicitly excludes participation by emerging market, developing countries—with their rapidly rising total emissions—and it has been rejected by the United States, historically the world's leading GHG emitter. The accord to initiate a more comprehensive dialogue was achieved only when the original proposed text was amended to delink, or segregate, the agreed consultations from the UNFCCC process itself. As is the custom in diplomatic circles, delegates and observers left Montreal spinning themselves into a mood of optimism and self-congratulation about what they had pulled from the embers of the negotiations. After COP-11 it is more incumbent than ever upon those who regard climate change as a serious threat to environmental and social stability to think beyond the Kyoto architecture.

To think beyond Kyoto implies both a reanalysis of why this first effort is failing and a reconception of what other regime or regimes might replace it. To that end, I divide this short essay into four parts. The first part focuses on the careful thought and process that resulted in the Kyoto architecture. I stress in particular that the problems experienced in the Kyoto process are neither the product of scientific uncertainties nor the consequence of a failure to think through and apply well-grounded orthodox forms of policy analysis. To the contrary, the real debates about climate science that currently demand research and resolution are largely confined to margins far removed from the low-level institutional steps being taken to found a multilateral climate regime. Nor has there ever previously been in any field of international policy a response to environmental risks so thorough and so crafted around an informed frame of theory.

In the second part I briefly describe the somewhat ironic outcomes of this idealized policy design process, with emphasis on why the Kyoto principles as now conceived cannot be incrementally extended to solve the far deeper and more inclusive reductions in GHG emissions needed to move toward stabilized atmospheric concentrations. In the third part I focus on reasons, drawn from political economy, organizational sociology, and international relations that suggest why the Kyoto architecture so quickly reached its limits and cannot serve the more ambitious needs of climate policy. In the fourth and final part I simply sketch the constitutive elements of an alternative approach to climate change that does not discard what Kyoto has accomplished but rather tries to address the asserted criticisms of the current architecture in order to reimagine a more effective set of responses to the several discrete issues that underlie the activities that have put the global environment under stress.

Architectural Elegance

The architectures of the UNFCCC and the Kyoto Protocol can be understood as evidence of the dominance of neoclassical economics at the close of the twentieth century. In spite of the strong tradition of moral absolutism that has long colored ecological thought and the associated critiques that penetrated at the margins of theory in evolutionary economics, the powerful influence of orthodoxy upon regime design was fully consistent with the tenor of the times. The years after 1990 were characterized by widespread adherence to the Washington consensus, which ratified the ideological triumph of markets in both the developed and developing worlds.

Among domestic economies, deregulation and privatization were the general order of the day. In the energy sectors, national oil companies were to be dismantled and monopolistic state utilities exposed to competition.[2] Environmental externalities were to be incorporated into price, whether by taxes, as in the European Union (EU), or by tradable permits, as in the U.S. Clean Air Act Amendments of 1990. At the international level, the same remedies and instruments were prescribed for transborder pollution problems, best illustrated by the successful negotiation of the Montreal Protocol in 1987 and by its coterie of subsequent agreements (London, Amsterdam, Copenhagen) reinforcing it throughout the decade. Whatever the later problems of the international climate change regime, it is foolish to attribute them to environmentalists riding roughshod over the prevailing consensus that law and normative economics are an integrated policy discipline.

Five elements of the Kyoto Protocol reflect its organization around economic orthodoxy. (A sixth element, differentiated responsibility, represented what was assumed to be a temporary accommodation to political realities.)

First, a stable climate is a global collective good. Because of pervasive and rapid atmospheric mixing, the introduction or removal of GHGs from the atmosphere has relatively the same impact on climate no matter where in the world emissions or sequestration takes place. A global collective good demands that inclusive institutions prevent leakage or free riding, and all nations, regardless of their interest in or opposition to emissions mitigation, were invited to join as equal members of the new multilateral order.

Second, the level of GHG concentrations aimed for by global controls is to be determined through cost-benefit analysis. The comprehensive summaries of the details of the outpouring of complex (and competing) modeling exercises to locate optimal outcomes can be found in reports by the Intergovernmental Panel on Climate Change (IPCC): these provide continuing testimony to the seriousness and competence with which this work has proceeded.[3]

Third, these optimization exercises would go forward under conditions of substantial, if diminishing, scientific and political uncertainty. The UNFCCC thereby incorporated both a broad principled statement of the regime's long-term objective and a largely aspirational and procedural initial framework treaty to provide an umbrella under which later protocols would be implemented. This was to accommodate learning into the definition of the UNFCCC's specific goals and the instruments through which best to reach them.

The fourth element, cap-and-trade mechanisms, and the fifth element, compliance mechanisms, were instituted as it became apparent after 1995 that global GHG emissions were rising faster than the original UNFCCC agreements had foreseen: the design of the Kyoto Protocol to impose mandatory regulations simply expanded the standard economic prescription for regime design. Although many economists would have preferred a first-best reliance on taxes (due to relatively large uncertainties about compliance costs and their effects on growth), a widespread political antipathy to additional taxes in many advanced industrial nations led planners to focus on tradable property rights as the fundamental instrument for emissions control. A total quantity of property rights or permits, which added up to the optimal emissions volume, or cap, in any given period, would be distributed among nations signatory to the inclusive treaty. These permits would then be tradable in financial markets, which would establish a single global price and provide incentives for those with the lowest possible costs of mitigation (or added sequestration) to undertake these measures first. Efficient global markets would require that noncompliance with the permit regime be punished by an international authority with hard legal powers, similar to those of nation-states.

Although Kyoto left the details of the cap-and-trade system and the compliance clause to be worked out between 1997 and 2000 through further negotiations, the greater economic concession to realpolitik came in the recognition that it would be impossible to conclude a uniform universal regime from the outset. Developing countries had, since the First Conference of the Parties to the UNFCCC in Berlin in 1995, made it unambiguously clear that they would not entertain discussion of mandatory caps (targets) that might constrain their economic growth. Attempts even to consider some process of graduation—the commitment to binding emissions targets by developing countries at some future point as their per capita incomes grew—were defeated at Kyoto (with citations to the need for industrial countries to demonstrate good faith by exclusive early actions and to the international law principle of differentiated responsibility for global collective goods).

Although the Kyoto Protocol therefore had no legal mitigation commitments for most of the nations that ratified it, a conceptually tricky surrogate trading instrument, the Clean Development Mechanism (CDM), was created to drive positive incentives for the exploitation of low-cost mitigation measures in developing nations. The mechanism would serve to capture some of the benefits of a comprehensive global market until the economic ideal of universal accession to full participation could be managed.

My argument, that the problems that now beset the multilateral climate change regime should not be attributed to ignoring good economic theory, should not obscure the residual difficulties of analyses implied by the UNFCCC architecture. A list of the problems associated with implementing the principles of design is quite easy to compile.[4] The considerable uncertainty about the cost functions of climate mitigation has contributed greatly to withdrawal from the Kyoto Protocol by key emitters like the United States and Australia. Controversy about valuing the marginal benefits of damages avoided, both from higher and lower probability climate risks, causes most measures to aim at least-cost solutions to politically specified targets rather than at true optimization. Negotiating parties have highly asymmetrical information about the supply and demand curves for climate mitigation of other nations, and that has forestalled bargaining solutions. There has never been a serious debate over the equity principles that would have to be agreed upon in order to define the initial allocation of property rights (and thereby income transfers) between rich and poor nations. Proposals that range from grandfathering existing emitters (most national cap-and-trade schemes) to per capita distributions based on wholly universal (cosmopolitan) and ahistorical (consequentialist) human rights claims present obstacles to practical discussion.

However, in the major part of this chapter I want to focus more upon a different type of disagreement with the UNFCCC-Kyoto architecture than the gap between theory and implementation. My concern is that the regime structure does not take into account what has been learned about political economy, organization theory, and international relations in the second half of the last century. Consequently, I focus less on implementing measures than on the political-economic point that international regimes have not been characteristically able to marshal such legal authority. I am less worried whether a smooth, single (carbon) price signal can be established across global markets than about whether it is politically possible to imagine a price signal high enough to provide the needed incentives for the diffusion and innovation of climate-favoring technologies. In other words, I suspect the problem is less analytical capacity to design an institutional architecture consistent with good economic principles than attention to the real prospects for implementing that design in time to deal with the pace of climate risks.

Kyoto Lite?

My argument about the future of the effort to mitigate climate risks centers on two key contentions: that the UNFCCC process will remain stuck in an unhappy deadlock during the negotiations of Kyoto's second period (2012–20) and that the Kyoto architecture must be reconceived with new attention to the political and organizational factors that describe how decisions that affect GHG emissions will be made in practice. To provide some bridge between them, I propose a schematic account of the journey that the multilateral climate regime traveled between the design of the Kyoto Protocol in 1997 and the opening of the second-period negotiations in Montreal in 2005. The outcomes of these debates over the implementing rules for the protocol have been caricatured as

Kyoto Lite, and an annotated guide to the literature might advise a reading with a strong dose of skepticism.

In one sense, only the easy parts of climate mitigation were confronted during these years. As noted herein, the harshly conflicting North-South claims about the equity of rights allocations (emission targets) were taken off the table by the Kyoto decision to postpone indefinitely the discussion of emerging markets' graduation. What was left in play was only the division of commitments among the Organization for Economic Cooperation and Development (OECD) economies, a group seemingly far less disparate in interests and outlooks than the general UNFCCC membership. Yet strong differences over the potential costs of compliance with national caps were immediately apparent, especially between the United States and the European Union. The EU argued that the pool of opportunities to reduce emissions and increase efficiency with the domestic economies of the richer nations was wide and deep. The United States did not deny this possibility but was uncertain about its scope and fearful of the consequences for growth of overestimation. The reasons the EU and U.S. models and cultures diverged on these matters are complex and interesting; the relevant concern for present purposes, however, is that each party constructed a negotiating strategy that reflected its perspectives on compliance costs.

The EU stressed the need for mitigation actions taken in the home country and sought agreement on policies and measures to stimulate the exploitation of the suggested pool of low-cost internal options. The United States, on the other hand, concentrated on flexibility measures that promised to hold down overall compliance costs should efficiency-enhancing emissions reductions run out quickly. These mechanisms included an aggressive interpretation of carbon sequestration in land use (Kyoto Protocol, article 3.4), extensive use of international trading mechanisms (Kyoto Protocol, articles 6, 12, and 17). More informally, to rescue the contested negotiations, the United States floated the idea of a price cap (escape clause) that allowed parties to issue all needed permits for a fixed ceiling price to ensure a maximum compliance cost. These expansive American proposals triggered a vigorous European response, supported by the bloc of developing countries, arguing to limit (make supplemental) the use of any and all of these flexibility mechanisms to a small and determined percentage of a party's mitigation actions.

EU analysts challenged several of the mechanisms, especially the CDM, claiming that it was environmentally incredible, unadministrable, and economically inefficient because it would undercut appropriate long-term price incentives to innovate. Despite the best efforts of negotiators from both sides of the Atlantic debate at The Hague in late 2000, the disagreements proved intractable, and the new U.S. administration withdrew from the Kyoto Protocol in March 2001.

The irony of the post-Hague, post–U.S. exit from the Kyoto Protocol is that much of what was agreed thereafter (Kyoto Lite) was closer to the discarded

American position than to the arguments of the parties that remained in the game. First, at the 2001 Conferences of the Parties at Bonn and Marrakech, in order to induce ratification by Japan, Canada, and Russia, the varieties of sequestration measures that would satisfy national commitments were pushed beyond afforestation and reforestation in the direction of conservation and improved carbon storage in soils. These same measures were those for which the United States had been vilified at The Hague. Second, the protocol was enacted with no supplementarity constraints placed on any of the three trading flexibility mechanisms. In fact, given the subtraction of the U.S. demand for permits (allowed allocations) and CDM certificates and the lack of clarity about the approval processes that would fix their total supply, those parties assuming commitments could almost unilaterally impose an effective price cap by choosing whether they would meet their Kyoto commitments by means of national mitigation measures or through purchases of inflated volumes of low-cost permits or certificates. Finally, continuing discord resulted in very weak sanctions for noncompliance, imposing only a deferred 30 percent interest charge on unfulfilled commitments in subsequent compliance periods, a remedy that would induce parties with prospective compliance problems in any one period to negotiate for increased forward targets as a hedge.

The dynamic of easing the burden of the more ambitious Kyoto obligations that had been demanded by the EU before the Hague deadlock was especially evident at the 2005 Montreal meetings. Diplomats and analysts there celebrated the success of trading markets for compliance in both the European Union Emissions Trading Scheme (EU ETS) and the central value of the CDM for developing country certificate sellers and the compliance goals of developed country buyers. Lower cost (EUR 5–15 per tonne of CO_2) CDM certificates had been made fully substitutable for higher priced (EUR 18–30 per tonne of CO_2) EU ETS permits by the EU's internal directives and dedicated funds. Faster evaluation procedures and favorable approval policies were endorsed in Montreal to ensure an increasing supply of CDM projects.

It is particularly ironic that this outcome provides precisely the insurance against any adverse impacts of Kyoto commitments on growth and competition once proposed by the United States. Especially in relation to the propositions advanced about the importance of a comprehensive regime, one that would give effective price signals as incentives for innovation, the EU and other proponents of action to mitigate climate risks cannot, in good faith, be sanguine about the state of climate regime as second-period negotiations begin post-Montreal.

Why are the results of Kyoto Lite not solid ground from which to go forward? The United States and Australia stand firmly and completely outside the second-period negotiations. Most of the signatories to Kyoto, whether developing countries or states of the former Soviet Union, face no positive price for carbon dioxide emissions and are only sellers of tradable instruments. Developing nations have ruled out discussion of second-period mandatory targets, and it is questionable whether Russia and Ukraine would reassume commitments without the headroom or excess of targets over emissions they have enjoyed until now. Heavy oil-rich Canada has severe compliance problems and, together with Japan, can only look toward a burgeoning CDM market, if it is to meet its obligations. In effect, the only parties in the Kyoto system looking at serious carbon prices are the few EU member states that took on substantial internal EU targets. They are increasingly lauding the merits of a broad CDM market to reduce compliance costs below the level at which EU ETS permits are trading—in what remains a thin initial market.

I do not present this bleak picture of the current condition of the Kyoto system to criticize the value of a low-level price signal as an element of a global climate system. In fact I think such a signal is a needed component of a differently structured approach. First, I only stress that EU ETS market prices, at least so far, have been consistently higher than those predicted if cheap mitigation options for the advanced industrial nations had been available to justify the limitations on flexibility that confounded an agreement at The Hague, one that might have included the United States. The presence of the United States would have increased the demand for tradable permits, generating a carbon price signal high enough to induce climate-favoring investment choices. American participation would also have reduced political demands in other Annex I nations to preserve their competitiveness, by pressing trading market regulators to generate very cheap offsets. (It remains hypothetical whether the U.S. Senate, under any administration, would have ratified the Kyoto Protocol because of the unresolved and unapproachable North-South issues, but this is a separate matter and one that will continue to plague ongoing negotiations in any inclusive regime model.)

Second, I argue that the actual experience of producing a Kyoto regime that will deliver only a noninclusive, low-level price signal is a far cry from the ambitious architecture that undergirded the UNFCCC—a convention that claims it can accomplish in future negotiations what it has, to this point, not accomplished. It is, of course, possible to spin out claims that any start in the general direction of carbon signals is to be lauded and, on that basis, a continuing ratcheting up of the stringency and breadth of commitments toward the ideal architecture can be expected. I want to suggest in the remainder of this essay why I am skeptical that an exclusive commitment to this regime will set us on the path to mitigating climate risks—and which other directions, in addition to what Kyoto has engendered, we ought to consider.

Political Economy and Climate Change

Because of the careful and theoretically informed analysis that marks the design of the UNFCCC, the current and prospective torpid state of the regime calls for explanation. The Kyoto Protocol has only a minimal number of nations and parties committed to a positive price for carbon. There is good reason to doubt that these parties will be able to comply with their commitments, unless (or even if) the global supply of tradable instruments is inflated to depress the carbon price to an environmentally insignificant level. Most states that are party to the UNFCCC show little enthusiasm to extend or deepen commitments in the negotiation of the second-period obligations. And if we look beneath multilateral diplomatic activities to the behavior of major developing and developed nations' key energy, transport, or land use sectors that constitute the principal inputs to GHG emissions, we can observe continuing growth in new coal-based power production, rapid development of private automobile transit, and ongoing destruction of tropical forests.

I do not want in any way to deny counterindications such as expansion of temperate forests, or the introduction of hybrid automobiles, or the decline in downstream costs of liquid natural gas production, any of which hold the promise of declining emissions. But I do want to stress the disconnection that now exists between the policy decisions made by sectoral authorities in national governments and the collective need to confront climate risks more immediately. Around the world, climate politics remains largely isolated in relatively less-powerful national agencies, agencies often perceived by commercial and political actors as just one more problem in a tough lineup of financial and regulatory constraints on development and growth. Only by confronting and understanding why there is such a confused picture of action, relative to the clear theoretical vision of how to manage climate, may we be able to reverse the present stagnant course and create an alternative package of international mandates, incentives, and programs that better fits the political landscape that climate policy confronts.

This section outlines why such explanations—now standard learning in political economy, organizational sociology, and international relations—must supplement orthodox economics, which has dominated climate analyses so far. The subject of the impact of noneconomic factors, like those described by political economy and organizational sociology, on GHG emissions trajectories has not been wholly absent from climate analysis. In the IPCC's Special Report on Emissions Scenarios (SRES) and in subsequent modeling exercises based on similar methodologies it is explicit that alternative development paths with widely variant associated emissions could arise in four hypothetical futures that diverge along two political and social (lifestyle) axes.[5]

In one set of scenarios the degree of integration of the global economy is allowed to vary. In a second set the variation centers on how many policies and consumer choices are dictated by noncarbon sustainability concerns. There is no attempt to account for probabilities or causal relations that might lead to the enactment of any of these scenarios, although the analysis makes clear that the magnitude of the impacts of these political and social factors on emissions trajectories could be far larger than specific climate policies. Even in this limited sense, the SRES marks a sharp distinction from the usual treatment of noneconomic issues in climate work. The more usual notations of political and social influences are phrased in terms of normative mistakes and labeled *barriers*.

All standard climate discussions point to the widespread presence of subsidies, especially in the energy sector, that favor carbon-emitting production. All demand that external environmental costs, including climate risks, be internalized through some appropriate policy instrument. Some even insist that regulators be made independent of political direction. In other words, that subsidies persist, that pollution remains uncharged, and that regulators are not technocrats are problems consigned to noneconomists whose mission is barrier removal. The fundamental climate analysis remains wholly normative, while the positive politics or organizational behaviors that forestall the desired actions are marginalized. The problem is that politics, organizational conduct, and the barriers they constitute are not realistically erasable because they derive from perfectly expectable behaviors, which result from interests and conflicts that have always and everywhere characterized social action. To push these behaviors beyond the boundaries of optimization analyses, which remain exercises in theory because of the persistence of these barriers, cannot be a plan for effective action. Instead, policy design must account for, and explicitly counter, the strategic and self-interested reactions that individuals, organizations, and nations in climate-central domains pursue. They will not be wished away.

Both political economy and organizational sociology should be approached as amendments to, not as repudiations of, standard economic analyses. Much of political economy grows out of the application of principal-agent theory to political systems, emphasizing the problems of contracting and monitoring information that arise in controlling the behavior of self-interested actors and groups. Organizational sociology adds institutional twists to neoclassical accounts of economic rationality by focusing upon the dilemmas of dealing with unavoidable uncertainties and cognitive limitations in markets.

Political economy predicts that states and other political organizations are likely to be imperfect agents of their sovereign principal (the people). Without binding legal constraints or efficient incentives, legislatures, courts, and other public agencies are as likely to pursue the particular interests of individuals and groups, inside and outside of government, as to pursue more abstract objectives like social welfare optima.[6] In addition, because public laws and regulations are always incompletely specified and only partially enforced, they create opportunities for informed actors to profit from strategically gaming or thieving around their edges. Political economy emphasizes less normative analyses of what ideally constituted governments should do than it does the incentives that explain how governments actually perform, how private actors adapt to these public

policies, and why the ostensible goals of legislation and regulation do not correlate well with observable outcomes.[7]

Organizational sociology argues that public and private agencies are rational
adaptations to complex environments that often manage (more efficiently than
contracts do) technical and transactional problems through specialization.[8] As
such (public) organizations evolve routinized behaviors and distinct missions or
identities to resolve problems of information costs, they fragment the social field
and multiply the number of self-interested agents with specialized missions that
resist assimilation into any comprehensive notion of the social good. Applied
economics under these circumstances must expect that individual and organizational performance will systematically deviate from normatively specified goals
and that there is no solution to socially complex issues that will not generate
dynamic, strategic reactions that will destabilize the intended outcomes. Let me
describe four implications particularly salient for climate analysis that arise from
political-economic and organizational factors.

First, most major economic sectors that generate significant GHG emissions
are regulated industries. Political economy suggests that state agencies, including independent regulators, are as regularly the objects of theft, gaming, and
capture as they are capable and loyal agents of the public good. Because they
concentrate on how decisions actually are made in practice rather than on how
they ought to be made, the focus of political-economy accounts is often more
on the informal play of interests in the interstices of policy processes than on the
formal characteristics of institutions. Nevertheless, as I suggest below in discussing the application of international relations theory to regime design, the
choice of formal rules sets the stage on which these informal interests are played
out. For instance, the European Union began with a set of rules (*acquis commu-
nitaire*) agreed to by a small number of original member states and, subsequently, offered admission only to those willing, or compelled, to come in
largely on those given terms. Had the EU constitution been negotiated among
the thirty-one nations it presently comprises, it would have had a quite different
structure. Or since the Clean Development Mechanism and the Global Environmental Facility operate under different voting rules, international climate
programs carried out by the one produce different outcomes than programs carried out by the other. Precisely because assignments of formal competence over
decisions about how resources will be used shape and constrain policy agendas
and the policy options in play, it is critical that most key decisions about the
sectors that generate GHG emissions are not assigned to competitive markets
but rather to regulatory agencies, wherein informality, discretion, and political
dependence are the norm.

Energy, transport, and land use continue to be handled by public authorities
that act as filters through which market factors, like price signals, must be transmitted. Consider energy policy. After more than a decade of attempted reforms

in both developed and developing countries, there is almost nowhere a competitive market in primary fuels or electricity generation. Tariffs remain controlled and cross-subsidized, service is mandated, incumbent national fuels are privileged, and corporatized former state monopolies retain market and political power.[9] Regulatory agencies are known to have particular institutional cultures, to have been captured or to have their rules made by their regulatees, to suffer from technical incapacities, and to become the objects of appropriation by politicians who distribute the regulated services as patronage goods. Once regulation allocates resources, private organizations will invest more resources in lobbying, corruption, soliciting appointments, and other modes of influencing its judgments. The point is not to argue for or against regulation as a normative matter. Good arguments exist on both sides of that debate. Rather, political economy teaches that regulatory decisions, like all organizational processes, will always give selective priority to a subset of policy options that are politically and organizationally most salient. The resulting patterns of institutionally particular choices will regularly distort external policy signals, like climate instruments, in normatively unintended directions.

Second, political-economic accounts stress the pervasive effects of distributive considerations that often dominate the international and national deliberation of climate-related policies. Standard optimization analyses assume that compensation is either directly given to groups whose legitimate interests are harmed by policy change or that such groups receive other transfer payments to ensure distributional equity. Because there is almost never certainty about either direct or indirect compensation, politically influential individuals and organizations will prefer inferior policy solutions that maximize their income at the expense of the more general welfare. Just as national competition laws tend to favor inefficient local producers over foreign consumers, or as agricultural trade policies subsidize local farmers at the expense of almost everyone else, climate-relevant choices are made on the same basis. National fuels dominate national systems. The United States permits ethanol only from corn (or in the future, switchgrass) that grows at home. The EU ETS defines its biofuels to exclude fish wastes from Norway. Asserted competitiveness considerations leak distributional preferences into the rules by which emissions permits are allocated to firms and sectors.[10] As argued above, an inability to agree on the facts or principles of distributional equity, over time or going forward, calls into question the entire enterprise of global climate regimes based on an initial allocation of property rights. Again, the point is positive. Climate policy will not be enacted or stable if it does not plan for and around deviations from normative designs that distributional politics predictably imposes.

Third, expected behaviors that impede the implementation of optimal climate solutions stem from the nature of organizations generally. Sociologists argue that organizations are formed around specialized tasks that define their core functions and rely on a portfolio of structural incentives and sanctions, as well as on internal cultural norms, to ensure quality performance of these tasks. The norms create a core identity that evolves from technical and operational programs to reinforce or legitimize the sense of coherence that helps to bind employees (agents) to the organization's core mission. Intrusion by rival organizations upon this core identity constitutes a threat to organizational integrity and elicits responsive defenses.[11] In addition, all organizations attempt to control their environment by building up, around the peripheries of their core mission, an overlay of formal, often symbolic, committees or task forces or departments that link them to external, demanding organizations.[12] Theorists emphasize that organizational behavior is largely predictable by a commitment to the particular routines and norms put in place to reduce the costs of uncertainty and control (path dependence) and by a willingness to sacrifice peripheral activities whenever they interfere with the performance of core function.[13]

Applied to the political economy of climate change, organizational sociology suggests that climate constraints will be viewed by political agencies traditionally charged with energy or transport policy as intrusions upon their core missions. The historic core missions of nation-states—when viewed as mere organizations with exceptional legal capacities to impose monopolies—are autonomy (sovereignty), security, and economic growth.[14] These core missions are regularly transmitted to functional line ministries in sectors like energy and agriculture, which have built identity and power on that foundation. When new authorities like climate agencies arise, various formal measures will be taken (such as interagency task forces) that are likely to afford more symbolic than effective commitment to the proposed changed agenda. In practice, organizational priorities that impose lexical rankings on the world climate well below the established order of development, security, and local environment are most likely to resist real climate compliance as a constraint on traditional goals.

Climate concerns are at best one more task added to a roster of tasks by which the sectoral agency and its superior state powers measure its performance. In the absence of technical or economic shocks to the governance system strong enough to disrupt embedded institutional arrangements, it is predictable that the routinized decision processes of established agencies will go on undisturbed by climate concerns. Only when attention to these concerns advances the interests of groups recognized in these same processes will climate management become relevant. Alternatively, to construct a climate regime that excludes from the negotiating table or from direct influence on that regime those national agencies that govern the key emitting sectors is to consign climate to the organizational margins from the outset.

Fourth, and finally, organization theory cautions that change in organizational fields is less likely to occur through adaptation by existing organizations than through building new and better-fit entities.[15] Yet none of the major GHG emitting sectors—energy, transport, land use—has undergone technological shocks comparable to those in telecommunications or information processing, which would call forth important restructuring of the currently dominant public institutions or private organizations in these fields. The organizational resources with which climate is to be confronted, then, are not selected for the character of the problem. Given the inertial proclivities of organizations adapted to an existing social, economic, or technical field, a theory of social change must be grounded in exceptional circumstances.

Consider the question of how effective changes in the governance structures of nations occur in the absence of overwhelming external shock. Executives at the top of the nation are primarily preoccupied with maintaining core performance levels. They normally have a limited amount of capital they can employ in reorganizational initiatives that cut across established routines and jurisdictions. They allocate the scarce resource of centrally coordinated innovation, which defines the identity of their administration, conservatively to that set of activities that combines exceptional organizational salience and high probabilities of success. Environmental goals are not likely to rise to this level in a political body with short time horizons, pressing internal problems, and numerous blocking interests. Climate policy alone (unless ancillary to security, growth, or domestic reforms) will rarely be an attractor for political entrepreneurship at the necessary level. If change can be expected only when there is an empowered agent whose particular interests will be strongly advanced by its improved prospects in the new environment, the incentives for firms in competitive markets to bear the agency costs of organizing innovation more often lead to effective reforms than do exercises of political will.

Another corollary of the stickiness of established organizational landscapes is the perpetuation of existing organizational boundaries. Policies are designed for and implemented by organizations that divide up political maps into known territories, drawn without reference to climate concerns, but imported into climate regimes. Spillovers that can contravene intended effects must be anticipated or they will lead to adaptive responses by affected organizations—and possible gaming. For example, London has imposed congestion charges within its city limits in part to reduce automobile driving and pollution, including GHG emissions.[16] However, if the effect of the charges is to encourage businesses to leave the city and relocate in exurban malls and offices, as now threatens to be the case, the emerging land use patterns will produce effects opposite to those intended.

While these perverse results may emerge through wholly uncoordinated action, they can also be brought about through intentional gaming. Imagine that on Russia's western borders, firms developed coal-fired power plants with high-voltage direct transmission to EU nations with climate constraints. The sale of such electric power would game the EU's decision not to buy Russia's excess GHG permits. The export of power from Russia to the European Union would count all generation emissions only against the headroom in Russia's Kyoto commitment, allowing the European importer to pay a premium that reflects its avoided cost of buying additional permits through the EU ETS. There is every reason to expect such arrangements to be considered in a world heavily populated by lawyers, brokers, and corporate developers who make good livings by discovering and exploiting such opportunities.

The optimal solution to scale problems, as all economics students know, is to create policy jurisdictions equal to the scale of the spillover, a program to which the UNFCCC aspires. An alternative political-economic question is to focus on how to minimize gaming created by policy when that ideal is organizationally infeasible. It is not necessarily mistaken to consider that multiple, suboptimal, and more ad hoc strategies tailored to cut off incentives for perverse gaming could dominate an elegantly designed, proactive, general regime. Moreover, different institutional arrangements, whether the number of players in a game or the organizational attributes of decisionmaking institutions (such as direct regulation versus market signals), may have variable vulnerabilities or capacities to manage prospective gaming dynamics. (I return to the question of the possible implications of gaming and countergaming for institutional design strategies with respect to international trading regimes and CDM markets.)

To summarize my case that political economy and organizational sociology ought to be central elements of climate analysis, let me resort to maxims that call attention to the types of insights I suggest are absent from orthodox accounts. If these simple formulations make sense in the light of the preceding discussion, they should provide some epigrammatic foundation for the post-Kyoto proposals that follow.

—Organizations do what they do.

—Local resources will be used.

—Economists think about margins; organizations think in step functions.

—Policy ratifies technology, economic, and political shocks; it does not lead them.

—Development and security dominate climate.

—All regulation will be gamed.

International Relations and Climate Change

Viewed as an exercise in international regime building, the life of the UNFCCC and the Kyoto Protocol reflects logic more than experience. The theoretical vision encompasses three beliefs:

—Rational policy planning and institutional design can be smoothly extended from national to multilateral, even global, levels.

—Regimes should be inclusive to forestall free riding and to increase the potential for productive trading.

—Regime rules and sanctions can be enforced multilaterally, as in any national compliance system.[17]

However, the utopian nature of these propositions is sharply contrary to the recent history of effective international regime formation. Examination of these regimes suggests that none of the propositions on which the UNFCCC is based is empirically well grounded. Four lessons emerge.

The first lesson is that, although international treaties have proliferated during the past half century, regimes that have been able to implement cooperative solutions through mandatory rules usually have only a few members. The mean international environmental regime has fewer than seven members.[18] Effective minilateral regimes are generally marked by coincident economic and geophysical conditions among their members, uniformity in their analytical approach to the collective problem, and participation by national actors who are politically empowered in the sectors regulated by regime norms. Mandatory international regimes work best as minilateral coalitions for two reasons. One, the rules to which their parties commit are credible without the need to build special-purpose institutions to monitor compliance. And two, minilateral coalitions require behavior close to the members' noncooperative preferences. In the absence of deep technical, price, or physical shocks that rip apart the reigning institutional equilibria that govern national policies, commitment to mandatory international rules is usually more the ratification and coordination of behavior close to existing practices than an innovative restructuring.

It is quite possible that a low-level price signal in the maximum range of U.S.\$15–\$30 per ton CO_2 may well constitute such a potential noncooperative solution within a minilateral group of advanced industrial nations that lack the ability to commit to the signal as a separate matter in the maelstrom of multiple and conflicting Kyoto arena debates. Current initiatives in many American states, proposals with broad and bipartisan support in the U.S. Congress, and the voluntary commitments of numerous corporations around the developed world to carbon neutrality all indicate that a low-level price signal will become accepted practice without the need for an integrated transnational regime.[19] Conversely, it is often when such noncooperative equilibria become apparent that further coordination between these multiple systems becomes practical and that more formal multilateral arrangements emerge.

Where mandatory transnational regimes become effective at a larger scale, they are likely to follow one of two paths. One path follows the model of the World Trade Organization and the European Union. A limited core of nations with largely coincident interests forms a minilateral body that defines the basic structures and rules of the collective. Once the minilateral system is in place, nations on its periphery find their interests have been altered by the costs they suffer through exclusion such that they are compelled to join the club under the rules of accession the minilateral regime has established. The negotiations to accede are asymmetrical, with the basic governance structure of the existing club (the *acquis*) constituting more or less a take-it-or-leave-it offer. Consequently, the final shape of the evolved multilateral regime is not the same as that which would have been agreed to by the enlarged membership had they been members of the club from the outset, when the consensus rules that characterize most incipient international decision processes would have afforded all parties a veto power over key choices. However, even though only six parties (United States, EU, China, Russia, Japan, and India) emit 65 percent of global GHGs—a proportion that will only expand in the future due to high growth in China and India—the initial constitution of the UNFCCC as an inclusive multilateral system never seriously entertained regime evolution along this pathway.

Another path to developing broad participation regimes is divorced from the UNFCCC experience in that it builds on soft law, or nonmandatory accords. Voluntary agreements that induce members to shift behavior toward collective goals are most often carefully structured around reporting, aspirational but realistic targets, the diffusion of best practices through benchmarking, and positive incentives and aid for compliant action.[20] These regimes will frequently be less the province of diplomats than of technically adept representatives who are immersed in the industries or policy agencies whose practices are marked for improvement. Soft law arrangements are also more likely to eschew the search for comprehensive solutions and general principles and to focus on specific opportunities and deals that advance in the broad direction of regime objectives. In particular, they remove the temptation to use the process of multilateral regime formation as an inclusive forum in which to raise philosophical or historical claims related to the principled equities of new international legal orders. While various elements of the UNFCCC negotiations might be segregated and treated as either voluntary or minilateral bargains, their interplay with the paralyzed efforts to agree on mandatory, general, and credible regime rules and procedures casts too long a shadow over their evolution to allow serious advance along a more fragmented agenda.

The second lesson is that the economic instinct to create large numbers of regimes in order to foster productive trading among disparate treaty members works poorly in the context of international diplomacy. The persons around the table in climate negotiations do not represent the agencies and interests in a position to deal on the particular issues of energy, transport, agriculture, forestry, and other sectors that contribute significantly to GHG emissions. The theoretical potential for trading does not match the political capacity of the negotiators, who are left with only the possibility to create financial markets in emissions permits, which are proving difficult to police and easy to game. At the same time, the elusive benefits of inclusive regimes are more than offset by the disadvantages of multiparty games. Large negotiations are characterized by historically constituted blocs that variably and arbitrarily package politicized demands, with multiple veto players within and between blocs. Strategic behavior pursued in the context of highly asymmetrical information among parties creates misperceptions of costs and benefits that lead to incorrect solutions. Multiparty commitments heighten concerns about expectations over extended time periods. International experience suggests rather that trading will be more efficient when it grows after a regime *acquis* (agreed property rights) is well established and after effective regulatory agencies have been chartered that are capable of managing the credibility of the (financial) assets being transacted. Until such a time, small groups—able to prevent gaming around a limited and flexible set of approved deals with transaction-specific definitions of contract terms and close monitoring—can provide a better route to trading between parties with widely variant mitigation costs.

The third lesson from international relations theory is that there is a broad expanse between compliance and effectiveness in international regimes. Most nation members of international regimes take their obligations seriously and prize compliance with their commitments. Precisely because formal compliance with treaties with mandatory rules is highly valued, there is a strong tendency for initial negotiators to restrict their regime commitments to targets they are quite certain they can achieve. This attitude was critical to the reluctance of U.S. negotiators to accept the ambitious Kyoto target of 7 percent below 1990 emission levels. It resulted in the U.S. insistence on ambiguously defined language on compliance through land use (Kyoto Protocol, article 3.4) and the several flexibility mechanisms (Kyoto Protocol, articles 4, 6, 12, 17) that later caused a breakdown in the Kyoto implementation bargaining at The Hague in 2000.

Alternatively, where events subsequent to regime commitment make formal compliance less probable, it is predictable that the rules of the system will be loosely interpreted to increase the likelihood of compliance. Each of these two propositions that favor compliance diminish the credibility or effectiveness of the agreement in reaching its substantive objectives. Broad compliance with minimalist mandatory standards accomplishes little. Watering down the regime to ensure compliance only contributes to an illusion of accomplishment among the wider public, whose ability to track the details is limited. Especially because there will always be financial interests in gaming the rules of any legal order to minimize compliance costs, the coincidence of political formalism and economic profit counsels a careful skepticism about the productivity of inclusive multilateral regimes.

Returning to the appraisal of practice under the UNFCCC Kyoto Protocol, I argue that the design of viable international regimes must account for the predictable dynamics of compliance. In relation to the first period of implementing the Clean Development Mechanism, I discuss the proposition that an effective climate strategy should be grounded less in elegant exercises of economic optimization than in the countergaming of expectable behaviors that will yield symbolic compliance more than substantive gains. In many ways, the CDM has been transfigured from an embattled and marginal afterthought to a central totem in the implementation of the Kyoto Protocol. Introduced as a concept by American advocates (under the name *joint implementation*) in the early days of the climate regime, and made politically acceptable by its sponsorship by Brazil before Kyoto, the CDM provides an instrument to allow trading between developed countries, with higher mitigation costs and mandatory targets, and developing countries, with lower mitigation costs and no hard reduction commitments. Its environmental credibility centers on the idea of additionality, or the assurance that the increased emissions permitted in the developed countries that buy CDM credits as offsets will be balanced by real emissions reductions that would not have occurred in the absence of the transaction in the developing nation CDM seller.

Determining whether a CDM transaction induces a reduction in GHG emissions that qualifies as *additional* to reductions expected under business as usual requires a counterfactual narrative that certifies what would have been the emissions path (baseline) in the selling country against which the mitigation can be measured. In the period between the Conferences of the Parties to the UNFCCC at Kyoto (1997) and at The Hague (2000), EU negotiators and environmental advocates opposed the extensive use of the CDM, arguing that the difficulty, if not impossibility, of baseline certification would lead to the proliferation of CDM projects of problematic credibility. In other words, the system was prone to gaming, which would avoid the regulatory controls that the international regime would create and lead to the declining environmental effectiveness of the Kyoto Protocol. However, in the final Kyoto agreements in Marrakech (2001), the CDM emerged as a relatively unrestricted compliance mechanism even after the withdrawal of its American advocates.

The apotheosis of the CDM as a dual-purpose development and environment tool has emerged in the evolution of the European Union's Kyoto implementation process. The two principal elements of that process are, one, regulatory policies and measures that require emissions reductions, imposed largely by the EU government in Brussels; and two, the EU Emissions Trading Scheme, which mandates emission quotas for four key industries in the electricity, heavy industry, and pulp and paper sectors. After considerable debate, CDM credits were made fungible with EU ETS permits on a one-to-one basis.[21] However, in early, thin, trading markets, the price paths of the CDM and the EU ETS have been far apart, with EU ETS permits trading in the high EUR 20s and the CDM in the EUR 5–15 range. While the sharp discount between legally fungible assets reflects current uncertainty about the ultimate delivery and recognition of the emission mitigations promised by CDM projects, arbitrage between the two financial markets is predictable. The final more unified price of compliance in the EU ETS will depend on the relative supplies of contractually credible CDM certificates available during the 2008–12 compliance period.

In effect, this means that the European Union's compliance cost for Kyoto is a function of how large a supply of CDM offsets will be approved by the

UNFCCC chartered regulator, the CDM executive board. To the extent that EU industries and governments resist being saddled with climate costs not shared by their competitors in the United States and in the developing world, I would expect increasing pressures on the regulators to expand CDM supplies by interpreting the additionality constraint liberally to permit formal Kyoto compliance at decreasing costs. Given the complementary incentives of credit sellers in developing countries to earn money by gaming the system rules to produce a quick, cheap, and ample supply of certified CDM offsets, I would worry that (as its former European and environmental critics once feared) the evolving dynamics of the CDM will both assist with formal compliance and damage the environmental credibility of the Kyoto regime.

The success of CDM markets has been surprising to even its zealous sponsors. After a brief initial period in which the executive board turned down all project proposals, the following months saw an enormous volume of potential credits set up for approval. However, rather than being concentrated in the fuel-switching or renewable power areas, in which CDM advocates expected its principal benefits, the vast bulk of projects in the regulatory pipeline are in the reduction of industrial gases and methane capture from landfills and flaring. Because these gases have global warming impacts that may be thousands of times more powerful than carbon dioxide (CO_2), even small volumes of reductions in existing industrial facilities, mostly in China and India, can produce a vast supply of low-cost CDM credits to EU trading markets. In effect, high-cost mitigation of CO_2 produced in the energy and transport sectors in the EU is being substituted by low-cost mitigation of more exotic industrial gasses in Asia. Economists would rightly insist there is nothing wrong with this substitution as long as the regulator can manage the quality of the assets in the trading scheme. And this is precisely what the scheme was set up to do, as long as its rules are not being gamed. The harder question is whether, under pressure to produce income in the South and formal compliance in the North, they are credible assets, because the scheme is well designed to forestall its predictable gaming.

The early experience of CDM markets has exposed several reasons for concern that the CDM is creating incentives to set up transactions that earn money for offset sellers and multiply supplies of low-cost compliance assets for buyers with either low environmental credibility or impolitic effects. Consider the major classes of CDM projects in the executive board's certification pipeline, since these constitute the great majority of the assets that will be available for use in the 2008–12 compliance period. A vast array of credits is scheduled to come from hydrofluorocarbon-23 (HFC-23) mitigation actions linked to the production of that potent gas (global warming potential = 11,000 times CO_2) released as a by-product of manufacturing the widely used refrigerant hydrochlorofluorocarbon-22 (HCFC-22). Mitigation of HFC-23 in existing HCFC-22 plants in developing countries is measured against a baseline of past production that well exceeds the levels of HFC-23 emissions in optimized man-ufacturing in the first world.[22] Market incentives to reconfigure production to yield the maximum quantity of HCFC-22 and cut the by-production of HFC-23 are limited when the CDM offers a price for HFC-23 production that exceeds the sales price of HCFC-22.

In effect, the CDM can discourage the use of best-practice technology. In addition, to the extent that CDM earnings are not taxed by host governments, producers may choose to lower the price of HCFC-22 products to capture mar-kets that are now contested with first world manufacturers.[23] The CDM will increase the probabilities or the speed of industrial relocation in the chemical sector. Finally, since the incremental cost of mitigating HFC-23 is well below even the current low trading price of CDM credits, the mechanism is an ineffi-cient mode of reducing HFC-23 emissions. Targeted programs that pay pro-ducers no more than an amount close to the actual costs of these reductions, rather than a price related to the higher costs of reducing CO_2 or less exotic pol-lutants, would expand the resource pool available to deal with climate problems more generally.

At present, the executive board has restricted HFC-23 reductions to past pro-duction levels. No new plants or expanded production for HCFC-22 in existing plants have been certified to generate CDM offsets. At Montreal the parties to the Kyoto Protocol tabled consideration of whether this policy should be revised in the future. Since global demand for HCFC-22 will increase, the temptation to allow the mitigation of rising HFC-23 emissions will be serious. If this were to occur, it is not difficult to project CDM prices that, if not heavily taxed by host governments, would encourage expanding HCFC-22 production (venting the release of the HCFC-22, which is not currently restricted by the Montreal Proto-col) for no reason other than to multiply the by-product of CDM sales. This horrific scenario highlights the perverse incentives that demand that regulatory authorities for CDM certification be completely and politically independent of the complementary interests of buyer and seller parties to make transfers that evade the compliance costs of Kyoto commitments. However, the regulator's treatment of other baseline issues magnifies the fear that CDM supplies are likely to become endogenous to the politics of implementation. In other words, CDM supplies will be allowed to grow and to function as an implicit price cap on compliance costs.

Setting a CDM baseline can create other subtle untoward incentives, because what counts as business as usual confers a political as well as a technical or eco-nomic status. Developing nation sellers have no incentives to impose local environmental controls on landfill gas collection or on flaring when the poten-tial emissions reductions from these controls can be sold as CDM offsets. The momentum behind these environmental regulations, which have been diffusing without reference to climate change, is undermined by the CDM, under which

landfill projects rank just below industrial gases as sources of tradable certificates. The same logic applies to developing nations' assumption of renewable
portfolio obligations in emerging markets.

A more subtle example of gaming around unintended incentives may characterize the rapidly expanding CDM market in nitrous oxide) emissions mitigation
in the production of fertilizers and adipic acid. Because of the huge potential
scale of this submarket, like HFC-23, CDM offsets are currently limited to
those associated with existing production of the primary product. But in the
developed nations, voluntary mitigation by all major chemical firms that produced adipic acid resulted in a very low emissions baseline. With the CDM we
will not be in a position to know whether such voluntary industrial measures
would have diffused to major developing country producers that will now maximize polluting by-products in order to sell reductions.

In none of these cases has the executive board looked to trends in domestic
regulation, to national commitments to cleaner energy policies, or to emerging
industrial actions in determining baselines or additionality for the CDM. The
consequence is that CDM prices will remain well below EU ETS or other more
CO_2-based mitigation prices in Kyoto-obligated nations. While this decline in
compliance costs will raise the probabilities of formal compliance, the low price
of mitigation will also lead CDM buying firms to turn toward offsets and away
from higher cost, longer term investments in energy or transport-related carbon
mitigation. Especially given the uncertainties about the permanence of the
Kyoto regime, inefficient transfers and, quite possibly, environmentally incredible trading behavior will dampen and displace economic pressures to change
more fundamental development paths.

A fourth lesson from international experience and social science more generally suggests that amendments to orthodox economic analyses center on the
proposition that it is a more effective regime-building strategy to adapt to existing
barriers than to hope for their elimination. As previously noted, public and private organizations will behave basically as in the past. They do what they do and
generally adapt poorly and only formally to changed contextual conditions. New
agencies and firms better selected to manage new problems can do so successfully
only when some shock to the system fractures the established political and market power of incumbents. It is always possible to do optimization analyses of
what should be done to adjust to unfamiliar problems, like climate change, and
to pronounce the embedded landscape of public policies and private practices a
barrier to what is normatively due.

An absence of political will, then, explains why what is optimal and what is
accomplished can diverge from one another. A strategy of adapting to embedded
barriers assumes that it is unlikely that organizational landscapes can change radically in the short run. It abandons a tactic of removing barriers in favor of understanding the goals and capacities of empowered organizations. It counsels a

program that differentiates policies across time as system adjustment becomes more feasible. It begins with actions that are more likely to fit with the established priorities and agendas of public and private actors. It also suggests concentrating political attention on agencies with the decision authority and resources to motivate change at the margins of their self-defined agendas. Successful change is most likely when incentives for reform surround already viable choices within the portfolio of policy options that appeal to those with the ability to enact and implement them.

The Kyoto process represents a regime-building strategy far removed from this injunction. None of the actors charged with energy development and security or agricultural and forestry policy are at the Kyoto table. The environmental authorities and activists who are there only magnify the sense of turf protection of embedded agencies and firms with normatively charged calls for regulatory and financial constraints. These can impede the central missions of those in national capitals facing a near-endless series of difficulties in carrying out the programs that define their core organizational identities. This situation is a recipe for the paralysis evident in the current context of climate concern. Intentions pronounced with fervor in one forum dissipate in later forums. Until a healthy climate becomes valuable to firms with both know-how and a climate-friendly asset base, the mitigation of climate risk will likely languish in the no-man's-land of fragmented adherence and formalistic compliance, which is where Kyoto now rests.

Building Blocks for a Post-Kyoto Architecture

This is not the occasion to describe the specific elements of a restructured approach to climate change, an approach that might better serve the post-Kyoto context. What I can do is stress some of the important implications of the prior critical discussion that draw on the heretofore missing attention to political economy, organizational sociology, and international relations theory. Thereafter, I sketch the dimensions of an alternative regime architecture—actors, problems, and pillars—more in tune with these implications. To end, I suggest three elements of such a regime that, with proper expansion, debate, and development, offer a foundation for reimagining how to go forward toward the article 2 goals of the UNFCCC. The elaboration of these elements I will have to promise elsewhere.

Ten Implications (for International Regimes)

Implied in the discussion above are the following points:

—Multiple clubs with limited members sharing local cooperative solutions are more likely to support international regime growth than comprehensive multilateral arrangements of parties with highly disparate interests and conditions.

—For regimes with a larger number of members, nonmandatory processes and mechanisms are more effective in setting and encouraging ambitious behavior targets than are regimes under which compliance is mandatory.

—Compliance is not equal to effectiveness.

—Climate change is a derivative problem of sectors that are already politically regulated.

—Policy in politically regulated sectors will be decided by agents with organizationally constrained priorities, which must be taken seriously and which must be framed in ways familiar to these established organizational cultures.

—The political priorities of empowered actors in these regulated sectors are nowhere, especially in developing countries, focused on climate.

—Environmental constraints on emitting sectors will be resisted by sectoral authorities unless these constraints advance the authorities' higher priority goals.

—In politically regulated sectors, shifting the institutional context for market behavior over time is more sustainable than imposing new forms of current regulation.

—All politically regulated sectors can and will be gamed.

—A price signal high enough to give appropriate signals for both short- and long-term aspects of the climate problem is not politically feasible in the absence of deep external shock.

Three Dimensions (of a post-Kyoto Architecture)

The post-Kyoto architecture can be seen in three dimensions: the actors, the problems, and the pillars.

Because climate change is overwhelmingly associated with emissions from energy, transport, and land use, sectors essential to growth and development that are not yet characterized by technological breakthroughs that allow substitution at large scale of nonemitting sources at costs comparable to fossil fuels, policy choices in these sectors that determine development paths are made by politically empowered actors, mostly in line ministries, dedicated agencies, and finance ministries. These actors are rarely represented in climate negotiations, which have thus far relied on output-based measures of allowable emissions and comprehensive environmental controls to manage climate risks. To engage the effective actors in climate action, it is important to switch to input-based policies that are better positioned to explicitly address the trade-offs and complementarities between higher priority sectoral policies and climate impacts. To separate climate from the broader policy agenda and portfolio of choices in play in these emitting sectors is to condemn climate amelioration to the political margins, where it will be resisted.

The mitigation of climate change risks can be broken down into three distinct problems. First, there is an immediate need for a low-level carbon price signal. A signal in the range of U.S.$15–$30 per ton CO_2 would provide incentives for firms to look for what are loosely termed no-regrets mitigation options, which save carbon through incremental behavioral changes, often involving the transaction costs of shifting organizational routines. Second is the midterm problem of diffusion (at a pace more rapid than that of business as usual) of proven commercial technologies into emerging economies with high rates of infrastructure investment. Because infrastructure in energy or transport is generally long-lived, investments made in the next decades will have deep climate consequences because they will determine which fuels, technologies, and land use patterns will be favored in commercial markets. Third is the long-term requirement to develop energy, transportation, and land use technologies that are not yet technologically available. In the longer run it is not contestable that carbon-free or carbon-sequestering technologies must and will become standard operations in all three carbon-emitting sectors. The relevant climate question is the pace and scale of their introduction, commercialization, and diffusion.

Each of these three problems implies different time scales, sequences, and solutions. The price signals necessary to exploit the pool of low-cost mitigation options would not produce adequate incentives for the more rapid diffusion of alternative commercial technologies and would not increase the rate of new technology development and commercial deployment. While it is unlikely that any politically viable solution can solve all three climate problems simultaneously, each problem individually may be amenable to tailored responses.

Following the model of the development of the European Union, this analytical division of climate mitigation might imply that a climate regime would be better built on multiple pillars. Europe first focused on the construction of an integrated economic market (first pillar), which appealed to only a limited set of six nations in a delimited set of collective functions. Over time the European Union expanded its transnational reach both by adding members to the economic union and by developing new cooperative institutions that EU members could join on a voluntary and conditional basis. The institutional rules and structures of the second pillar (foreign and security affairs) are distinct from those of the third pillar (home affairs and justice). Member states that choose these institutions and structures are also distinct. Similar individuation marks adherence to the European Monetary Union and to social policy agreements. Pillarization as regime development implies a collection of clubs, with variable membership determined by acceptance of differentiated cooperative solutions.

The Kyoto Protocol could be reconceived as a first pillar in an architecture of climate institutions, a pillar designed to provide a low-level price signal whose reach would be constitutionally limited to this particular task. The development of different forms of comparable price signals in nations not party to the Kyoto Protocol would more complement than compete with the effectiveness of this pillar. Such a restructured protocol would be supplemented by pillars tailored to the diffusion and technology innovation problems. Each pillar would vary as to

member nations and as to actors, time lines, and policy instruments. Pillarization could get the right actors to the table and eliminate players bent on imped-
ing the design and implementation of collective solutions; instead, the actors
would represent a coherent, small number of cooperating nations with capabilities and interests relevant to the climate problem addressed.

Three Elements (of a post-Kyoto regime)

The elements of a post-Kyoto regime include a low-level price signal, straight-
ahead deal making, and technology innovation.

A low-level price signal will be the least controversial element of a multipillar
post-Kyoto regime because it involves only amendment and confinement of the
Kyoto Protocol. Its reach would be essentially the same as those parties with
current Kyoto mitigation commitments, supplemented by the United States
and Australia, which could individually enact a comparable price signal within
or beside the Kyoto agreements. There is a good likelihood that a low-level price
signal would constitute a cooperative solution agreeable to the advanced industrial countries. Price signals have not yet been adopted by the industrial nations
because there is no credible cap on the signal. In other words, the fear of continuous escalation of the initial signal to deal with climate problems (other than
the no-regrets pool) deters empowered interest groups from accepting a climate
price they would otherwise be willing to pay. While there are questions of how
to set a constrained price signal and how to structure a trading market that pre-
cludes the perverse incentives of incipient CDM markets, these issues are hardly
problematic for standard diplomacy.

There is only a limited number of emerging markets whose growth is fast
enough to raise substantial concerns about climate-damaging infrastructure
being put in place with long-standing effects. It seems futile either to count on
these rapidly developing nations to undertake mandatory mitigation targets or to
design a comprehensive trading scheme that can marshal the financial and regulatory capacity to induce sectoral policies more consistent with both development
and climate objectives. Instead, it would make better sense to abandon the quest
to build inclusive trading markets and just cut specific political deals, acceptable
to the parties involved, that favor relatively climate-friendly technologies and that
are consistent with national development and security priorities.[24] Such deals
could be focused on a package of policy changes, investment financing arrangements, risk-sharing measures to influence infrastructure, and other one-of-a-kind
costs in restructuring markets in fast-growing economies. They would demand
the engagement of sectorally knowledgeable actors from government ministries,
government regulating bodies, and firms with industry experience.

Deals would not need to follow general principles of additionality or observe
project baselines—which the CDM has revealed to be inevitably political—
because the deal itself would define the programs to be undertaken by sectoral

regulators, the nature of the external contributions from bilateral aid, international financial institutions, private firms, or climate-specific cooperation mechanisms, any of which would be needed to facilitate such choices. Deals that affect the development of markets with the potential for emissions reduction at large scale would foster industry and policy standards that could be emulated and made cost-effective in later-developing nations.

Nor should deals limit their scope to targeted sectoral policies or programs. Changes in macroeconomic practices, financial liberalization, security arrangements, international trade reform, or other indirect influences on important climate input markets could have a far greater impact on climate-relevant choices than more direct and obvious policy measures. It is not possible to say in the abstract whether the development of liquefied natural gas markets in East and South Asia, of biofuel and plantation agriculture in the Amazon or West Africa, of implementation of currently unenforced energy efficiency regulations in China and India, or of regional hydroelectricity in Southern Africa will be the stuff of game-changing deals. But it seems clear that reducing the number of self-interested players who explore, broker, agree, implement, and monitor such specific deals is a more practical solution to fast diffusion of proven technologies than the present architecture is.

The recent history of technology policies chronicles both successes and cautionary tales. Common pitfalls include premature selection of winners, underestimation of development costs, overestimation of the declining slope of learning curves, and failure to anticipate the tenacity of existing technologies, which undercuts the promise of new entrants. The usual difficulty with technology projections is not the engineering feasibility so much as the scale, speed, and scope in the commercialization and diffusion of innovations. Technology initiatives, especially at the international level, must contend with multiple national systems for research and development, patents, one-of-a-kind costs that impede market development, first-mover risk allocations, and the lack of a policy or institutional environment adapted to the issues posed by technology deployment. Although most national technology policies include all phases of development, from scientific conceptualization through demonstration projects, new noncommercial, climate-favoring technologies will still face delay and unforeseen costs. These will occur in later stages of the technology pipeline and can be worked through only by the industrial engineers, bankers, regulators, and lawyers in the trenches where commercial feasibility is defined and money is made or lost.

It is likely that the search space within a particular technology pipeline is as great as the search space between alternative technologies and that this search space is well downstream of publicly funded demonstration projects or even subsidized niche installations. This search space is also more likely to be explored by experienced industrialists, financiers, and policymakers than by pure scientists. An innovation that directly addresses the pace and scale of technology innovation must meet the expectations of these actors. Both across-the-horizon technology and the impediments to realizing this technology are predictable. The biggest challenge is institutional.

Conclusion

The first years of building a regime for climate change may be at once disappointing and instructive. We have experienced a period in which carefully crafted institutions with enormous theoretical appeal have bogged down. It is tempting to assert that these institutions are simply experiencing growing pains and that, with patience on our part, the kinks will be worked out. I do not hold this optimistic opinion. It skips over, in its quest for analytical elegance, the less appealing project of implanting an effective regime in the inescapable details of politics, organizational rivalries, and the entrepreneurial power of self-interest. To continue to ignore the less idealized and less appealing sides of social life in pursuit of our higher potential ironically only increases our environmental vulnerability.

Notes

1. UNFCCC, article 2 (www.unfccc.int/resource/docs/convkp/conveng.pdf); Kyoto Protocol (www.unfccc.int/resource/docs/convkp/kpeng.pdf).
2. Thomas Heller and David Victor, *The Political Economy of Power Sector Reform: Experiences in Five Major Emerging Countries* (Cambridge University Press, 2006), chap. 1.
3. IPCC, *Climate Change 2001: Synthesis Report,* Contribution of Working Groups I, II, and III to the Third Assessment Report, edited by R. J. Watson and the Core Writing Team (Geneva: 2001); IPCC, *Climate Change 1995: Synthesis Report* (Geneva: 1996).
4. The gaps between economic theory and diplomatic practice that appeared in the negotiations of the Kyoto Protocol have led good economists to be critical of the economics of the final protocol. See Joseph E. Aldy, Scott Barrett, and Robert N. Stavins, "Thirteen Plus One: A Comparison of Global Climate Policy Architectures," *Climate Policy* 3 (2003): 373–97.
5. IPCC, *Climate Change 2000: Emissions Scenarios,* edited by Nebojsa Nakicenovic and Rob Swart (Cambridge University Press, 2000).
6. James M. Buchanan and Gordon Tullock, *The Calculus of Consent: Logical Foundations of Constitutional Democracy* (University of Michigan Press, 1962); James Buchanan, Robert D. Tollison, and Gordon Tullock, *Toward a Theory of a Rent Seeking Society,* Economics Series 4 (Texas A&M University Press, 1980); Mancur Olson Jr., *Power and Prosperity: Outgrowing Communist and Capitalist Dictatorships* (New York: Basic Books, 2000).
7. For an extensive discussion of these issues in another field of international law, see Mariano-Florentino Cuellar, "The Tenuous Relationship between the Fight against Money Laundering and the Disruption of Criminal Finance," *Journal of Criminal Law and Criminology* 93 (2003): 311–464.
8. For general introductions to the literature on organizational theory and its applications to institutional economics, see W. Richard Scott, *Organizations: Rational, Natural, and*

Open Systems (Englewood Cliffs, N.J.: Prentice-Hall, 1987); Walter W. Powell and Paul J. DiMaggio, *The New Institutionalism in Organizational Analysis* (University of Chicago Press, 1991).

9. Heller and Victor, *The Political Economy of Power Sector Reform,* chap. 7.

10. For discussion of the disarray caused in the market of the EU Emissions Trading Scheme by the political overallocation of emission permits in the first phase (2005–07) of trading, see *Petroleum Intelligence Weekly,* July 10, 2006, p. 2. For initial discussion of the political economy of EU member states' national allocation plans in the second period (2008–12), see Karsten Neuhoff and others, "Emissions Projections 2008–2012 versus NAPs II" (www.climate-strategies.org).

11. "Once particular sets of social arrangements are in place, they embody sunk costs—economic and psychological—that cannot be recovered. Shared expectations arise that promote psychological security, reduce the cost of disseminating information, and facilitate the coordination of diverse activities. Efforts at change are resisted because they threaten individuals' sense of security, increase the cost of information processing, and disrupt routines. Moreover, established conceptions of 'the way things are done' can be very beneficial; members of an organizational field can use these stable expectations as a guide to action and a way to predict the behavior of others. These are not necessarily stories about inefficiency or maladaptation, but rather plausible accounts of how practices and structures reproduce themselves in a world of imperfect information and increasing returns." Walter W. Powell, "Expanding the Scope of Institutional Analysis," in *The New Institutionalism in Organizational Analysis,* edited by Powell and DiMaggio p. 194.

12. For discussion of organizational techniques for managing external environments, see Scott, *Organizations,* pp. 181–200, 206–08.

13. Organizations in the same field become isomorphic over time because—in the face of uncertainty about how best to manage core functions, deal with internal problems of agency, and respond to external demands—managers mimic the practices of perceived leaders in the field. The ease with which professional or standards bodies share information or benchmarking processes across the organizational field can result in rapid informal diffusion of best practices in the absence of formal regulation. John Meyer and Brian Rowan, "Institutional Organizations: Formal Structure as Myth and Ceremony," in *The New Institutionalism in Organizational Analysis,* edited by Powell and DiMaggio. This point can be applied to the mechanisms by which voluntary international regimes can be effective with a large number of players in the absence of formal compliance institutions. David Victor, Kal Raustiala, and Eugene Skolnikoff, editors, *The Implementation and Effectiveness of International Environmental Commitments: Theory and Practice* (MIT Press, 1998).

14. Thomas C. Heller, "African Transitions and the Resource Curse: An Alternative Perspective," *Economic Affairs* 26, no. 4 (2006): 24–33.

15. See discussion of adaptation versus selection in organizational ecology in Scott, *Organizations,* pp. 200–05.

16. Transport for London, *Central London Congestion Charging: Impacts Monitoring,* Third Annual Report (London: 2005).

17. The concept that international governance and law can and should mirror the structure of formal statelike law and regulation is long-standing in Western public international law but is now challenged on various grounds. H. Patrick Glenn, "The Nationalist Heritage," in *Comparative Legal Studies: Traditions and Transitions,* edited by Pierre Legrand and Roderick Munday (Cambridge University Press, 2003).

18. Peter M. Hass and Jan Sundgren, "Evolving International Environmental Law: Chang-ing Practices of National Sovereignty," in *Global Accord,* edited by Nazli Choucri (MIT Press, 1995); for discussion of the relatively greater effectiveness of regional, bilateral, and local legal measures compared to those of international regimes, see Richard Hildreth, "Achieving Fisheries Sustainability in the United States," *Environmental Law Reporter* 36 (2006): 10004–15.

19. Barry G. Rabe, *Race to the Top: The Expanding Role of U.S. State Renewable Portfolio Standards* (Arlington, Va.: Pew Center for Global Climate Change, 2006).

20. David Victor, " 'Learning by Doing' in the Nonbinding International Regime to Manage Trade in Hazardous Chemicals and Pesticides," in *The Implementation and Effectiveness of International Environmental Commitments,* edited by Victor, Raustiala, and Skolnikoff.

21. Directive 2004/101/EC of the European Parliament and of the Council of 27 October 2004.

22. HFC-23 waste streams (http://cdm.unfccc.int/methodologies); AM0001 and inputs received on approved meth AM0001 (http://cdm.unfccc.int/inputam0001/index.html).

23. China taxes 65 percent of CDM profits from sales of HFC-23 certified emissions reduc-tions, which is then said to be dedicated to alternative energy subsidies. Although the World Bank has relied on this use of the proceeds of the tax to explain its investment in HFC-23 offsets, it would surely expand the definition of *additionality* to look to the pur-ported environmental uses of the funds earned through the CDM rather than the envi-ronmental impact of the project itself to justify the CDM's environmental credibility. See "HFC-23 China Projects Answers and Questions" (http://carbonfinance.org/docs/HFC23_q-and-a_12-18-05.pdf).

24. For preliminary discussion of the concept of deals, see Thomas C. Heller and P. R. Shukla, "Development and Climate," in *Beyond Kyoto: Advancing the International Effort against Climate Change,* edited by J. E. Aldy and others (Arlington, Va.: Pew Center on Global Climate Change, 2003).

9

An International Policy Architecture for the Post-Kyoto Era

ROBERT N. STAVINS

After seven years of uncertainty, the Kyoto Protocol (1997) to the United Nations Framework Convention on Climate Change (UNFCCC, 1992) came into force in February 2005 but without participation by the United States. With Russian ratification late in 2004, requirements for implementation were met, namely ratification by a minimum of 55 nations (127, in fact), including—importantly, since this was the binding constraint—Annex I (industrialized) countries representing at least 55 percent of 1990 industrialized world emissions of carbon dioxide (CO_2).

The impacts of the Kyoto Protocol on emissions of greenhouse gases, targeted for the compliance period 2008–12, will be much less than originally anticipated. Nonparticipation by the United States is quantitatively important, and the rules written at the Conferences of the Parties (COPs) of the UNFCCC in Bonn and Marakesh in 2001 had the effect of significantly relaxing the aggregate target. But a scientific consensus has continued to form regarding the likelihood of future climate change due to anthropogenic emissions of greenhouse gases;[1] and economic analysis increasingly points to the wisdom of some kind of

This chapter draws upon Robert N. Stavins, "After Kyoto: Climate Change Strategies for the United Nations," paper prepared for United Nations Secretary General Kofi Annan, April 24, 2002; Robert N. Stavins, "Forging a More Effective Global Climate Treaty," *Environment* 46, no. 10 (2004): 23–30; Robert N. Stavins, "Beyond Kyoto: Getting Serious about Climate Change," *Milken Institute Review* 7, no. 1 (2005): 28–37. It has benefited from comments by conference participants.

policy action.[2] Thus there is a dilemma. The Kyoto Protocol has come into force without U.S. participation; its effects on climate change will be trivial; but the economic and scientific consensus points to the need for a credible international approach. What can be done?

A reasonable starting point is the UNFCCC, which was signed by 161 nations and ratified by 50—including the United States—and which entered into force in 1994. Among other things, the UNFCCC established the principle of "common but differentiated responsibilities," meaning that all nations should engage in the solution (because of the global-commons nature of the problem) but that different countries could participate in different ways.[3]

If the UNFCCC provides a reasonable starting point, can the Kyoto Protocol provide the way forward? It is helpful to examine the protocol in terms of its major architectural elements. Its targets apply only to industrialized nations; it contains ambitious, short-term emissions reduction targets but no long-term targets; and it provides flexibility through market-based mechanisms such as tradable permits. This architecture has been widely criticized, chiefly because it would impose high costs, fail to provide for full participation by developing countries, and generate modest short-term climate benefits while failing to provide a long-term solution. On the other hand, the argument has been made that the Kyoto Protocol is essentially "the only game in town" and that, instead of suggesting alternatives, analysts "should concentrate on convincing policymakers how to get the long-term climate policy instruments right that build on Kyoto's foundations."[4]

Thus some analysts see the agreement as deeply flawed.[5] Others see it as an acceptable first step.[6] But virtually everyone agrees that the Kyoto Protocol is not sufficient to meet the overall challenge and that further steps will be required. As Eileen Claussen, president of the Pew Center on Global Climate Change, wrote in 2003, "whether or not the Protocol enters into force, the same fundamental challenge remains: engaging all countries that are major emitters of greenhouse gases in a common long-term effort. We need a durable strategy that can take us beyond Kyoto."[7]

A Three-Part Policy Architecture

I outline the basic features of a post-Kyoto international global climate policy agreement, which contains three essential elements: a means to ensure that key nations, both industrialized and developing, are eventually involved; an emphasis on an extended time path of targets (employing a cost-effective pattern over time); and inclusion of market-based policy instruments. This architecture is consistent with fundamental aspects of the science, economics, and politics of global climate change.

Expanding Participation

Broad participation by major industrialized nations and key developing countries is essential to effectively and efficiently address the global-commons problem of climate change. The share of global emissions attributable to developing countries is significant and growing, and developing countries are likely to account for more than half of global emissions by the year 2020, if not before.[8] But it certainly can be argued on an ethical basis that industrialized countries should take the first emission reduction steps on their own. The simple reality, however, is that developing countries provide the greatest opportunities for relatively low-cost emissions reduction.[9] It would therefore be unnecessarily costly to focus emissions reduction activities exclusively in the developed world.

A reasonable response to this observation about cost-effectiveness is that industrialized countries, almost by definition, are responsible for the bulk of anthropogenic concentrations of greenhouse gases in the atmosphere. Hence industrialized countries should be first with emissions reductions, with developing countries taking action only later. Although sensible arguments can be made in support of this position on grounds of distributional equity, there is a serious problem.

If developing countries are not included in an agreement, comparative advantage in the production of carbon-intensive goods and services will shift outside the coalition of participating countries, making developing countries' economies more carbon intensive, through "emissions leakage," than they otherwise would be. Rather than helping developing countries move onto less carbon-intensive paths of development, the industrialized world would be pushing those nations onto more carbon-intensive growth paths, increasing their cost of joining the coalition later. Still, on equity grounds, it is unreasonable to expect developing nations to incur significant emissions-reduction costs in the short term, because it would retard their economic development.

This poses a policy conundrum. On the one hand, for purposes of environmental effectiveness and economic efficiency, key developing countries should be participants in an international effort to reduce greenhouse gas emissions. On the other hand, for purposes of distributional equity (and international political pragmatism), they cannot be expected to incur the consequent costs. The solution is that these countries must get on the global climate policy "train" without necessarily paying full fare. How can this be accomplished?

A trigger mechanism appears to be required, whereby developing countries would be obligated to take on binding commitments only when their per capita gross domestic product reached agreed levels. But there is no reason to limit thinking to such a simple, dichotomous instrument. Rather, a preferable approach would be growth targets that become more stringent for individual developing counties as those countries become more wealthy.[10] Such indexed targets could be set at business-as-usual (BAU) emissions levels. In other words, a growth target is not a number but an equation that relates targeted emissions to per capita income and possibly other variables. Two necessary characteristics of a growth target formulation are that it not create perverse incentives that would encourage nations to increase their emissions and that it be relatively simple so as not to create impediments to negotiation.[11]

Note that the short-term targets for developing countries could even be set at emissions levels that are above BAU levels. If combined with an international trading program (discussed later), such headroom would provide a direct economic incentive (subsidy) for developing country participation. Developing countries could fully participate without incurring prohibitive costs (or even any costs in the short term). That is, cost-effectiveness and distributional equity could both be addressed.

An Extended Time Path of Targets

Global climate change is a long-term problem, due to the fact that the relevant greenhouse gases remain in the atmosphere for decades and even centuries. The Kyoto Protocol fails to reflect this fundamentally important reality, namely, the cumulative, stock-pollutant nature of the problem. The protocol has only short-term targets, an average 5 percent reduction from 1990 levels by the 2008–12 compliance period. This sounds like a modest reduction, but it translates into a severe 25–30 percent cut for the United States from its BAU emissions path. The reason for this is that the United States economy grew at an exceptionally rapid rate during the 1990s, exhibiting a remarkable 37 percent increase in real GDP from 1990 to 2000.

Thus the Kyoto Protocol's targets are too little, too fast: they do little about the problem but are unreasonable for countries that enjoyed significant economic growth after 1990. Two elements are needed to ameliorate this problem: firm but moderate targets in the short term to avoid rendering large parts of the capital stock prematurely obsolete, and flexible but more stringent targets for the long term to motivate (now and in the future) technological change, which in turn is needed to bring costs down over time.[12] Specifically, emissions targets ought to start out at BAU levels, then gradually depart from these, so that emissions targets in the short term would, in fact, be increasing over time but at rates below the rate of increase exhibited by BAU levels. Importantly, these intertemporal emissions targets should not be monotonically increasing but should reach a maximum level and then begin to decrease, eventually becoming substantially more severe than the constraints implied by the Kyoto Protocol's short-term targets.

It is important to recognize that the word *target* should be taken generically to refer not only to emissions targets (as in the Kyoto Protocol and as described above) but also to intensity targets, that is, emissions per unit of gross domestic product. For that matter, the proposal I offer here is also consistent with a time path of targets denominated in purely financial units, that is, carbon prices (levels of taxes on the carbon content of fossil fuels).

In any event, the pattern I suggest is consistent with estimates of the least-cost time path of emissions for achieving long-term greenhouse gas concentration targets: short-term increases in emissions (slightly below the BAU path) and subsequent emissions reduction.[13] Such a time path of future targets, put in place now, would be consistent with what is often denigrated as politics as usual. That is, politicians are frequently condemned for the fact that in representative democracies there are strong incentives to place costs on future, not current, voters and, if possible, future generations. It is typically the politically pragmatic strategy. In the case of global climate policy, it can also be the scientifically correct and economically rational approach.

Market-Based Policy Instruments

The final component of the three-part policy architecture is in principle part of the Kyoto Protocol: working through the market rather than against it. There is widespread agreement that conventional regulatory approaches cannot do the job, certainly not at acceptable costs. To keep costs down in the short term and bring them down even lower in the long term through technological change, it is essential to embrace market-based instruments as the chief means of reducing greenhouse gas emissions.[14]

On a domestic level, in some countries systems of tradable permits might be used to achieve national targets. This is the same mechanism that was used in the United States to eliminate leaded gasoline from the market in the 1980s, at a savings of more than U.S.$250 million a year.[15] The same mechanism is now being used to cut sulfur dioxide (SO_2) emissions (a precursor of acid rain) in the United States by 50 percent, at a savings estimated to be U.S.$1 billion a year.[16] Of the two systems, the better model for climate change policy is the upstream, lead rights system (analogous to trading based on the carbon content of fossil fuels), rather than the downstream, SO_2 emissions trading system.

For some countries, systems of domestic carbon taxes may be more attractive. Another promising market-based approach is a hybrid of tax and tradable permit systems: an ordinary tradable permit system plus a government promise to sell additional permits at a stated price.[17] This creates a price (and thereby cost) ceiling and has hence been labeled a safety valve system.

International policy instruments are also required to solve this fundamentally international problem. The Kyoto Protocol includes in article 17, a system whereby the parties to the agreement can engage in trading their "assigned amounts," that is, their reduction targets, translated into quantitative terms of emissions.[18] In theory, such a system of international tradable permits—if implemented only for the industrialized countries (as under the Kyoto Protocol)—

could reduce costs by 50 percent. If such a system also included major develop-ing countries, costs could be lowered to 25 percent of what they otherwise would be.[19]

In an emissions permit-trading system, sources that have low costs of con-trol have an incentive to take on added reductions so they can sell their excess permits to sources that face relatively high control costs and wish to reduce their control efforts.[20] An undisputed attraction of an international trading approach, in theory, is that the equilibrium allocation of permits, the market-determined permit price, and the aggregate costs of abatement are independent of the initial allocation of permits among countries. However, this is only true as long as particularly perverse types of transaction costs are not prevalent and individual parties—be they nations or firms—do not have market power.[21] The latter concern is a real one in the Kyoto context. In any event, the initial allocation can be highly significant in distributional terms, implying possibly massive international wealth transfers. Some analysts highlight this as a major objection to an international carbon trading regime,[22] but it is essentially because of this feature that a permit system can be used to address cost-effectiveness *and* distributional equity.

If an international trading system is used, it must be designed to facilitate integration with domestic policies that nations use to achieve their respective domestic targets. In the extreme, if all countries use domestic tradable permit systems to meet their national targets (that is, allocate shares from the interna-tional permit system to private domestic parties), then an international system can in theory be perfectly cost-effective. But if some countries use nontrading approaches, such as greenhouse gas taxes or fixed-quantity standards (which seems likely), cost minimization is not ensured.[23] Thus individual nations' choices of domestic policy instruments to meet their targets can substantially limit the cost-saving potential of an international trading program. In this realm, a trade-off exists between the degree of domestic sovereignty and the degree of cost-effectiveness.

Not long ago most observers would have predicted that few if any European countries would employ tradable permit systems, given the European Union's strenuous opposition to such approaches dating back to the time of the Kyoto Protocol. But the European Union has now launched its own continentwide trading system.[24] Furthermore, by the time of the COPs in Bonn (summer 2001) and Marrakech (fall 2001), China and the G77 (the coalition of developing nations) had in effect dropped their opposition to international emissions trading. Combined with the strong U.S. preference for trading, these realities represent important political arguments for this element of a future international climate policy architecture.

International permit trading thus remains a promising approach to achiev-ing global greenhouse targets, despite the challenge that any program must be integrated carefully with domestic policies. It is probably fair to state that the more one studies international tradable permit systems to address global climate change, the more one comes to believe that this is the worst possible approach—except of course for all the others (bringing to mind Winston Churchill's famous observation about democracy).

Conclusion

The three-part global climate policy architecture outlined above builds upon the UN Framework Convention on Climate Change and can serve eventually as a successor to the Kyoto Protocol. For such an approach to work, key nations have to be involved, including major developing countries, through the use of economic trigger mechanisms such as growth targets. In addition, cost-effective time paths of targets are required: firm but moderate in the short term and in the long term much more stringent and flexible. Finally, market-based policy instruments ought to be part of the package, whether they be emissions trading, carbon taxes, or hybrids of the two.

This overall approach can be made scientifically sound, economically rational, and politically pragmatic. There is no denying that the challenges facing adoption and successful implementation of this type of climate policy architecture are significant, but they need not be insurmountable, and they are not necessarily any greater than the challenges facing other approaches to the threat of global climate change.

Notes

1. IPCC, *Climate Change 2001: Synthesis Report,* Contribution of Working Groups I, II, and III to the Third Assessment Report, edited by Robert T. Watson and the Core Writing Team (Geneva: 2001); Rajendra K. Pachauri, "Re-Examining the Evidence," paper prepared for meeting, "Global Warming: Looking beyond Kyoto," Yale University, October 21–22, 2005.

2. Jay F. Shogren and Michael A. Toman, "Climate Change Policy," in *Public Policies for Environmental Protection,* 2nd ed., edited by Paul R. Portney and Robert N. Stavins (Washington: Resources for the Future Press, 2000); Charles D. Kolstad and Michael Toman, "The Economics of Climate Policy," Discussion Paper 00-40REV (Washington: Resources for the Future, 2001), forthcoming in Karl-Goran Mäler and Jeffrey Vincent, eds., *Handbook of Environmental Economics,* vol. 2 (Amsterdam: Elsevier Science).

3. United Nations, "United Nations Framework Convention on Climate Change, 1992."

4. Axel Michaelowa, "Global Warming Policy," *Journal of Economic Perspectives* 17, no. 3 (2003): 204–05.

5. David G. Victor, *The Collapse of the Kyoto Protocol and the Struggle to Slow Global Warming* (Princeton University Press, 2001); Richard Cooper, "The Kyoto Protocol: A Flawed Concept," Working Paper 52.2001 (Trieste: Fondazione Eni Enrico, Mattei, 2001); Warrick McKibbin and Peter Wilcoxen, "The Role of Economics in Climate Change Policy," *Journal of Economic Perspectives* 16, no. 2 (2002): 107–29; Warrick McKibbin

and Peter Wilcoxen, "Estimates of the Costs of Kyoto: Marrakesh versus the McKibbin-Wilcoxen Blueprint," *Energy Policy* 32, no. 4 (2004): 467–79.

6. Michael Grubb, "The Economics of the Kyoto Protocol," *World Economics* 4, no. 3 (2003): 143–89; Michaelowa, "Global Warming Policy," 204–05.

7. Eileen Claussen, foreword to *Beyond Kyoto: Advancing the International Effort against Climate Change,* edited by Eliot Diringer (Arlington, Va.: Pew Center on Global Climate Change, 2003), p. ii.

8. IPCC, *Climate Change 2000: Emissions Scenarios,* edited by Nebojsa Nakicenovic and Rob Swart (Cambridge University Press, 2000); I. Pies and G. Schröder, *Causes and Consequences of Global Warming: How Rational Is Our Policy on Climate Change?* (Munich: Policy Consult, 2002).

9. IPCC, *Climate Change 2001.*

10. Randall Lutter, "Developing Countries' Greenhouse Emissions: Uncertainty and Implications for Participation in the Kyoto Protocol," *Energy Journal* 21, no. 4 (2000): 93–120.

11. Joseph E. Aldy, R. Baron, and L. Tubiana, "Addressing Cost: The Political Economy of Climate Change," in *Beyond Kyoto: Advancing the International Effort against Climate Change,* edited by Diringer.

12. Lawrence H. Goulder and Stephen H. Schneider, "Induced Technological Change and the Attractiveness of CO_2 Abatement Policies," *Resource and Energy Economics* 21, nos. 3–4 (1999): 211–53; Adam B. Jaffe, Richard G. Newell, and Robert N. Stavins, "Energy-Efficient Technologies and Climate Change Policies: Issues and Evidence," Climate Issue Brief 19 (Washington: Resources for the Future, 1999), reprinted in Michael A. Toman, ed., *Climate Change Economics and Policy* (Washington: Resources for the Future Press, 2001); J. Pershing and F. Tudela, "A Long-Term Target: Framing the Climate Effort," in *Beyond Kyoto: Advancing the International Effort against Climate Change,* edited by Diringer.

13. Thomas Wigley, Richard Richels, and Jae Edmonds, "Economic and Environmental Choices in the Stabilization of Atmospheric CO_2 Concentrations," *Nature,* January 18, 1996, pp. 240–43; Alan Manne and Richard Richels, *On Stabilizing CO_2 Concentrations: Cost-Effective Emission Reduction Strategies* (Stanford University Press for the Electric Power Research Institute, 1997).

14. Robert N. Stavins, "Policy Instruments for Climate Change: How Can National Governments Address a Global Problem?" *University of Chicago Legal Forum* (1997): 293–329.

15. Robert N. Stavins, "Experience with Market-Based Environmental Policy Instruments," in vol. 1, *Handbook of Environmental Economics,* edited by Karl-Goran Mäler and Jeffrey Vincent (Amsterdam: Elsevier Science, 2003).

16. Richard Schmalensee and others, "An Interim Evaluation of Sulfur Dioxide Emissions Trading," *Journal of Economic Perspectives* 12, no. 3 (1998): 53–68; Robert N. Stavins, "What Can We Learn from the Grand Policy Experiment? Lessons from SO_2 Allowance Trading," *Journal of Economic Perspectives* 12, no. 3 (1998): 69–88; Denny Ellerman and others, *Markets for Clean Air: The U.S. Acid Rain Program* (Cambridge University Press, 2000).

17. Mark Roberts and Michael Spence, "Effluent Charges and Licenses under Uncertainty," *Journal of Public Economics* 5, nos. 3–4 (1976): 193–208; Raymond Kopp and others, "A Proposal for Credible Early Action in U.S. Climate Policy," in *Flexible Mechanisms for Efficient Climate Policy: Cost Saving Policies and Business Opportunities,* edited by K. L. Brockmann and M. Stonzik (Heidelberg: Physica-Verlag, 2000); William A. Pizer, "Combining Price and Quantity Controls to Mitigate Global Climate Change," *Journal of Public Economics* 85, no. 3 (2002): 409–34; McKibbin and Wilcoxen, "The Role of Economics in Climate Change Policy."

18. United Nations, "Kyoto Protocol to the Convention on Climate Change, 1997."
19. J. Edmonds and others, *Return to 1990: The Cost of Mitigating United States Carbon Emissions in the Post-2000 Period* (Richland, Wash.: Pacific Northwest National Laboratory, 1997).
20. Jeremy B. Hockenstein, Robert N. Stavins, and Bradley W. Whitehead, "Crafting the Next Generation of Market-Based Environmental Tools," *Environment*, May 1997, p. 12.
21. Robert N. Stavins, "Transaction Costs and Tradable Permits," *Journal of Environmental Economics and Management* 29, no. 2 (1995): 133–48; Robert W. Hahn, "Market Power and Transferable Property Rights," *Quarterly Journal of Economics* 99 (1984): 753–65.
22. Richard Cooper, "Toward a Real Treaty on Global Warming," *Foreign Affairs* 77, no. 2 (1998): 66–79.
23. Robert W. Hahn and Robert N. Stavins, *What Has the Kyoto Protocol Wrought? The Real Architecture of International Tradable Permit Markets* (Washington: American Enterprise Institute Press, 1999).
24. J. A. Kruger and W. A. Pizer, "Greenhouse Gas Trading in Europe: The New Grand Policy Experiment," *Environment*, November 2004, p. 8.

PART FIVE

Climate Policy in the Industrialized Countries

10

Controversies of Russian Climate Policy and Opportunities for Greenhouse Gas Reduction

ALEXANDER GOLUB

Russia is an important player in the international effort to address climate change. Its share in global carbon dioxide (CO_2) emissions declined from about 11 percent in 1990 to about 6.4 percent in 2003.[1] Despite the sharp decline, Russia remains among the world's largest polluters, ranking third in the world after the United States and China and before Japan and India. This chapter presents the history of Russian climate policy since the Kyoto Protocol was adopted at Conference of the Parties (COP-3) until the present day.

This chapter also presents an analysis of the driving forces behind Russia's CO_2 emissions and offers discussions on future emissions scenarios. Until now there were no specific incentives to reduce carbon emissions. Any improvements in carbon efficiency were the result of general economic reforms and the integration of Russia into the world economy. Nevertheless, after Russia recovered from its economic crisis, carbon emissions grew four times more slowly than its gross domestic product. Russia will definitely meet its Kyoto target and, with high probability, will be able to supply nearly 3 billion tonnes of CO_2 allowances to the international carbon market, especially as Russia's carbon emissions will remain below its 1990 levels.

Introduction

Russia holds about a third to a half of the world's natural gas reserves, has abundant coal resources (about 20 percent of the world's reserves), and large crude oil resources (10 percent of the world's reserves). Thus Russian climate policy, combined with its energy and export-import policies, will significantly influence its long-term carbon emissions levels. As for the near future, the progress of Russia's climate policy will, to a large extent, determine the success or failure of the Kyoto Protocol to the United Nations Framework Convention on Climate Change (UNFCCC).

Since ratified by Russia, the Kyoto Protocol has entered into force; Annex B countries (except Australia and the United States) now face the challenges of its implementation. For the European Union (EU), Japan, and Canada, whose carbon dioxide emissions are expected to rise above Kyoto targets, the major challenge is how to close the gap between actual emissions and emission targets. According to various projections, the cumulative shortfall for the five-year commitment period could be equivalent to 3 billion to 5 billion tonnes of CO_2. Kyoto's flexible mechanisms, especially emissions trading, are options that could be used to establish the balance.

Russia and Ukraine have the reserve capacity to supply the amount of required carbon allowances and, therefore, appear as essential to the compliance reserves of Annex B countries. In the first Kyoto commitment period, 2008–12, Russia alone will have a large enough surplus carbon allowance to cover the deficits of the other Annex B countries just mentioned. To be a player in the carbon market, Russia should build institutions for managing its carbon emissions budget. Russia made some progress in this field but is still far from being ready to meet all the necessary conditions for participation in emissions trading as stipulated by the Marrakech rules adopted at the COP-7.[2] Despite the fact that Russia is an obvious beneficiary of the Kyoto Protocol, it took the country six years to ratify it. After U.S. withdrawal from the protocol, Russia's ratification became the primary bargaining tool in negotiations with the European Union over Russia's entrance into the World Trade Organization (WTO). The debates about the ratification decision best illustrate the controversies among Russian climate policymakers. Russia faces a big challenge to overcome these controversies.

Another and perhaps more important challenge is for Russia to pursue a macroeconomic policy optimizing the role of the energy sector in its economy. Energy resources already play a critical role in the Russian economy. High oil prices in the world market were one of the important factors contributing to the economic growth that started after the financial crisis in 1998. Obviously, Russia will use these abundant energy resources to its advantage. The question then becomes how Russia plans to reconcile the management of these resources with the demands of the Kyoto Protocol.

In this chapter the history of Russian climate policy is presented, the forces that contribute to carbon emissions in Russia are analyzed, and finally some insights into the future of carbon emissions are offered. Alternative scenarios for Russia's future carbon dioxide emissions are proposed, which argue that there is great potential for Russia to combine economic growth with carbon limits.

History of Climate Policy and Ratification of the Kyoto Protocol

In 1997 Russia's carbon dioxide emissions trajectory was unclear. There was a lot of speculation surrounding the greenhouse gas (GHG) emissions scenarios. The *First Russian National Communication to the UNFCCC* (1995) presented three scenarios for CO_2 emissions. According to one of them, Russia was at risk of reaching 1990 levels of emissions around 2010. Projections for the *First National Communication* were oversimplified and did not take into account endogenous changes in the Russian economy induced by general economic reforms, which included price liberalization and the liberalization of international trade.[3] Other projections, including two scenarios for the *First National Communication* as well as other studies, were more optimistic.[4] Nevertheless, all of these studies considered the possibility that Russia could overshoot its 1990 emissions some time between 2008 and 2012.

Russia negotiated an emissions target in 1997 equal to 100 percent of 1990 levels. However, for Russian officials it was still not clear how Russia would fulfill its Kyoto obligations. To address these concerns, the Russian government and the World Bank agreed to conduct a national strategy study on Russia's GHG emissions policy. This study was completed in 1998 and presented to the Russian government. Preliminary results were available in 1997, just before COP-3.

This study demonstrates that energy-saving, economic incentives (including the gradual increase of energy prices and the phasing out of hidden energy subsidies) could curb Russia's GHG emissions. Further incentives to reduce carbon emissions could be created through the application of Kyoto's flexible mechanisms, such as emissions trading.[5] The impact of market reforms, including price liberalization, followed by structural changes and technological innovations and improvements of energy efficiency, could add roughly 1 billion tonnes of CO_2 emissions to Russia's trading potential; and additional incentives could be created by international emissions trading by adding another billion tonnes.[6] In case of slow market reforms as well as slow diffusion of new technologies, Russia is still expected to have a moderate surplus, equal to 700 million tonnes of CO_2.[7] A rapid increase of coal in the mix of Russian fuel consumption is projected as the only threat to Russia's GHG emissions Kyoto target.

There were a few more studies whose conclusions were consistent with this assessment. Among these studies was an official forecast presented in the *Third*

National Communication.[8] This document presents GHG emissions forecasts approved by the Russian government and represents the official position of the Russian Federation.

Taking into account all the benefits offered to Russia from its participation in the Kyoto Protocol—including potential revenues from emissions trading, the future increase of prices for natural gas in Europe, and other ancillary benefits—Russia had every reason to ratify the treaty several years ago.[9] However, that did not happen until recently—October 2004 to be precise. By this time a number of experts and politicians were ready to pronounce the Kyoto Protocol a failure. In the meantime, Russia was sending out mixed signals regarding its intention to proceed with the Kyoto Protocol. While the Ministry of Economic Development and Trade, among other governmental agencies, gave assurances that Russia was on its way to ratification, Andrey Illarionov, the economic adviser to President Vladimir Putin, tried to convince the world that Russia would never ratify the Kyoto Protocol, alluding to the unreasonable burden the protocol would place on the Russian economy.

Bargaining with the European Union

When President George W. Bush announced in early 2001 that the United States was not going to ratify the Kyoto Protocol, Russian officials in charge of climate policy came to two realizations: one, that Russia would lose the United States as a client on the international carbon market; and two, that Russia would gain leverage with its bargaining power through the ratification issue. To enter into force, the treaty had to be ratified by a sufficient number of Annex B countries to reach 1990 CO_2 emissions of at least 55 percent of the total Annex B CO_2 emissions. A Russian ratification of the protocol was the only way to meet this condition.

Russia, in turn, anticipated receiving something in exchange for its ratification of the treaty, most likely from the EU, since the EU was known to be a strong proponent of the Kyoto Protocol. During the bargaining process, Russia tried to find the "right price," which included transit to Kaliningrad, visas for Russian citizens to Europe, and membership in the WTO. Eventually, a compromise was found within the field of energy and trade. In April 2004, at an EU-Russian summit, the EU agreed to waive its requirement for Russia to rapidly increase domestic natural gas prices as a precondition to supporting Russia's accession to the WTO. In turn, Russia agreed to increase its domestic prices gradually so as to make sure that such an increase would not harm the Russian economy. At the same time, President Putin promised to speed up ratification of the Kyoto Protocol.[10]

Dual Pricing of Natural Gas

Russian domestic energy prices are significantly lower than those of Western European states. For example, the average domestic price of natural gas in 2003 was about 4.5 times lower in Russia than in Germany.[11] Such a difference in price raises questions about hidden subsidies in Russia, and the elimination of hidden subsidies has become a precondition for Russian WTO membership.

Hypothetically, elimination of subsidies should lead to elimination of market distortions, an increase in energy efficiency, and a reduction in global and local air pollution. However, one precondition for successful subsidy elimination is an increased investment in new production facilities and structural changes to the GDP. If these preconditions are not met, subsidy elimination could in fact be harmful to the economy and the environment. Immediate elimination of hidden subsidies for natural gas, for example, may result in an increase in coal consumption. Russia's weak environmental policy would not address the emission increases that would result from more coal combustion, specifically emissions of sulfur dioxide, nitrogen oxide, and particulate matter. The substitution of coal for natural gas, using outdated combustion facilities without appropriate abatement, would increase conventional pollution—with a substantial impact on human health. Subsidized natural gas thus acts as a kind of short-term substitute for a more environmentally friendly policy in Russia, at least until it adopts and executes a well-articulated environmental policy. Annual benefits to public health in Russia from its policy of subsidized natural gas are about 110,000 avoided years of life lost and 173,000 avoided cases of child morbidity and chronic bronchitis. In monetary terms, economic damage avoided is around U.S.$8.2 billion. Also about 60 million tonnes of CO_2 emissions annually are prevented. These environmental arguments were important in the debate over dual gas prices.

The Last Attack on the Kyoto Protocol

While promising EU leaders that Russia would speed up its ratification of the Kyoto Protocol, President Putin did not set a time frame. In turn, his economic adviser, Andrey Illarionov, made one last effort to attack the treaty. It is hard to believe that this was a very well orchestrated show. Most likely Illarionov acted alone in an attempt to at least postpone ratification. Nevertheless, his anti-Kyoto campaign had a negative impact on Russian bureaucrats, and a further delay in Russia's ratification efforts loomed on the horizon.[12]

On August 18, 2004, the Institute of Economic Analysis, run by Illarionov, presented the report *Economic Consequences of Possible Ratification of the Kyoto Protocol by the Russian Federation.* It was the first attempt by the Kyoto Protocol's opposition to conduct comprehensive research with regard to the standards established by other publications, including the analysis of the Ministry of Economic Development, the Institute for Energy Studies (Russian Academy of Sciences), the Institute for the Economy in Transition (Russia), Environmental Defense (U.S.), and the Royal Institute for International Affairs (U.K.). To predict Russian carbon emissions, protocol opponents attempted to apply econometrics and conducted a wide, cross-country, analysis to support their claims. They failed, however, to explain the dynamics of CO_2 emissions in Russia in the period 1990–2003 or to offer a consistent story about projections for the near future. This problem, along with serious methodological and technical mistakes, significantly discounted the value of the institute's results and raised concerns about the validity of its conclusions.

A few weeks later, the Center for Russian Environmental Policy and Environmental Defense presented a comprehensive review of Illarionov's report, detailing the report's methodological and technical mistakes.[13] Both reports—Illarionov's and the center's—were available to the Putin administration, the Russian government, parliament, and the analytical centers involved in research on climate change and the economics of the Kyoto Protocol. In September the Russian government decided to send the treaty to the parliament for ratification. It was ratified by both chambers of the Russian parliament and entered into force in February 2005.

Illarionov's major technical mistake was related to the misreporting of 1990 CO_2 emissions levels, which were essential to calculating the Russian emissions budget under the protocol. The Institute of Economic Analysis failed to report the 1990 baseline of CO_2 emissions as that of the Annex B Kyoto targets. Instead of applying the figure presented in the *Third National Communication,* the authors used International Energy Agency data, which were slightly lower.[14] Although the *Third National Communication* reports 2,600 million metric tonnes of CO_2 emissions and the *First National Communication* reports 2,373 metric tonnes, the authors cite 2,000 metric tonnes of CO_2 emission.[15] As a result of this misrepresentation, the Russian budget for the first Kyoto period was instantly reduced by 3 billion metric tonnes of CO_2 emissions allowances.[16] The application of the correct 1990 data led to the conclusion that, even under Illarionov's emissions scenario, Russia would surely meet Kyoto's emissions targets.[17]

Later Developments

Two years after the decision was made and the Kyoto Protocol entered into force, Russia did not demonstrate significant progress in implementation of the treaty. Domestic institution building occurred at a slow, even very slow, pace. By May 2007 Russia did not have the infrastructure in place to allow for complete participation in Kyoto's flexible mechanisms. At the end of May 2007 the Russian government adopted a joint implementation procedure. It is an important, but obviously insufficient, step for Russian participation in the global carbon market. It is hard to understand why Russia has still not taken the necessary steps to collect the benefits allowed by the protocol.

These developments, as well as the debates surrounding the protocol's ratification in 2004, lead one to believe that Russian policymakers in charge of climate change consider neither the benefits that Russia can get from emissions trading as tangible nor the local economic and environmental ancillary benefits related to GHG emissions control. The only important question debated on the eve of Russian ratification was whether Russia would be able to double its GDP within ten years without breaking its Kyoto commitments. Illarionov's central argument was that Russia would exceed Kyoto targets as a result of doubling its GDP. However, even with GDP doubling, the Kyoto commitments would be met with probability equal to one.[18] Still, nobody can predict Russia's emissions profile and what headroom it would have for emissions trading. Russian officials may be reluctant to give a green light to emissions trading until they get answers to this question. In the next sections, the driving forces behind Russian GHG emissions in the past are analyzed, and the major factors that will determine emissions pathways in the future are examined.

Driving Forces behind Russian Carbon Emissions

All Eastern European, former socialist countries faced economic crises in the beginning of their respective transition periods, followed by a period of recovery growth. By now, the nature of the transition is well described in the economic literature.[19] The crisis in the former Soviet Union was if anything even more profound than in the other transition countries (figure 10-1).

Figure 10-1. *GDP as Percent of 1992 Level, Selected Countries (Central and Eastern Europe, Former Soviet Union), 1992–2003*

Percent of 1992

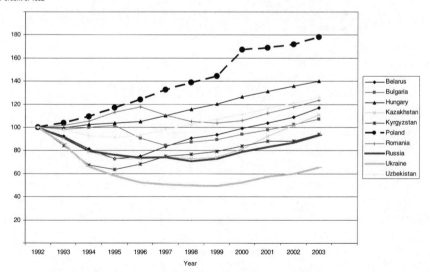

Source: Based on data from U.S. Energy Information Administration (www.eia.gov).

GDP Dynamics and Carbon Emissions

Carbon dioxide emissions did follow the path of GDP—but not closely. During the economic crisis, carbon emissions declined more slowly than the rate of GDP; so they also grew more slowly during the recovery growth period (figure 10-2). An analysis of CO_2 and GDP dynamics demonstrates that, since 1998, the real elasticity of CO_2 by GDP has been about 0.25. In fact GHG emissions elasticity has been slightly lower, since other fractions of GHG emissions (small gases) were growing more slowly than CO_2.

Structural Economic Changes and Energy Efficiency

In 1999 Russia's industrial sector accounted for about 55 percent of the country's carbon emissions; this share has been nearly the same over several years. Since carbon emissions per Russian industrial output are about three times higher than in the rest of the economy, even minor changes in the industrial share of GDP could lead to notable changes in CO_2 emissions.

The carbon intensity of production among industrial sectors is, however, quite diverse. Therefore, structural changes in industry during the economic crisis, along with an increase in the industrial share of GDP, were the most important factors in decoupling GDP and carbon emissions. The highest share of

Figure 10-2. *Carbon Emissions, Carbon Intensity, and GDP as Percent of 1992 Levels, Russia, 1990–2004*

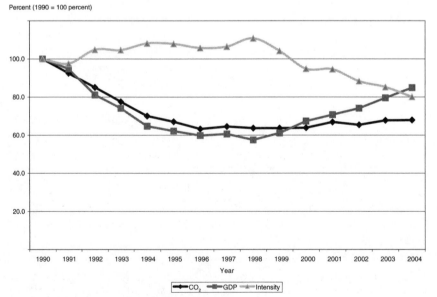

Percent (1990 = 100 percent)

Source: Based on data from U.S. Energy Information Administration (www.eia.gov/environment.html).

Figure 10-3. *Carbon-Intensive Industries, Share in Total GDP, Russia, 1990–2003*

Percent

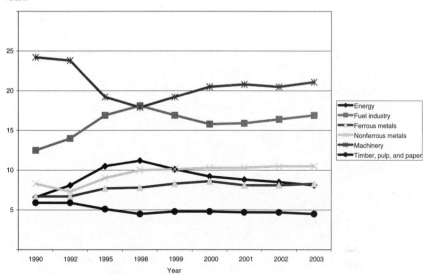

Source: Author's calculations based on Roscomstat data.

most carbon-intensive industries was reached in 1998, when the carbon intensity of GDP was the highest (figure 10-3).

During the recovery period, further reductions in carbon emissions by industry were an important factor in determining overall carbon emissions. After 1998 the share of these sectors gradually declined. Therefore, in 1999–2004 the carbon intensity of industrial production dropped from 11.4 to 9.7 tonnes of CO_2 per U.S.$1,000 market exchange rate, while in other sectors carbon intensity declined from 4.3 to 3.1 tonnes of CO_2 per U.S.$1,000, or about an 18 percent decline in the industry sector (versus a 40 percent decline in other sectors). At the same time, the industry's share in GDP decreased slightly. This decline, along with the structural changes within the industrial sector, was one of the important factors in the further decoupling of carbon emissions and GDP growth. In other words, the tendencies that determined the increase of carbon intensity of GDP during the crisis reversed during the recovery period. As a result, two types of decoupling have been in play in the dynamics of GDP and carbon emissions.

During the recovery period there was a slight improvement in carbon efficiency in most economic sectors (figure 10-4). Although the contribution of this factor to overall carbon emissions was not as significant as the structural changes discussed earlier, nevertheless the combined effect of efficiency and structural changes allowed for the avoidance of a significant amount of emissions. If the

Figure 10-4. *Metric Tonnes of CO_2 Emissions per U.S.$1,000 of GDP, Russia, 1999–2004*

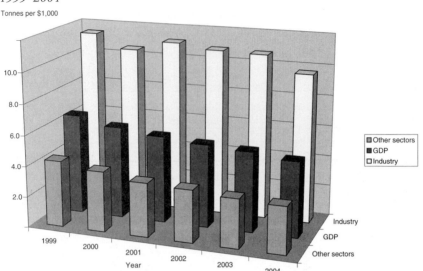

Source: Author's calculations based on Roscomstat data.

GDP structure and carbon intensity both held on the 1999 level, then 2004 emissions would have been about 2,130 megatonnes instead of actual emission estimates of 1,610 megatonnes. Thus if structural changes and carbon intensity dynamics in the industrial sector as well as the rest of the economy accounted for 520 megatonnes of avoided CO_2 emissions in 2004, then CO_2 emissions could have been 1,680 megatonnes. Thus only 70 megatonnes of avoided emissions would have been attributed to efficiency improvements, while 450 megatonnes of avoided emissions were a result of structural changes in GDP, namely the substitution of less carbon-intensive sectors for energy- and carbon-intensive industries.

Fuel Mix

Despite abundant resources of coal, its share in the fuel mix did not significantly change between 1992 and 2003 (figure 10-5). Moreover, the share of natural gas increased slightly, and as a result carbon emissions per unit of fossil fuel energy declined by about 2 percent. During the economic crisis, the carbon intensity of the fuel mix declined from 68.4 million metric tonnes per terajoule in 1992 to 66.6 metric tonnes per terajoule in 1998. During the recovery period, it increased to 67.0 metric tonnes per terajoule, the result of a slight increase of coal in the fuel mix. Natural gas was the main substitute for oil. This fact can best be explained by foreign trade liberalization: it is easier to export oil than

Figure 10-5. *Share of Oil, Coal, and Natural Gas in Total Fuel Use, Russia, 1992–2003*

Percent

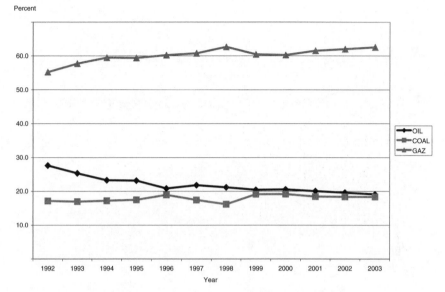

Source: Based on data from U.S. Energy Information Administration and Insitute for Economy in Transition (Russia).

natural gas, since the latter's transport is limited by existing pipelines, whose capacities cannot be increased quickly.[20]

The downward trend in primary energy consumption, especially oil products, was characteristic of all the industrial sectors in Russia during the period. Consumption of heavy oil (*mazut*) decreased from 1999 to 2003 by 32.2 percent.

Incentives

Analysis of carbon emissions and fuel consumption leads to the conclusion that carbon emissions are strongly determined by fuel consumption. Namely, there are no specific factors in carbon emissions other than those that determine fuel consumption: the index of CO_2 emissions closely follows the index of energy consumption (figure 10-6).

Energy consumption in Russia has mainly been determined by structural changes in the Russian economy, which were the result of general market reforms and integration into the world economy. There was no significant investment in energy efficiency during this time. Therefore, slight improvements are explained mainly by no-regret options to cut energy consumption. With the exception of oil, energy demand appears to be not very sensitive to existing price signals. At the same time, more research is needed to quantify

Figure 10-6. *Energy Consumption and Carbon Dioxide Emissions as Percent of 1992 Levels, Russia, 1992–2003*

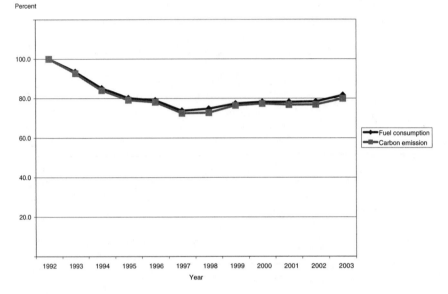

Source: Based on data from U.S. Energy Information Administration and Insitute for Economy in Transition (Russia).

consumer response to energy prices, which have continued to rise since 1998. Fuel price signals and additional incentives to cut GHG emissions created by emissions trading will determine Russian carbon emissions in the near future.

At the moment, the conclusion is that the decline in the carbon intensity of GDP and the decoupling of CO_2 and GDP are the result of general market reforms and the integration of the Russian economy into the world economy. The pollution haven effect, which is considered in environmental and economic literature as a possible outcome of trade liberalization, is more than offset by the shrinking of most energy-inefficient sectors and the realization of the simplest efficiency improvements economywide.

The Future of Carbon Emissions

The future of the emissions path for Russia is uncertain because it is not clear how long existing determinants will drive carbon emissions and when and how new incentives, like energy prices and incentives brought on by Kyoto's flexible mechanisms, will influence the emissions pathway. Some factors determining Russian carbon emissions in the future are summarized in table 10-1. It is difficult to quantify the factors in the table with respect to forecasting the future.

Table 10-1. *Factors Determining Carbon Dioxide Emissions, Past and Future*

Factor	Past	Future
GDP dynamics	Carbon dioxide emissions followed GDP but not closely	Carbon dioxide emissions will increase
GDP structure	Decline	Carbon dioxide emissions will decline
Fuel mix	Decline	Carbon dioxide emissions may increase
New technologies	Moderate decline	This factor may be the major source of carbon emissions reduction
Energy price elasticity	Moderate decline	This factor has not been explored. Price signals will create additional incentives for innovations, so carbon dioxide emissions may decline
Incentives created by emissions trading	No incentives	This factor will promote low-carbon fuels and renewables, so carbon dioxide emissions may decline

Much depends on the diffusion of new technologies, which will be induced by gradual reforms in energy prices and incentives created by international carbon emissions trading.

Short-Term Projection

For the short-term projection, a very simple methodology is applied. The CO_2 emissions in the time period t (CO_{2t}) are calculated by the formula

$$CO_{2t} = CO_{20}(1+\alpha\beta/100)^t ,$$

where α denotes the elasticity of CO_2 emissions growth with respect to GDP growth and β denotes GDP growth calculated as a percentage. This approach was applied as a short-term projection.[21] Many forecasts have been created for Russian emissions based on a similar method. The forecasts were also presented in the various *National Communications* to the UNFCCC. All of these rely on this simple approach, which is easy to implement.

However, few researchers will use such simplification when considering the uncertainties of exogenous parameters such as the current level of emissions, projected GDP growth, and of course the elasticity of CO_2 growth with respect to GDP growth. All these uncertainties significantly influence the results. Sensitivity analysis addresses some of these. The Monte Carlo method allows simulation of different combinations of exogenous parameters (independent variables)

Figure 10-7. *Estimated Carbon Dioxide Emissions as Percent of 1990 Level,*
Russia, 2010

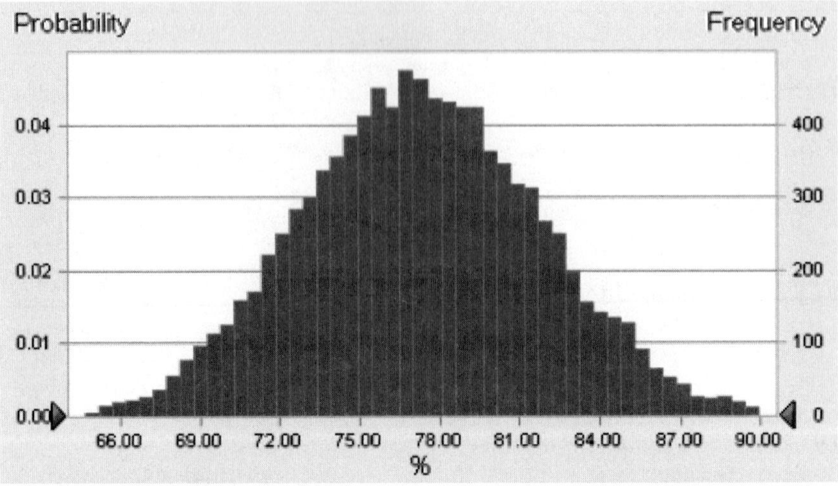

Source: Author's calculations.

and evaluations of possible variations of the outcomes (such as CO_2 emissions
during the coming years).

For the simulation, carbon dioxide emissions in 2004 were assumed to be
normally distributed, with a mean of 1,610 megatonnes of CO_2 and a standard
deviation of 5 percent, while GDP annual growth and the elasticity of CO_2
emissions growth with respect to GDP growth were assumed to be distributed
uniformly on the interval of 5–7 percent for GDP and 0.2–0.5 for elasticity.
The results of the Monte Carlo simulation are presented in figure 10-7. Mean
emissions in 2010 (or the average during the Kyoto commitment period) are
about 77 percent of 1990 levels; the standard deviation is about 4.5 percent.
The minimum is 60 percent and the maximum is 95 percent. With a probability of 0.9, Russia's 2010 CO_2 emissions will be less than 83 percent of the
Kyoto target. Thus the mean surplus of allowances over the five-year commitment period will be about 2,700 megatonnes of CO_2; with a probability 0.9,
this surplus will be not less than 2,000 megatonnes.

Long-Term Perspectives

Annual emissions growth is most sensitive to the elasticity of carbon dioxide
emissions with respect to GDP. The methodology just presented works to
answer the question of whether Russia will be in compliance with the Kyoto
Protocol and what its surplus allowances will be. However, the methodology is
not reliable for making more precise projections, since elasticity itself could be

Figure 10-8. *Three Scenarios for Carbon Dioxide Emissions, Russia, 2004–20*[a]

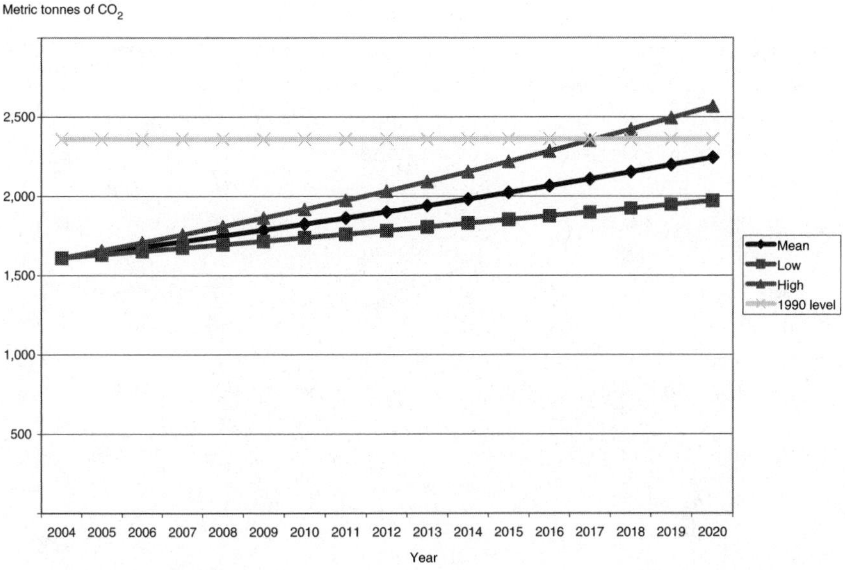

Metric tonnes of CO_2

Source: Author's calculations.
a. Confidence interval of 90 percent.

presented as an endogenous parameter, determined by various factors, including energy price elasticity, incentives for carbon emissions reduction that could be created by emissions trading, and saving rate. The next important factor is annual GDP growth. A mean and two marginal (within 90 percent confidence interval) scenarios are presented in figure 10-8 to illustrate the possible deviation of CO_2 emissions projected from 2004 until 2020. The difference between two marginal scenarios in 2020 is about 500 million tonnes of CO_2 emissions. This difference illustrates what could be achieved if market incentives to reduce energy consumption and carbon emissions were in place.

Nevertheless, there are some rules determining the future dynamics of carbon emissions that could be useful for future projections. Since elasticity is the major determinant of future carbon emission dynamics, I focus on this parameter. By definition, elasticity, e, is equal to the derivative of CO_2 emissions by GDP multiplied by GDP and divided by CO_2 emissions:

$$e = \frac{\partial C}{\partial G} * \frac{G}{C} = \frac{\partial C}{\partial G} \bigg/ I,$$

where C is carbon emissions (in CO_2 equivalent); G is GDP; I is carbon intensity of GDP, and $I = C/G$.

This formula suggests that there is a link between elasticity and the carbon intensity of GDP. Countries with higher carbon intensity will demonstrate lower elasticity. Russia's carbon intensity is among the highest. Therefore, one could expect relatively lower elasticity of CO_2 emissions by GDP.

The derivative of CO_2 emissions with respect to GDP is another component that explains the elasticity of CO_2 emissions. An analysis of carbon emissions and GDP for EU countries and major developing countries demonstrates the decarbonization of economic growth.[22] It implies that $\partial^2 C/\partial^2 G < 0$. Therefore, on the one hand, elasticity should be declining along with GDP growth. On the other hand, it will increase as intensity declines. Taking into account a very high initial intensity, it is reasonable to predict that elasticity will remain low during the next several years. Most likely, carbon emissions will be closer to the lower frontier of the 90 percent confidence interval than to the upper one. In any case, it is difficult to quantify this theoretical conclusion. More sophisticated analytical tools are needed to provide a detailed analysis of the effect of market incentives on Russian CO_2 emissions.

Conclusions

Despite the obvious benefits to Russia from its signing of the Kyoto Protocol, it took several years for Russian politicians to ratify the treaty. The protocol was a bargaining tool in the WTO negotiations, and Russian leaders promised to speed up ratification after the European Union withdrew its request for Russia to sharply increase its domestic natural gas prices. Hidden subsidies for natural gas allow Russia to keep a significant share of natural gas in the fuel mix. With regard to the absence of any other meaningful environmental policy, the subsidies for gas consumption are the only way to prevent the sharp increase of conventional pollution and carbon emissions.

During the economic crisis of 1991–98, Russian carbon emissions declined along with GDP, but the emissions reduction was not as large as the GDP reduction. Likewise, the increase of CO_2 emissions during the recovery period was not as sharp as the GDP increase: elasticity of CO_2 emissions with respect to GDP was about 0.25. The major factor determining carbon emissions was structural change in GDP. The industrial sector contributes a substantial share of CO_2 emissions; changes in total industry production significantly influenced carbon emissions and help to explain the decoupling of CO_2 and GDP. The GDP share of industry increased during the economic crisis and then declined during the recovery period.

Structural changes within the industry are important as well. The variation of carbon intensity across industrial sectors declined. Decline in the share of most carbon-intensive sectors led to a decrease in aggregated carbon intensity. In the industrial sector the combined effect of these factors allowed for the avoidance of a significant amount of emissions. If the GDP structure and carbon intensity held, then 2004 emissions would have been about 2,130 megatonnes instead of their actual 1,610 megatonnes. All structural changes and improvements of efficiency were the result of the integration of the Russian economy into the world economy and the general effect of economic liberalization.

As of now there are no specific incentives for CO_2 emissions reduction. Thus all improvements in carbon efficiency can be explained by the alteration in energy efficiency of the economy. CO_2 emissions closely follow energy consumption. Therefore, some additional incentives could be created by the Kyoto Protocol, which will help determine CO_2 emissions in the future.

The future of carbon emissions is uncertain. Nobody can tell exactly how long the existing forces driving carbon emissions will determine these dynamics and when new factors will take over. To address these uncertainties, the Monte Carlo method to predict the range for CO_2 emissions was applied. Surely, Russia will meet its Kyoto target, and with 90 percent confidence, will have a cumulative surplus of assigned amount units equal to 2,000 megatonnes of CO_2. Most likely Russian CO_2 emissions will remain below 1990 levels during the next decade. A more precise projection requires the application of a general equilibrium model with endogenous technological changes, because technological changes and further improvements in efficiency will be important factors for GHG emissions.

Notes

1. This calculation is based on data from the U.S. Energy Information Administration (www.eia.doe.gov/environment.html); and on data from the *Third Russian National Communication to the United Nations Framework Convention on Climate Change* (www.eia.doe.gov/environment.html).
2. Russia obviously has great potential to build these institutions. For example, the Russian state power company, RAO UES Russia, which supplies about 90 percent of power and is responsible for about a third of Russian carbon dioxide emissions, has completed its emissions inventory. Dan Dudek and others, "Emission Inventory on Company Level: Lessons from Russia," *Mitigation and Adaptation Strategies for Global Change* 7 (2002): 155–72. The company is on the way to building a companywide GHG management system. Archangelsk Pulp and Paper Plant completed an emission inventory and voluntarily announced its emission target. Alexander Golub and others, "Breaking through Barriers in Russia," *Environmental Finance,* May 2004. This experience could be replicated, and that would help to build the relevant institution for carbon emission management in Russia.
3. Alexander Golub and Elena Strukova, "Russia and the GHG Market," *Climatic Change* 63 (2004): 223–43.
4. David Victor, Nebojsa Nakicenovic, and Nadeja Victor, *The Kyoto Protocol Carbon Bubble: Implications for Russia, Ukraine, and Emission Trading,* Interim Report IR-98-094 (Laxenburg, Austria: International Institute for Applied Systems Analysis, 1998); Evsei Gurvich and others, *Greenhouse Gas Impacts of Russian Energy Subsidies: Reforming Energy and Transport Subsidies* (Paris: OECD, 1998).

5. Alexander Golub and others, *The National Strategy Study on GHG Mitigation* (Washington: World Bank, 1999).

6. Golub and Strukova, "Russia and the GHG Market," p. 235. All calculations are for CO_2 only and reflect the cumulative surplus over the five-year commitment period. Under a scenario that assumes successful market reforms and additional incentives created by carbon emission trading, this potential is equal to 2.7 billion tonnes of CO_2. Other gases, as well as additional allowances that could be generated under articles 3.3 and 3.4 of the Kyoto Protocol, are not included.

7. Golub and Strukova, "Russia and the GHG Market," p. 235.

8. *Third Russian National Communication to the United Nations Framework Convention on Climate Change.* The communication includes three scenarios for GHG emissions based on a methodology similar to the one applied for the projections in the *First* and *Second National Communications.*

9. Increases in the price of natural gas would be induced by EU domestic policies aimed at meeting Kyoto emissions targets.

10. There is no publicly available evidence that this was the deal, but indirect evidence is convincing.

11. Dan Dudek, Alexander Golub, and Elena Strukova, "Should Russia Increase Domestic Prices for Natural Gas?" *Energy Policy* 34, no. 13 (2006): 1659–70; Dan Dudek, Alexander Golub, and Elena Strukova, *Environmental Aspects of Dual Pricing for Natural Gas in Russia* (New York: Environmental Defense, 2004).

12. For more details, see Alexander Golub and Benito Müller, "Kyoto's Future Lies in Putin's Hands" (www.oxfordenergy.org/pdfs/EV33.pdf).

13. Sergei Bobylev and others, "Comments on *Economic Consequences of Possible Ratification of the Kyoto Protocol by the Russian Federation*" (New York: Environmental Defense, 2004).

14. International Energy Agency, *CO_2 Emissions from Fuel Combustion, 1971–2003* (Paris: 2004), figure 35.

15. The statistics from the International Energy Agency are reproduced in Bobylev and others, "Comments on *Economic Consequences,*" table E.

16. It is not clear why the authors used International Energy Agency data, since the agency warned that the discrepancy could result from incomplete information on Russian fuel consumption in 1990. International Energy Agency, *CO_2 Emissions from Fuel Combustion 1971–2003*, pp. xliv–xlvi.

17. Bobylev and others, "Comments on *Economic Consequences.*"

18. Ibid.; Golub and others, "Breaking through Barriers in Russia."

19. See for example Jan Svejnar, "Transition Economies: Performance and Challenges," *Journal of Economic Perspectives* 16, no. 1 (2002): 3–28.

20. Dudek, Golub, and Strukova, "Should Russia Increase Domestic Prices for Natural Gas?"

21. Golub and others, "Breaking through Barriers in Russia."

22. Alexander Golub, Anil Markandya, and Dominic Marcellino, "Will the Kyoto Protocol Cost Too Much and Create Unbreakable Barriers for Economic Growth?" *Contemporary Economic Policy* 24 (October 2006): 520–35.

11

Climate Policy in the United Kingdom

HOWARD DALTON

The United Kingdom has been at the forefront in the response to climate change. For two decades it has regarded climate change as a critical issue facing humankind, one with the potential for profoundly affecting the global environment, its flora and fauna, and global society. As evidence began to emerge through a number of assessments in the 1980s, against the background of rising air pollution, acid rain, and ozone depletion, governments were faced with how to deal with the growing threat. In her speech to the Royal Society in September 1988, Prime Minister Margaret Thatcher noted: "For generations, we have assumed that the efforts of mankind would leave the fundamental equilibrium of the world's systems and atmosphere stable. But it is possible that with all these enormous changes (population, agricultural, use of fossil fuels) concentrated into such a short period of time, we have unwittingly begun a massive experiment with the system of this planet itself."[1]

Shortly afterward the United Kingdom was a key mover in the formation of the Intergovernmental Panel on Climate Change (IPCC), and in 1990, building on existing modeling capabilities of the Met (Meteorological) Office, formed the Hadley Centre for Climate Prediction and Research. Successive British administrations have placed climate change at the heart of their environmental policy and have taken a lead on the international stage in tackling climate change. In more recent years, much effort has been invested in integrating climate and energy policies: the publication of the Energy White Paper in 2003 and the placing of climate change at the center of the U.K.'s presidency of the Group of Eight (G-8) in 2005.

The U.K. has taken a leading role in climate science, in domestic policy for reducing greenhouse gas emissions, and in international negotiations. It is on track to meet its Kyoto target on emissions reduction, was the first to introduce economywide greenhouse gas emissions trading, has committed to a long-term emission reduction goal (down 60 percent by 2050), and is one of the leaders in the development of adaptation responses. The U.K. sees not only the threat of climate change but also the potential for the introduction of new, low-emission technology and its associated economic benefits. The country is also working with others in the developed and developing world to achieve an effective and equitable global response to climate change.

Evidence-Based Policy

An important element of the U.K. approach is the recognition of the need to base policies on good science and to take seriously the clear message coming from the scientific community. Science has a crucial role to play in providing necessary evidence to understand, predict, and prepare for the changes that are likely to happen and to devise policies to prevent what is still preventable. The U.K. has therefore accepted the assessments of the IPCC as providing the most authoritative picture of climate change, and it is prepared to act on them.

Science is at the heart of policymaking in the Department for Environment, Food, and Rural Affairs (DEFRA)—providing evidence for decisionmakers, finding solutions, and identifying future issues. During 2005 DEFRA scientists and policymakers mapped out in detail the information needed from science, economics, social research, and statistics to deliver in its priority policy areas. In 2006 DEFRA published its *Approach to Evidence & Innovation.*[2] These followed the first *Science and Innovation Strategy,* published in 2003, and *Evidence and Innovation: DEFRA's Needs from the Sciences over the Next 10 Years,* published in July 2004. The latter set out DEFRA's science needs, including increasing research into priority areas such as climate change, rural communities, and sustainable consumption and production.

The Nature of the Threat and the Rationale for Action

There is good evidence that climate change due to human activities is happening. The Hadley Centre provides strong evidence that greenhouse gases are primarily responsible for recent global and regional warming.[3] The Hadley Centre used its climate model to simulate the general trend in twentieth-century temperature climate, using various combinations of external influences as input to

Figure 11-1. *Observed and Modeled World Temperature Change, Three Combinations of Possible Influences on the Climate System, 1850–2000*

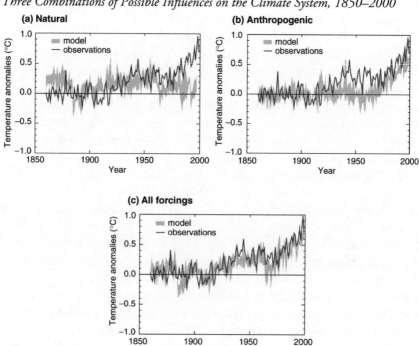

Source: IPCC, *Climate Change 2001: Synthesis Report*, Contribution of Working Groups I, II, and III to the Third Assessment Report, edited by Robert T. Watson and the Core Writing Team (Geneva: 2001).

the calculations. Three experiments were undertaken (figure 11-1). The first, labeled *natural*, simulates the observed global temperature of the past 150 years, taking into account only natural changes (solar and volcanic) but keeping anthropogenic influences, such as greenhouse gases, constant; it also shows the observed warming in the early part of the century but not the warming in the latter part. The second experiment (labeled *anthropogenic*) keeps natural influence constant and includes the historic increase in greenhouse gas levels. The result reproduces recent warming but is a poor fit to the middle of the record. The third experiment, *all forcings*, combined natural and human influences and shows the best fit over the whole record. Statistical tests show that it is impossible to explain the recent warming with natural changes only.

The indications are growing that the almost universal warming seen over the past century is affecting the natural world and society. Heat waves led to the deaths of over 26,000 people across Europe in 2003; there is a worldwide melting of glaciers, a downward trend in Arctic sea ice in the summer, widespread melting of permafrost, earlier spring activity of plants and animals across the northern hemisphere, rising sea levels, and increases in extreme rainfalls, droughts, and storms.

The IPCC in its Third Assessment Report (2001) indicates that greenhouse gas concentrations will continue to grow through this century, leading to temperature increases of between 1.5°C and 5.8°C.[4] Such changes will have dramatic effects. The uncertainty range is large due in part to the underlying uncertainty about how human societies will develop without specific climate policies and how this will affect greenhouse gas emissions. There is also uncertainty over the sensitivity of the climate system to increasing greenhouse gas concentrations. Assessing impacts adds another level of uncertainty.

But despite these uncertainties, estimates can be made. Drawing on IPCC reports and on work presented at the "Avoiding Dangerous Climate Change" conference in Exeter in February 2005, table 11-1 summarizes the impacts that we might expect with various levels of temperature change.[5] Up to 2°C the greatest impacts will be upon the natural world: ecosystems and species. Increasing extreme weather will also result. The irreversible loss of the Greenland ice sheet may begin to occur with a global temperature rise of only 1.5°C, although work being carried out by the Hadley Centre and Reading University suggests that the threshold may be a bit higher. Even so, the threat cannot be ignored. Societal impacts tend to become more severe above a 2°C rise, although this ignores possible collateral impacts on society from ecosystem disruption. The risks of large-scale climate disruption also increase with temperature, but identifying trigger points is very difficult. Note that all of these impacts fall within the temperature range predicted by the IPCC.

Table 11-1. *How Much Climate Change Is Too Much?*

Degrees above normal	Impact
1°–2°C above preindustrial	Major impacts on ecosystems and species; wide-ranging impacts on society
1.5°C	Greenland ice cap starts to melt (7 meters)
2°–3°C	Major loss of coral reef ecosystem; considerable species loss; large impacts on agriculture, water resources, health, economies
	General increase in droughts and extreme rainfalls as temperature increases. Up to 88-centimeter sea-level rise in next 100 years
2°–3°C	Terrestrial carbon sink becomes a source
1°–4°C	North Atlantic circulation collapses
2°–4.5°C	West Antarctic ice sheet collapses (5 meters)

Source: Adapted from R. Warren, "Impacts of Global Climate Change at Different Annual Mean Global Temperature Increases," in *Avoiding Dangerous Climate Change,* edited by H. J. Schellnhuber and others (Cambridge University Press, 2006).

In considering such threats, the European Union proposes that action be taken to prevent global temperatures from rising by more than 2°C. This is not risk free and will not avoid all climate change damage, so 2°C is really a conservative limit. The EU also notes that a 2°C limit would mean keeping CO_2 concentrations well below 550 parts per million (ppm), double preindustrial levels. The level of greenhouse gas stabilization chosen depends on climate sensitivity, which is uncertain and which recent studies suggest could be higher than has been quoted in the Third Assessment Report of the IPCC.

The key question, then, is what would a 450–550 ppm limit mean for emission limitations? Figure 11-2 shows total accumulated emissions of CO_2 for three scenarios since the beginning of the industrial revolution (1750) up to 2100. The key points that the figure illustrates are

—Without concerted action to reduce CO_2 emissions, the world could easily emit more CO_2 by the year 2030 than has been emitted since the industrial revolution.

—The United Kingdom could use up more than 60 percent of its CO_2 emissions allowance to meet 450 ppm stabilization by 2030; that number is twice what the country should emit to be on track. Even with a 550 ppm target, the U.K. will use nearly 40 percent of its allowance in 30 percent of the time.

—A 550 ppm scenario is unlikely to deliver a 2°C limit. Indeed, according to the IPCC, at stabilization the temperatures could be between 2°C and 5°C higher than today's values, carrying a substantial risk of damaging impacts and climate system disruption.

—It would be decidedly risky to allow emissions to continue to rise unchecked when there is a considerable risk of damage and little headroom for

Figure 11-2. *Cumulative Carbon Dioxide Emissions (GtC) by 2100, Three Scenarios*

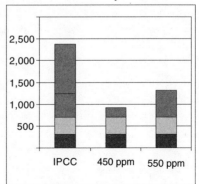

■ IPCC high scenario, 2030–2100

■ IPCC low scenario and stabilization scenarios, 2030–2100

□ IEA projection, 2000–2030

■ Historic, 1750–2000

Source: Institute of Economic Analysis, *World Energy Outlook, 2004* (Paris: 2004); IPCC, *Emissions Scenarios: Summary for Policymakers*, Special Report of Working Group III (Geneva: 2000).

maneuver. Early actions to limit emissions are essential to significantly reduce the risk of damage from climate change.

The United Kingdom faces a major challenge. Growing populations, industrial development, and basic energy needs in the developing world will raise the demand for energy by some 60–70 percent between 2002 and 2030, according to the International Energy Agency. If these needs are largely met through the use of fossil fuels, then emissions will rise by a similar amount. Such growth would put the world on an emissions track far higher than would be prudent given our understanding of the risks of climate change. And delay will only lead to the need to catch up. Furthermore, inertia in both the climate system and energy structures may mean that, by the time the damage becomes apparent, it may be too late.

This is the challenge of climate change and the rationale for immediate action. The risks of considerable damage and disruption suggest constraints on carbon emissions, which run counter to the underlying aspirations of societies around the world. Yet society does have many options to reduce emissions, such as energy efficiency, renewable energy, and combined heat and power among others. In addition, carbon capture and storage are technologically possible. Global institutions need to implement these measures immediately and to accelerate research and development, which will deliver new systems to meet this challenge.

Climate Change and the U.K. Presidency of the Group of Eight

The U.K. held the presidency of the G-8 in 2005; throughout that year Prime Minister Tony Blair made climate change a major G-8 focus. The prime objectives were to position climate change as a matter deserving the urgent attention of G-8 heads of government and to promote an international consensus on the need for further action to control emissions. In his speech to the World Economic Forum in Davos, Switzerland, Blair stated three broad climate change aims for the G-8 under the U.K. presidency to achieve:

—To set a direction. Whether because of the risks associated with climate change or related issues of security of energy supply, there is a need to send a clear signal that, while the group continues to analyze the science, it is united in moving in the direction of greenhouse gas reductions.

—To develop a package of practical measures, largely focused on technology, to cut emissions of greenhouse gases.

—To engage countries outside the G-8, like China and India, on how their growing energy needs can be met sustainably and how they can adapt to the impacts of climate change.

Because the U.K. wanted the G-8 heads of government to have access to the most up-to-date scientific information regarding climate change, it hosted a science conference to consider the long-term implications of different levels of climate change for different sectors and for the world as a whole. Major themes included the key vulnerabilities of the climate system and the critical thresholds, the socioeconomic effects both global and regional, the emission pathways to climate stabilization, and the technological options available to achieve stabilization levels.

At the conference it was noted that, compared with the IPCC's Third Assessment Report, there was now greater clarity and reduced uncertainty about the impacts of climate change across a wide range of systems, sectors, and societies. In many cases the risks were more serious than previously thought. As well as climate impacts, the conference noted that CO_2 could result from increasing the acidity of the ocean, which would likely reduce the capacity of the ocean to absorb CO_2 from the atmosphere, affecting the entire marine food chain.

A range of emission pathways can be followed to avoid certain temperature levels. Probability analysis provides a quantitative estimate of the risk that a particular temperature level will not be exceeded. For example, limiting warming to 2°C above preindustrial levels with a relatively high certainty requires the equivalent concentration of CO_2 to stay below 400 parts per million. Conversely, if concentrations were to rise to a 550 ppm CO_2 equivalent, then it is unlikely that the global mean temperature increase would stay below 2°C. Delaying action would require greater action later, and even a delay of five years could be significant. In terms of achievability, the technological options for significantly reducing emissions over the long term already exist. Large reductions can be attained using a portfolio of options, whose costs are likely to be smaller than previously considered.

The findings from the science conference were reinforced by the unprecedented joint statement issued just before the G-8 summit by the science academies of the G-8 countries as well as those of Brazil, China, and India. According to these independent scientific institutions, "the scientific understanding of climate change is now sufficiently clear to justify nations taking prompt action," and they urged nations to "identify cost-effective steps that can be taken now to contribute to a substantial and long-term reduction in net global greenhouse gas emissions."[6]

On July 8, 2005, at Gleneagles, the heads of government of the G-8 and the president of the European Commission signed a communiqué that includes the following:[7]

—A statement on the importance of climate change, including an agreement that human activity does contribute to climate change. It also agreed that greenhouse gas emissions need to slow, peak, and reverse and that nations need to act to make "substantial cuts" in emissions. In addition the G-8 agreed to "act with resolve and urgency now." This is the first time that G-8 leaders have agreed that human activity is a major contributory factor to climate change.

—A plan of action on climate change that builds on existing work in order to increase the speed with which greenhouse gas emissions are reduced. The plan of action highlights the need to improve energy efficiency in appliances, buildings, transport, and industry and to move to lower carbon options for power generation, including the use of carbon capture and storage and renewable energy. It also looks at cross-cutting issues, including the need to promote broader participation in research and development and in financing the transition to clean energy (principally through public and private investment driven by market-based policy instruments and regulatory signals).

—Agreement to a new dialogue on climate change, clean energy, and sustainable development among G-8 countries and other interested countries with significant energy needs, a dialogue that allows continuing informal discussion of the issues around climate change and measures to tackle it, such as those agreed at Gleneagles. The dialogue is to create the conditions for more constructive negotiations within the United Nations framework.

The discussions at Gleneagles included a session with the heads of government of Brazil, Mexico, South Africa, China, and India. These countries issued their own joint statement on issues of sustainable development and the global economy, including a call for new approaches to international cooperation on climate change for the future. This is particularly significant for climate change, as emissions in these countries are set to rise substantially as they develop and their economies grow. Their communiqué states its overall objectives as

—Addressing the strategic challenge of transforming their energy systems to create a secure and sustainable future.

—Monitoring the implementation of the Gleneagles plan of action and exploring how the countries can build on that progress.

—Agreeing to share best practices.

The World Bank and the International Energy Agency were to play an important role in supporting the dialogue. The World Bank's role was to create a framework for investment in cleaner energy technologies and in measures necessary for adaptation, involving the private sector and the regional development banks. The International Energy Agency was to analyze alternative energy strategies and to support work on best practices in energy efficiency and cleaner coal technologies.

The Gleneagles communiqués make clear that dialogue is not a substitute for negotiations. The U.K. remains of the view that the UNFCCC is the only appropriate forum to negotiate commitments beyond 2012, when the first Kyoto commitment period ends. The first meeting of the dialogue took place on November 1, 2005, and was chaired by Margaret Beckett, secretary of state for Environment, Food, and Rural Affairs; and by Alan Johnson, secretary of state for Trade and Industry. It was attended by energy and environment ministers from up to twenty countries with significant energy needs and focused on how to make the transition to a secure and sustainable energy future.

Future International Action on Climate Change

In consideration of what needs to be done to combat climate change, the European Council of Ministers, drawing on the communication, "Winning the Battle against Global Climate Change," concludes that[8]

—There is increasing scientific evidence that the benefits of limiting the overall global surface temperature increase to 2°C above preindustrial levels outweigh the costs of abatement policies.

—Immediate and effective implementation of agreed policies and measures is important, and there is a need to foster increased public awareness and a need for better focused research and the promotion of stronger cooperation with developing countries.

Further, the European Union's future climate change strategy should

—Strive for the widest possible cooperation by all countries,

—Include all important greenhouse gases, sectors, and mitigation options,

—Drive technological innovation, employing an optimal mix of push and pull policies, in particular in the transport and energy sectors,

—Promote the transfer of technologies to appropriate markets,

—Provide for the continued use of market-based and flexible instruments,

—Support the adaptation to unavoidable climate change in all countries, particularly in the most vulnerable developing countries.

Public funding channeled inter alia through development banks needs to be used to leverage private sector funding toward climate-friendly investments, particularly in the low greenhouse gas–emitting energy technologies.

In Montreal in November and December 2005 the Conference of the Parties to the UNFCCC met for the eleventh time. In parallel, and for the first time, there was a meeting of the parties to the Kyoto Protocol, which had recently come into force. At these meetings the European Union's objective was to secure the start of negotiations on further international action for the period beyond the Kyoto commitment period, that is, post-2012.

The international debate on what the framework post-2012 should be is still at an early stage. It is important that the parties remain flexible in looking at the options; any future regime needs to be

—Realistic (relevant to countries with different national circumstances),

—Robust (capable of being adjusted in the light of experience), and

—Durable (will not become irrelevant after a few years).

For any such framework to be effective, it needs to achieve a wide global acceptance and to deliver results in terms of significant emissions reductions.

Long-Term U.K. Emission Goals

Considerations similar to those mentioned earlier led the U.K. government to commit, in an energy white paper, to reducing its emissions of CO_2 by 60 percent below 1990 levels by 2050, with real progress by 2020.[9] The white paper also contains important commitments to maintain the reliability of U.K. energy supplies, to promote competitive markets in the United Kingdom and beyond, and to ensure that every home is adequately and affordably heated.

The domestic U.K. goal to cut emissions of CO_2, the most important greenhouse gas, had been recommended by the U.K. Royal Commission on Environmental Pollution in June 2000.[10] The Royal Commission advised that a reduction in CO_2 emissions of 60 percent would be necessary to limit atmospheric concentration of CO_2 emissions globally to 550 parts per million, assuming that an atmospheric concentration of 550 ppm of CO_2 should be regarded as an upper limit that ought not be exceeded.

By placing in the white paper a specific commitment to a 60 percent reduction in CO_2 emissions by 2050, the United Kingdom set a clear goal for domestic policy, committing it to a national program to reduce emissions. It also led the way internationally by highlighting the need to address the long-term challenge of climate change. By setting a precedent in terms of adopting a long-term target, the U.K. has been in a position to exert greater influence internationally by setting out and promoting more clearly what approach it favors in terms of an international framework for reducing carbon emissions. The government also committed the country to make "real progress" toward achieving its goal of a 60 percent reduction in emissions by 2020. The goal was reaffirmed in the Labour Party's 2005 election manifesto, which states that "a 60% reduction by 2050 remains necessary and achievable."

The four goals of the energy white paper (reducing CO_2 emissions, maintaining the reliability of U.K. energy supplies, promoting competitive markets, and ensuring the affordable heating of every home) can be achieved. Rather than the use of a simple mechanism to determine the relative weights of differing objectives, the following considerations should guide the implementation of the white paper's measures:

—Significant harmful climate change and effects on local air pollution are environmental limits that should not be breached.

—Reliable energy supplies are fundamental to the economy as a whole and to sustainable development.

—Liberalized and competitive markets will continue to be a cornerstone of energy policy.

—Policies should take into account impacts on all sectors of society; specific measures will be needed for particular groups of people (for example, for the fuel poor).

There will, of course, be a cost to the U.K. economy in implementing the white paper's measures, but modeling studies suggest that these are likely to be relatively small. The cost of making a 60 percent cut in carbon dioxide emissions by 2050 is estimated at 0.5–2.0 percent of U.K. GDP. In the worst-case scenario—in which other countries take no action to reduce carbon emissions—U.K. industries facing intense international competition (some chemicals sectors, man-made fibers, paper; iron, steel, and nonferrous metals) could experience overall cost increases of 1 percent or more. The estimated cost increases would occur over the period to 2020. Energy efficiency measures could successfully reduce energy use and mitigate the energy cost increases faced by these sectors.

The economic aspects of climate change are important for the policy response, and in July 2005 the chancellor of the exchequer, Gordon Brown, announced a review of the economics of climate change. It is a further demonstration of the importance that the U.K. government attaches to the issue of climate change.

The U.K. Climate Change Programme

The United Kingdom's commitment under Kyoto is to reduce the emissions of the basket of greenhouse gases by 12.5 percent between 2008 and 2012, relative to 1990. In addition, the U.K. has a domestic goal to reduce its CO_2 emissions by 20 percent by 2010 relative to 1990. The long-term goal of a 60 percent CO_2 reduction by 2050 provides a useful context for the U.K.'s Climate Change Programme.[11]

The U.K. was one of the first countries to publish a program setting out how it planned to meet its Kyoto Protocol target. The program is a statement of how the U.K. government and the administrations of Scotland, Wales, and Northern Ireland seek to tackle climate change; the statement includes a framework of policies and measures to reduce emissions across all sectors of the economy. It also explains how the U.K. will adapt to some of the changes that could result from climate change.

The United Kingdom has already met its Kyoto target for all greenhouse gases (figure 11-3). Carbon dioxide emissions alone have fallen since 1990. In 2004 they were about 4 percent lower than 1990 levels due to reductions in emissions from the energy sector and across industry, despite increases from residential fossil fuel use and transport. It is also estimated that the U.K. Climate Change Programme, started in 2000, has succeeded in reducing CO_2 levels by about 4 percent compared to what would have happened otherwise. Increases in both 2003 and 2004 were mainly due to increases in industrial and transport sector emissions. Estimates suggest that, based on current policies and measures, CO_2 emissions in 2010 will be 11.0–11.5 percent below 1990 levels, without taking into account the impact of the first phase of the European Union Emissions Trading Scheme (EU ETS).

Figure 11-3. *Emissions of All Greenhouse Gases and Carbon Dioxide, Million Tonnes, 1990–2012*

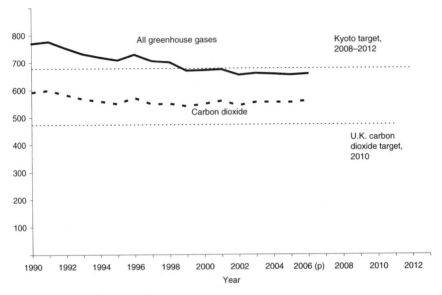

Source: S.L. Bagott and others, "UK Greenhouse Gas Inventory 1990 to 2005: Annual Report for Submission under the Framework Conventon on Climate Change," AEAT/ENV/R/2429, 13/04/2007 (www. nael.org.uk/reports.php); 2006 figure is provisional but typically accurate to within 1 percent (www.defra.gov.uk/environment/statistics/globatmos/kf/gakf05.htm).

Emissions of methane, nitrous oxide, and the fluorinated compounds have declined significantly (41 percent since 1990) due to integrated pollution prevention and control, diversion away from landfill for waste, increased utilization of landfill gas, and the United Kingdom Emissions Trading Scheme (U.K. ETS). The scheme encompasses six principal areas for reducing emission of greenhouse gases: business, transport, agriculture, power generation, domestic use, and building.

Improvement in business's use of energy is being promoted through a number of measures, including the climate change levy, which taxes the use of energy in industry, commerce, and the public sector. Energy-intensive sectors affected by this levy were given the opportunity to sign up to ten-year negotiated agreements covering energy use or emission reductions in return for an 80 percent discount on the levy. By October 2005 there were forty-four sectors with over 10,000 facilities covered by these agreements. Both the U.K. ETS and the EU ETS are proving very effective in lowering emissions from industry. Both schemes are discussed in more detail in the following paragraphs.

Stimulation of new and more efficient sources of power generation is addressed in the U.K. Climate Change Programme by an obligation on electricity suppliers to increase the proportion of electricity provided by renewable sources to 10 percent by 2010 and a target to double the U.K.'s combined heat and power capacity by 2010. Emissions reductions by the transport sector should be realized through a European-level agreement with car manufacturers to improve the average fuel efficiency of new cars by at least 25 percent by 2008–09. The ten-year transport investment plan (2000–10) is worth £180 billion. Domestic energy efficiency is being promoted via energy efficiency commitments, through which electricity and gas suppliers assist their domestic customers, particularly the elderly and those on low incomes, to save energy and cut their fuel bills. Increasing energy efficiency is regarded as one of the most cost-effective approaches to lowering emissions.

Better enforcement of building regulations, largely to reduce energy loss, is regarded by the government as essential. The 2010 review of building regulations will provide an opportunity for the government to tighten existing regulations. In the agricultural sphere, better countryside management, cuts in the use of fertilizers, and the protection and enhancement of forests are key objectives. The public sector can also play a major role by reducing emissions from its buildings and by leading initiatives to combat climate change at a local level. Existing policies are projected to save about fourteen megatonnes of carbon dioxide annually by 2010.

The government established the U.K. Climate Impacts Programme in 1997 to coordinate a stakeholder-led assessment of the impacts of climate change at regional and national levels and to help organizations prepare strategies to adapt to the impacts of climate change. The Climate Change Programme has been reviewed to examine how existing policies are performing and the range of policies that might be put in place to help achieve the U.K.'s domestic goal of 20 percent reduction. The review focused on emissions from key sectors of the economy: business, households, energy supply, agriculture, forestry and land use, the public sector, and transport.

The review process includes a consultation exercise to seek stakeholder views on how existing measures are working, how they might be improved, and whether any of them should be discontinued. As part of this consultation process, the government held a number of events focused on particular sectors. A robust analytical process was used to evaluate the impacts, costs, and benefits of existing policies and measures and to appraise possible new policies. Each possible new policy was evaluated in terms of its overall annual carbon reductions—the net present value to 2010, to 2020, and over the lifetime of the policy, both with and without ancillary impacts. The impact of each policy was also considered in terms of the effect it would have on U.K. competitiveness, security of supply, air quality, fuel poverty, and innovation. On the basis of this work, a package of policies and measures has been designed to form the revised program.[12]

The Role of Emissions Trading

Emissions trading gives industry a clear incentive to reduce carbon emissions and enables it to do so at least cost. The emergence of a market price for carbon stimulates savings from increased efficiency and drives forward the development and implementation of new technologies. The U.K. ETS and the EU ETS are an important part of U.K. policies and measures designed to drive down greenhouse gas emissions.[13]

The U.K. ETS, a voluntary scheme and open to nearly all organizations in the United Kingdom, was the first economywide emissions trading scheme anywhere in the world. The scheme was launched in April 2002 to run for five years. Thirty-three direct participants entered the scheme by bidding annual, cumulative emissions reductions targets set against a 1998–2000 baseline. At the start of the scheme, direct participants committed to deliver 11.88 million tonnes of CO_2 equivalent in emissions reductions over the life of the scheme in return for a share of government incentive money. Indications so far are that these participants exceeded targets.[14] Companies participating in the scheme have gained both a greater understanding of how they can reduce emissions and practical experience in using the emissions market. The scheme has also helped to establish brokerage and verification services in the U.K. market. Their experience places these companies in a strong position to gain further business, as European and international emissions trading develops. The U.K. ETS led also, in 2001, to the development of the world's first electronic greenhouse gas emissions trading registry, which has since been refined and licensed to thirteen other EU member states.

The EU ETS was established across Europe in 2003 and came into force at the beginning of 2005. All twenty-five member states agreed in their national allocation plans to certain emission reductions to be achieved over the following three years. The U.K. national allocation plan commited to a reduction on the order of 65 million tonnes of carbon dioxide, or 8 percent below estimated emissions for the first phase of the scheme (2005–07).[15] The EU ETS is a key component of the U.K.'s wider strategy for tackling climate change beyond its Kyoto Protocol target of 20 percent carbon dioxide reduction. Phase 2 of the scheme (2008–12) represents a change in the level of effort required by the National Allocation Plan.

Clear incentives for industry to reduce emissions will occur only if a thriving and competitive carbon market is established. Consequently, to ensure the successful development of the carbon emissions market, the United Kingdom looks to the European Commission and other member states to address any competitive distortions, gaps, or anomalies in the coverage of carbon dioxide emissions that may have arisen during phase 1. The U.K. is gathering and analyzing evidence relating to the shape and the scope of the scheme in phase 2. As part of this process, a public consultation was held to explore a number of areas, including possible expansion to include additional carbon dioxide emissions, the treatment of small installations, and the use of joint implementation and Clean Development Mechanism credits, among others. The carbon emissions market showed much progress through 2005—but also volatility, with allowance prices having risen from approximately EUR 7 a tonne of CO_2 at the beginning of 2005 to a peak of over EUR 29 in July 2005; on October 31 it was trading at around EUR 22.

However, the market for EU ETS allowances is still emerging; the majority of trades to date have been forward trades between limited numbers of market participants. The carbon market is still a young market, but it is developing rapidly. Market commentators estimate that the global carbon market could be worth some EUR 5 billion in 2005, with the EU ETS accounting for some 88 percent. I expect that the liquidity of the market will improve as the scheme develops and as players in the market gain a better understanding of its workings. The early experience provided by the U.K. ETS has helped develop London as a center of carbon trading expertise. The establishment of the London Climate Change Service Providers Group is a sign that U.K. industry is prepared to embrace market mechanisms for tackling climate change.

The United Kingdom is fully supportive of emissions trading as an effective means of reducing greenhouse gas emissions, and it is committed to linking to other schemes with a view to global industry-level emissions trading in the near future. This can assist the development of a more comprehensive future framework to tackle climate change, as participants will have a vested interest in the continuation of the regime once markets have been developed.

Adaptation to Climate Change

All U.K. government departments have undertaken an examination of the implications of climate change for their policy responsibilities. The U.K. Climate Impacts Programme (U.K. CIP) encourages private and public sector organizations to assess their vulnerability to climate change so they can plan their own adaptation strategies. Research into the impacts of climate change and adaptation is ongoing in many countries, but few if any have drawn stakeholders into the research activity as successfully as has the CIP.[16]

A report integrating findings from all studies under the U.K. CIP was published earlier in 2005. This work indicates that every region in the United Kingdom will feel the impacts of climate change, although these impacts may be different. In addition, every economic sector will be influenced by the changing climate. In some sectors, detailed quantitative research has brought the potential costs of climate change into sharper focus. Perhaps because they will arguably be hardest hit by climate change, the flood management and water resources sectors seem to have advanced the most along this path, giving detailed assessments of both the impacts and the adaptation options in hand.

Researchers at the Tyndall Centre completed a study for DEFRA assessing adaptations in practice across the U.K.[17] The study finds that in every sector investigated adaptation was already happening, albeit at an early, capacity-building stage. The study also shows that weather impacts or climate change itself often have a minor influence on adaptation decisionmaking compared to other drivers for change, such as cost savings and regulation. Few adaptations were undertaken solely in response to expected climate change. This finding reinforces the approach that the U.K. has taken so far, which is that adaptation to climate change needs to be built into many policies and programs and incorporated into existing networks and partnerships, such as those initiated by the U.K. CIP. Only this kind of integration will place climate change adaptation alongside all of the other drivers that influence behavior.

Such a range of activity can make adaptation to climate change seem unmanageable. In fact every action and decision plays a part in adaptation, which means that individuals have the key role in preparing the U.K. for climate change. To help raise public awareness of climate change, DEFRA announced in February 2005 a package of at least £12 million to be spent on climate change communications over the following three years. In addition, inputs to a public consultation (November 2005 to January 2006) on adaptation, along with other policy proposals, will help develop a U.K. adaptation policy framework.

The impacts of climate change will fall disproportionately upon developing countries and upon the most vulnerable people in those countries, exacerbating existing inequalities in health status and access to adequate food, clean water, and other essential resources. The U.K. is giving increasing attention to the need to understand this impact on the poor and to support developing countries to evaluate the potential impacts of climate change and to develop adaptation measures. Specific measures are

—Building on research programs funded through DEFRA's Global Atmosphere Division, to investigate the impacts of climate change in India, China, and Bangladesh (with the U.K. Department for International Development) and initiating new projects, including some in Africa.

—Supporting development of a regional climate model (PRECIS) that can be easily applied to any part of the world to generate detailed climate change predictions; and providing PRECIS training workshops to interested developing countries.

This work involves developing new approaches to vulnerability assessment and adaptation; building capacity through the transfer of methods and technology from the U.K.; and supporting training in the wider use of the PRECIS model in developing countries.[18]

Conclusions

It is the firm view of the U.K. that climate change constitutes a major threat to the environment and human society, that urgent action is needed now across the world to avert that threat, and that the developed world needs to show leadership in tackling climate change. This chapter outlines the case for action and summarizes the U.K.'s international and domestic environmental activities. The country believes that the scientific case for action is strong and that remaining uncertainties do not justify a wait-and-see policy but rather point to the need to act urgently to reduce risk and create room for maneuver.

Notes

1. Prime Minister Margaret Thatcher, Speech to the Royal Society, London, September 27, 1988. Margaret Thatcher Foundation archive (www.margaretthatcher.org/speeches/displaydocument.asp?docid=107346).
2. Department for Environment, Food and Rural Affairs, *Our Approach to Evidence & Innovation,* PB 12245 (Norwich, U.K.: Stationery Office, 2006).
3. Met Office Hadley Centre, "Climate Change and the Greenhouse Effect: A Briefing from the Hadley Centre" (Exeter, U.K.: 2005).
4. IPCC, *Climate Change 2001: The Scientific Basis,* Contribution of Working Group I to the Third Assessment Report, edited by J. T. Houghton and others (Cambridge University Press, 2001).
5. See R. Warren, "Impacts of Global Climate Change at Different Annual Mean Global Temperature Increases," in *Avoiding Dangerous Climate Change,* edited by H. J. Schellnhuber and others (Cambridge University Press, 2006).
6. Joint Science Academies, "Global Response to Climate Change" (www.royalsoc.ac.uk/displaypagedoc.asp?id=20742).
7. Gleneagles communiqué (www.g8.gov.uk/servlet/Front?pagename=OpenMarket/Xcelerate/ShowPage&c=Page&cid=1119518704554).
8. European Council of Ministers, "Winning the Battle against Global Climate Change" (Brussels: Commission of the European Communities, 2005).
9. Department for Trade and Industry, *Our Energy Future: Creating Low Carbon Economy,* Energy White Paper (Norwich, U.K.: Stationery Office, 2003).
10. Royal Commission on Environmental Pollution, *Energy: The Changing Climate* (Norwich, U.K.: Stationery Office, 2000).
11. Department of the Environment, Transport, and the Regions, *Climate Change Programme 2000,* CM 4913 (Norwich, U.K.: Stationery Office, 2000).
12. Department for the Environment, Food and Rural Affairs, *Climate Change: The UK Programme 2006,* CM 6764 (Norwich, U.K.: Stationery Office, 2006).

13. For further information on both the U.K. and European Emissions Trading Schemes, please see http://defraweb/environment/climatechange/trading/index.htm.

14. See www.defra.gov.uk/environment/climatechange/trading/uk/index.htm.

15. Department for Environment, Food, and Rural Affairs, EU Emissions Trading Scheme, Approved National Allocation Plan 2005–2007 (Norwich, U.K.: Stationery Office, 2005).

16. U.K. Climate Impacts Programme (www.ukcip.org.uk/).

17. E. L. Tompkins and others, "Linking Adaptation Research and Practice," a report submitted to DEFRA as part of the Climate Change Impacts and Adaptation Cross-Regional Research Programme, May 2005 (www.defra.gov.uk/science/project_data/DocumentLibrary/GA01077/GA01077_2664_FRP.pdf).

18. R. G. Jones and others, *Generating High Resolution Climate Change Scenarios Using PRECIS* (Exeter, U.K.: Met Office Hadley Centre, 2004).

12

Canada's Approach to Tackling Climate Change

JOHN M. R. STONE

I n this short chapter I attempt to bring together the thinking of the Canadian federal government of the time on tackling the climate change issue. It is based on publicly available material. I am not representing the government of Canada, and so I include some of my own observations and interpretations. I first describe the history of Canadian attempts to address the issue, then review existing programs and policies, and finally outline some of the thinking regarding future actions, in particular for the Eleventh Conference of the Parties (COP-11) under the United Nations Framework Convention on Climate Change (UNFCCC), which took place in Montreal at the end of 2005.

The last section is a postscript, written in 2007 as an update on the events reported in the rest of the chapter.

Historical Background

Canada's political attention to the issue of climate change was demonstrated by its hosting of the conference, "The Changing Atmosphere," in Toronto in 1988. The conference was intended to discuss a variety of atmospheric issues, including acid rain. It featured such eminent speakers as Gro Harlem Brundtland, who the previous year had completed the report, *Our Common Future,* under the auspices of the UN World Commission on Environment and Development.[1] However, the conference coincided with unusually hot weather, and in consequence much of the discussion focused on climate change. The conference may best be remembered by the target it set in its concluding statement: a 20 percent reduction by 2005 of 1988-level emissions of carbon dioxide.

Perhaps less well known is that, following the First World Conference on Climate Change in 1975, the organization within the Canadian federal government responsible for weather predictions had set up a climate modeling group. This wise initiative produced extremely useful information and a climate model considered among the best in the world. The model gave Canada a certain credibility when it came to negotiating regimes to tackle the threat of climate change—a credibility that has sadly diminished, in part as a result of reduced government resources for science.

Canada was fully engaged in the negotiations of the UNFCCC and subsequently ratified the Framework Convention on Climate Change. It was similarly engaged in the negotiations of what became known as the Kyoto Protocol, being particularly articulate in arguing for the extensive inclusion of carbon sinks in forests and agriculture. In preparation for the final negotiations, Canada arrived at an agreement with the provinces to go no further than stabilizing emissions at the 1990 levels. However, as a result of a last-minute telephone call from the prime minister's office to the head of the Canadian delegation to keep close to the U.S. position, Canada accepted a reduction of 6 percent, a target that, at the time, it had no idea how to achieve. After a subsequent and very noisy discussion in the media and elsewhere regarding the economic costs of reaching the Kyoto target, the prime minister, Jean Chrétien, in one of his last acts before stepping down, made the decision to ratify the Kyoto Protocol because, as he said, "It is the right thing to do."

Since the signing of the Kyoto Protocol the government of Canada has made incremental investments in addressing climate change, totaling some Can$3.7 billion. However, only half of this had been spent by 2005, and several audits by the Treasury Board, the Auditor General of Canada, and others show that the results of these investments were disappointing. It is not an unusual observation that many of the departments that were charged with administering these resources were more interested in enhancing the size of their budgets than in the objective of beginning to reduce Canadian emissions. For example, programs intended to develop new energy technologies were primarily supply driven and not related to the demands of those who had to make the reductions. As a result, the government undertook a full review of all of its climate change programs with the intention of effecting significant reallocations.

The Challenge

Canada's emissions reduction target under the Kyoto Protocol is 6 percent. Its 1990 emissions were about 590 megatonnes of carbon dioxide (CO_2) equivalent. Unfortunately, emissions in Canada have been increasing, although by

2003 there was an energy efficiency improvement of some 13 percent since 1990.[2] The net result is that the difference between projected business-as-usual emissions and the Kyoto target is now estimated to be at least 270 megatonnes of CO_2 equivalent. This amounts to a 45 percent reduction, or about ten tonnes for every Canadian.

This is clearly a considerable challenge, and it is questionable whether it can be achieved within the Kyoto time frame. The increase in emissions is mainly due to unexpected growth in the Canadian economy and particularly in fossil fuel production (mainly from oil sands). But Canada is not alone. The European Commissioner for the Environment has suggested that only two European Union (EU) members, the United Kingdom and Germany, were on track to meet their targets. If rich, developed countries are not able to show that they have made progress in reducing their emissions, it is very unlikely that developing countries are going to be willing to take on any such commitment.

Project Green

Project Green was part of the federal government's budget in the spring of 2005.[3] The project was the latest plan "honouring" Canada's Kyoto commitment. The choice of the word was deliberate; in previous documents the government was to "respect" Canada's commitment. The word *honour* subtly recognized that Canada may not meet its target. Project Green, at the time of this writing, was a work in progress in that many of the details of the initiatives were not yet fully elaborated. It again seemed to assume that money would be sufficient to achieve the commitment, an assumption that was not supported by the progress to date. Project Green incorporates a significant shift by putting the 2008–12 Kyoto emissions reduction into the longer-term framework of tackling climate change. Thus the project recognized the need for a long-term approach to address the threat of climate change and still maintain technological and economic growth and achieve sustainability.

The estimates of the potential of each of the initiatives in Project Green were somewhat optimistic, if not flawed. One of the initiatives addressed the reduction of emissions from large point sources like oil, gas, electricity generation, mining, and manufacturing, which account for roughly 50 percent of Canadian greenhouse gas emissions. Previous initiatives using covenants proved to be inadequate. The new initiative covered some 700 companies and was intended to achieve reductions of 45 million tonnes of CO_2 equivalent. Authority was to derive from the Canadian Environmental Protection Act, which was designed to tackle toxic substances but was to be amended by adding greenhouse gases to the list of controlled substances. Reductions were to be based on improvements in emission intensities.

Almost all operations had a 15 percent reduction target; the exception was fixed-process operations such as cement production, which had a 0 percent reduction target. In addition, the government committed to honor a previous commitment to cap reduction costs at Can\$15 per tonne CO_2 equivalent. Informal discussions with western Canadian oil and gas interests suggest that the targets were not regarded as onerous: they could be met through in-house reductions, purchases from other companies, domestic offsets, and international "green" credits. In addition, credits could be earned through investment in a greenhouse gas technology investment fund.

A novel initiative was the establishment of a climate fund designed to broaden the participation of the private sector in emission reductions. Its purpose was to create a permanent federal institution for the purchase and retirement of emission reduction credits. Purchases were to be made through a competitive process. The climate fund was to be an arm's-length operation under the authority of the minister of environment but with its own chief executive officer. Any initiative that reduced greenhouse gas emissions below the business-as-usual level was to be eligible for the fund. These initiatives include agricultural soil carbon enhancement, improved forest management, and energy-efficient urban and property development. Establishment of the climate fund was consistent with the government's policy not to invest in green projects abroad and to achieve the majority of reductions in Canada. The climate fund was to have a minimum of Can\$1 billion over five years and was expected to yield a reduction of 75–115 million tonnes of CO_2 equivalent annually. Some observers were concerned that the administrative burden of having to deal with the potentially large number of small projects could overwhelm the initiative.

Canada is a federation, and many powers, especially relating to natural resources, rest with the provinces. Hence it is imperative that, on greenhouse gas reduction, the two levels of government work together. To facilitate this, a further initiative was a partnership fund to share the costs of large initiatives. Such initiatives could also involve the private sector and include, for example, promoting the use of carbon capture and storage in connection with existing or planned electricity-generating plants, the building of an east-west electricity grid across Canada, and the development of more energy-efficient, intermodal transport. Initially, the partnership fund was to have access to Can\$250 million over five years and was expected to yield a reduction of 55 million to 85 million tonnes of CO_2 equivalent annually.

A final example of the initiatives included in Project Green is government promotion of renewable energy. The government was to expand its wind power production incentive to include a further 4,000 megawatts of power. It was also to expand its renewable power production incentive with an additional 150 megawatts of power from small, electricity-generating plants using hydropower, biomass power, and tidal power. Cogeneration was to be encouraged through tax measures such as larger capital cost allowances. These initiatives were expected to yield some 15 megatonnes of CO_2 equivalent annually.

Post-2012 Regimes

Canada hosted the Eleventh Conference of the Parties under the UNFCCC (COP-11). The First Meeting of the Parties under the Kyoto Protocol (MOP-1)—at which all the draft decisions taken on implementing the protocol (known as the Marrakech Accords, after the COP that took place in this Moroccan city) were to be adopted—also took place. This meeting began to discuss possible post-2012 regimes, as foreseen under the protocol. As Canada was the host country, Stéphane Dion, the Canadian minister of environment, chaired these meetings.

To facilitate the discussions, Dion used the framework of the three I's: implement, improve, and innovate. *Implement* referred to adopting the Marrakech Accords and establishing the basis for the operation of the Kyoto Protocol. *Improve* referred to streamlining the operation of the Clean Development Mechanism and addressing some of the shortcomings of the protocol. *Innovate* referred to beginning the process of negotiating a post-2012 regime and looking for solutions that would lead to the engagement of all large emitting countries and an eventual stabilization of atmospheric concentrations of greenhouse gases. The Kyoto Protocol at the time was estimated to cover only some 35 percent of global greenhouse gas emissions.

Dion also developed a discussion paper, which he shared with other governments, both bilaterally and multilaterally, in an exhaustive round of meetings.[4] His paper discusses six elements:

—Effectiveness: A long-term framework involving real reductions, guided by science, and contributing to other environmental objectives.

—Participation: A regime that allows for the broadest participation, including the largest emitters, possibly based on a sectoral approach.

—Sustainability: A regime that contributes to the development goals of all countries, that considers climate change in all development decisions, that is consistent with economic growth, and that mobilizes private investment.

—Carbon market: Maximization of market forces through such mechanisms as an international carbon market (although the Canadian government has repeatedly said it will not introduce a carbon tax).

—Technology: The deployment of existing technology and the development of new transformative technologies as well as common standards.

—Adaptation: Recognition that in both developed and developing countries some impacts are inevitable and other stresses cannot be ignored; establishment of a mechanism to further assist developing countries.

The idea of sectoral strategies was relatively new. These strategies were seen as a means of integrating the six elements and possibly shifting the focus away from governments. Targets would be set for each sector. These would not necessarily be emissions targets, but they could be framed around technology. Electricity generation was considered a suitable sector to begin with.

Some Considerations

Canada put a huge amount of effort and energy into preparing for COP-11, which over a two-week period in 2005 brought the issue of climate change to the attention of Canadians. Unfortunately, it had to compete for attention with a federal election campaign. But of greater concern was the question of Canadian credibility in providing leadership, given that Canadian emissions had been growing and that it was very unlikely that an internal carbon market would be in place soon.

COP-11 has been declared a success by many of those who participated. The perception of Canadians is important if the government is to realize Project Green's goals. Canada's credibility in Montreal may have spilled over into domestic credibility, but many Canadians are quite cynical about climate change and have adopted a wait-and-see attitude, believing that ratifying the Kyoto Protocol was sufficient. Also, many Canadians, with the exception of those living in the Arctic, have not personally experienced climate impacts.

Is Canada on the right track? Some criticize the Kyoto Protocol for being convoluted, arbitrary, and short term. It is perhaps significant that the chairman of the Intergovernmental Conference that produced the Kyoto Protocol said: "We should not be fixated on Kyoto but on the climate change problem itself and what comes after Kyoto." Several leaders have stated that the UNFCCC forum is the appropriate mechanism to discuss future climate change regimes. Yet we now have several parallel initiatives such as the Group of Eight (G-8) dialogue and the Asia-Pacific Partnership on Clean Development and Climate. The COP-11 was just one of many healthy policy discussions. It is possible that, rather than one globally inclusive regime, we might end up with several regional regimes.

It has also been argued that climate change cannot be solved if it is seen solely as a single environmental issue. Indeed, this is one of the criticisms that has been made of the Kyoto Protocol and its focus on emission reduction targets. There is a growing realization that climate change must be factored into every development decision, whether it is rural development, technology development, energy development, or northern development. This notion is often couched in terms of mainstreaming climate change considerations into all development and security concerns. If indeed the debate needs reframing, it is not clear that those who have been involved in the negotiations have the right mind-set to elaborate a new approach.

A further question that needs to be explored is the future role of the Inter-governmental Panel on Climate Change (IPCC). It can be fairly claimed that science put the issue of climate change on the political agenda and was the driving force for the establishment of the IPCC in 1988. Some argue that the problem has now been well defined and that more attention needs to be directed to solutions. However, many governments, and certainly large sections of the electorate, do not yet fully appreciate the demands on them that will be necessary if atmospheric concentrations are to be stabilized at a level that many scientists believe is necessary to avoid significant threats to society and the environment. Thus greater demands will be put on the science behind this view (levels of confidence will have to be higher), and more efforts will have to be made to secure the science.

Postscript

Since the Eleventh Conference of the Parties in Montreal in 2005 there have been some politically significant developments in Canada. This postscript is intended to bring the reader up to date on the current situation regarding the government of Canada's attempts to address the issue of climate change.

On September 19, 2005, Federal Environment Minister Stéphane Dion unveiled Project Green, "a broad environmental vision that links Canada's economic competitiveness and prosperity to a sustainable future." This was the Liberal government's fourth plan in less than a decade to address climate change and other environmental issues. As discussed above, Project Green contained initiatives to improve energy efficiency and waste management practices, conserve biodiversity, protect fresh water, improve air quality, and reduce greenhouse gas emissions. The clean air component was a response to the growing concern in some Canadian cities with the health consequences of increasing smog levels. Measures included regulatory actions covering emissions from vehicles, engines, and fuels. Climate change initiatives included a proposed large final emitters system, the addition of the six greenhouse gases to schedule 1 of the Canadian Environmental Protection Act, and the creation of a climate fund to purchase reductions in greenhouse gas emissions. The main elements of Project Green were developed by a small number of trusted advisers in the prime minister's office. Department heads were brought in later to work out the details.

The government was in a minority position and suffering from a series of accountability scandals. The day of reckoning came on November 28, 2005, with the passing of a nonconfidence vote. Canadians in general felt that the government needed to be punished for what they saw as arrogant behavior—and the government fell. Unfortunately, this coincided with the Conference of the Parties (COP-11) under the UNFCCC that Canada was to host in Montreal.

Stéphane Dion, who was still the minister of the environment, was in a relatively safe seat and was determined to fulfill his responsibilities as chair of COP-11. Indeed, he worked tirelessly to achieve a positive result from a meeting in which it was uncertain that any progress in maintaining momentum in the UNFCCC process would be made. Prime Minister Paul Martin took advantage of being the meeting's host to deliver a hortatory speech, which received national attention, in part because of some derogatory remarks aimed at the U.S. administration.

Despite some limited attention to climate change during COP-11, particularly in Quebec, there was virtually no mention of the environment during the election of January 23, 2006. The election brought in another minority government, this time under the Conservative leader Stephen Harper, who had a significant base in oil-rich Alberta. One of the first acts of this new government was to cancel all of the climate change initiatives of the previous government (although short-term funding has been quietly restored to some of these initiatives). Indeed, it seemed that the new government would have preferred not to have to deal with this issue: the environment was not among its first five priorities. The new environment minister, Rona Ambrose, who took over as chair of the Conference of the Parties, made only a token appearance at the May meetings of the UNFCCC subsidiary body meetings. She also announced that Canada will not meet its Kyoto targets, maintaining however that Canada was still part of the Kyoto "process." Canada missed several of the deadlines for submissions to the UNFCCC.

Nowhere more than in Canada have the climate change naysayers received attention in the media. They have been able to influence the new government (which at the time of this postscript has yet to receive a briefing from its own scientists). However, the view of most Canadians is that environmental degradation is real and that the government should act to ameliorate the damage done and to prevent more. Indeed, in a recent poll 85 percent of Canadians agreed that Canada should maintain its commitment to the Kyoto Protocol.

In a maneuver of realpolitik the new government unveiled its approach to clean air and climate change on October 19, 2006. Interestingly, the prime minister identified himself with this initiative. In fact, the initiative is primarily run out of his office. The announcement included a long-term emission reduction target of between 45 percent and 65 percent by 2050, but shorter-term targets are quite vague. Perhaps surprising for a right-wing party, it has said it will regulate all industrial sectors, but it seems to be shying away from a cap-and-trade system that would create a market for carbon emissions. Some of the other components are a modification of previous Liberal government programs. Because of opposition from other parties, this initiative may be dead on arrival, and there might be more life in a private member's bill to stick to Canada's Kyoto commitment.

There is every prospect that the environment, and climate change in particular, will be an issue at the next election. Meanwhile, greenhouse gas emissions are continuing to rise such that Canada could see levels reach 28 percent above 1990 levels during 2008–12.

Notes

1. UN Commission on Environment and Development, *Our Common Future* (Oxford University Press, 1987).
2. "Canada's Greenhouse Gas Inventory 1990–2003" (http://unfccc.int/national_reports/annex_i_ghg_inventories/national_inventories_submissions/items/2761.php).
3. "Moving Forward on Climate Change: A Plan for Honouring our Kyoto Commitment" (www.climatechange.gc.ca/kyoto_commitments/report_e.pdf).
4. United Nations Climate Change Conference, "Action on Climate Change: Considerations for an Effective International Approach for the Preparatory Meeting of Ministers for Montréal 2005" (www.montreal2005.gc.ca/96A244AE-5A90-4823-A9CF-112E50B46243/DiscussionPaper.pdf).

PART SIX

Linking Climate Change Control and Development Policies

13

India and Climate Change: Mitigation, Adaptation, and a Way Forward

JYOTI PARIKH

The problem of climate change poses challenging issues to almost all countries, and India is no exception. Along with global problems like ocean pollution and species extinction, and local problems such as pollution of air and water as well as the degradation of soil and forests, the problem of climate change has to be addressed in the context of sustainable development. Development activities and poverty alleviation programs also increase emissions of greenhouse gases (GHGs). The 1992 United Nations Framework Convention on Climate Change (UNFCCC) recognized the need for the development of developing nations while expecting contributions from all signatory nations.

Given that 75 percent of global GHG emissions were emitted by the 25 percent of the world's population who live in developed countries (these are listed in UNFCCC Annex I and hence called Annex I countries), the UNFCCC required the developed countries to lead the efforts to reduce GHG emissions.[1] Developing countries were exempt from any commitment to reduce emissions but were asked to do their best. Since then, emissions of developing countries, which have risen, now pose challenges and cause concern. One should not lose the perspective that accumulated emissions, and not annual emissions, should

I am grateful to Ayan Pujari for his valuable assistance in completing this chapter. I cherish my time at Yale University and thank Professor Ernesto Zedillo for his invitation to write this chapter and Haynie Wheeler for her help.

be the criterion for reductions in the near term of twenty years—because, once emitted, greenhouse gases remain in the atmosphere for centuries.

The 1997 the Kyoto Protocol brought developing countries closer to the ambit of GHG reduction by making it attractive for them to reduce emissions by providing carbon credits under the proposal of the Clean Development Mechanism (CDM). Each year, numerous training programs, workshops, and consultations take place involving Annex I states, non–Annex I states, policy-makers, experts from public and private sectors, nongovernmental organizations (NGOs), and academic organizations.

The discussion in this chapter covers the following:
—India's efforts to reduce GHG emissions,
—The problems of India's adaptation to climate change,
—Future scenarios on India's GHG emissions, especially carbon dioxide (CO_2),
—Suggestions for resolving the impasse about developing countries' partici-pation in the UNFCCC Framework,
—Concluding remarks.

India's Efforts to Reduce GHG Emissions

India has been trying to reduce emissions through various measures:
—Emphasis on energy conservation,
—Promotion of renewable energy,
—Abatement of air pollution,
—Afforestation and wasteland development,
—Economic reforms,
—Fuel substitution policies,
—Recycling.

Energy conservation has been emphasized for many decades to conserve scarce resources as well as to reduce GHG emissions. The scarcity of resources, lack of capital for new projects, scarcity of nonrenewable fossil fuels, increased oil imports, and the concern about air pollution are the important factors behind India's energy conservation. To fill the gap in energy supply, renewable energy sources are being promoted.

A number of organizations have been set up in India to handle these prob-lems. Its Petroleum Conservation Research Association (PCRA) aims to explore oil sources and raise production as well as reduce oil imports. India's Bureau of Energy Efficiency (BEE) is set up for training and research in alternative energy sources and the implementation of standards. Moreover, its Power Finance Cor-poration (PFC) has been entrusted to take care of supply-side efficiency. Addi-tionally, policies are in place to address the following:
—Promotion of renewable energy: to make energy conservation effective, renewable sources serve as potential alternatives. India is working to promote its

renewable sources. This can help to avoid emissions of greenhouse gases and, hence, the adverse effects of climate change.

—Abatement of air pollution: several policies have been formulated for air pollution abatement. Most of these measures either avoid or reduce emissions. The main polluters (industries, the transport sector) have been directed to control their pollutants. Several technologies have been provided to check pollution. The introduction of compressed natural gas engines shows that there has been improvement in technology as well as in fuel substitution.

The following efforts can check pollution to a great extent:

—Recycling: resource conservation through reusing or recycling such items as clothing, furniture, paper, and bottles can contribute considerably to reduction of GHG emissions.

—Afforestation and wasteland development: those involved in afforestation are state government organizations, private organizations, and NGOs.

—Fuel substitution: several types of fuel substitutions are simultaneously taking place. Coal is being replaced by gas in the power-generating sector and by diesel and electricity in railway locomotives. Traditional biomass (fuel wood, crop residue, animal dung) is gradually being replaced by fossil fuels such as kerosene and liquefied petroleum gas. But the use of sustainable biomass through biogasification, improved stoves, efficient kilns, and such biofuels as biodiesel and ethanol is gaining ground. Other low-carbon technology and renewable energy sources include, for example, the use of hydro, solar, and wind power. Figure 13-1 presents the change in share of six fuels in India's primary energy supply over the period 1953–2004.

India's Adaptation to Climate Change

The Eleventh Conference of the Parties (COP-11) at Montreal in 2005 focused on adaptation, in addition to mitigation, as a response to climate change. By then 800 billion tonnes of greenhouse gases, nearly 80 percent of which were emitted by the industrial countries, had accumulated in the atmosphere. Gustave Speth observed that 0.6°C of warming had already taken place, resulting in increased frequency and severity of extreme weather events.[2] Arctic melting has begun, and coral bleaching and species loss are taking place. Even though some scientists hesitate to link these phenomena with climate change or human activities, it may be too late if one waits for concrete evidence beyond any doubt. Therefore, many scientists, and especially technologists, believe in taking such mitigating measures as energy efficiency and a shift to renewable energy immediately. These are inevitable: save coal, oil, and gas and encourage conservation.

India is especially vulnerable to climate change due to its large population, temperatures that already reach above 42°C (108°F) in many parts of the

Figure 13-1. *Shares of Primary Commercial Supply, Six Fuels, India, 1953–2004*

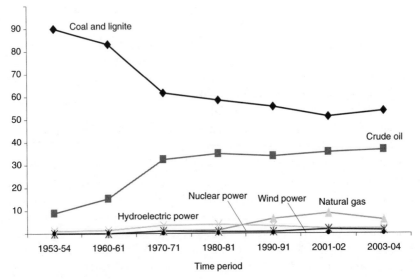

Source: Based on energy statistics from the Planning Commission, Government of India, 2006, personal communication.

country, a coastline of about 7,000 kilometers (about 4,300 miles), and thirty-two islands, where 1 meter (39 inches) of sea-level rise will displace 7 million persons.

The International Institute for Sustainable Development has carried out adaptation case studies in Peru, Mexico, Sudan, Kenya, Bangladesh, Bhutan, and small islands such as Samoa and Kiribati. The case studies involved community participation projects in rural development, in which check dams were built, land and water management skills were transmitted, and concepts of crop and livestock management and resource allocations were applied. It is possible that the most important outcomes of any rural development project are poverty alleviation and capacity building. A well-networked community with local knowledge can survive difficult conditions. Even though extreme climate change may see these communities move on or die out, it is to be hoped that their accumulated knowledge will live on. These community projects are small and often focus on sustainable development; adaptation on this scale can mitigate the effects of climate change and is often climate friendly.

But large-scale adaptation measures, such as widespread use of air-conditioning in response to global warming, can lead to a significant rise in GHG emissions. Air-conditioning was considered a luxury not long ago in poor countries like India as well as in rich countries like Canada, but now it is considered a necessity. The construction of buildings and coastal embankments to withstand storms, for example, although an adaptation measure, is costly and can increase GHG emissions.

India's Future Scenarios

Mitigation is expensive beyond a certain point, as it requires expensive technologies and high-end renewables. However, with less mitigation, there would be high adaptation costs forced on people, and the consequences and costs of these need to be taken into account; they can also lead to a loss in GDP.

After lengthy debates since 1997 on the issues and options, a broad consensus seemed to emerge in regard to operationalizing the CDM. India has embraced the CDM and is looking beyond small-scale projects, such as renewables, and thinking of large emission reduction projects in such sectors as cement, power, and transport. India holds considerable potential for CDM projects, which can be realized only if an appropriate policy environment is created at local, national, and global levels.

John Weyant and Jyoti Parikh's analyses of India in various global models are shown in figure 13-2. All of the global models show that ratios of CO_2 to GDP will consistently fall over the next few decades. This fall could be because of a rise in GDP or because of a fall in emissions—or because of a

Figure 13-2. *Carbon Dioxide Emissions per GDP, India, 2000–10*[a]

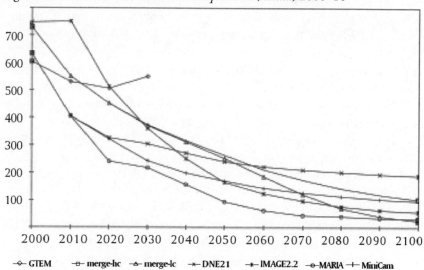

Source: John Weyant and Jyoti Prikh, India, *Sustainable Development, and the Global Commons* (Hyderabad: ICFAI, 2004).

a. GDP is measured in million metric tonnes of carbon dioxide per U.S.1990$ trillion.

slower rise in emissions than in GDP. The latter scenario, unfortunately, is the more probable. Given the pace of development, emission reduction technologies are likely to be improved, so that a downward trend in the ratio of emissions to GDP could be experienced.

Using a multisectoral, intertemporal, economywide model for India over a thirty-year horizon (1996–2026), Jyoti Parikh and B. K. Chandra Kiran present a few simulation results with respect to CO_2 emissions.[3] The whole economy is represented by eight commodities or goods. The focus is on specific options of the power generation and transportation sectors (as large parts of India's CO_2 emissions occur in these sectors, policy options here need to be clearly understood). Industrial output is produced by two alternatives: using coal boilers and using oil boilers. Technical progress and energy efficiency gains over time are prescribed exogenously and remain the same across all scenarios. Income distribution is endogenous and depends on total consumption, exogenously projected total population, and a specified Lorenz ratio. Thus population belonging to each consumption expenditure class is determined in the model. The composition of aggregate consumption, therefore, changes nonlinearly as the economy grows and people move from one income class to another. Fifteen consumption bundles are provided for each class to represent approximately the indifference curve of the class, which permits substitution across commodities as relative prices change. The bottom class corresponds to those below the poverty line and provides an indication of the number of poor in each period.

The Parikh/Kiran model maximizes social welfare (aggregation of utilities) with respect to various constraints, such as those on domestic oil and gas production. Capital constraints are imposed to keep the model and its results realistic, while on the trade side a balance-of-payments constraint is imposed. There is also a wedge between export price and import price to reflect international trade and transport margins. Restrictions are imposed on exports and import growth rates by sector to keep the model, and its results, realistic. Import of agricultural commodities is restricted (to reflect a self-sufficiency requirement). Finally, the model is run for an extra five years to account for the post-terminal period and to smooth composition results.

The main scenarios from the model are business as usual, carbon emission restrictions of 10 percent, carbon emission restrictions of 20 percent, and oil shock. The general observation from the model scenarios is that CO_2 emissions reduction imposes costs in terms of lower GDP and higher poverty. In fact the authors find that these impositions have impacts similar to those of an oil shock. They also report that emissions grow at a lower proportion with regard to population growth. Therefore, developing countries like India have a long way to go to reach the level at which there should be binding commitments for GHG emissions reduction.

Encouraging Developing Country Participation in the UNFCCC

Global pressure on India, China, and Brazil is mounting for these states to take on some obligations to reduce GHG emissions from the use of coal, oil, and gas, which cause climate change, or global warming. However, the UNFCCC, having established multilateral frameworks, should not abandon the framework to focus on those three countries alone. A more logical way should be found. Why should Korea, South Africa, OPEC countries, Saudi Arabia, and others be off the hook if their per capita emissions and growth rates are much larger than those of India, China, and Brazil? If we do not address the issue in a multilateral framework, there could be problems ahead. The following sections argue a case for the alternatives.

CO_2 Emissions (per Capita and per GDP) of Relevant Countries

Table 13-1 provides some information on per capita CO_2 emissions and their growth. India's annual per person emissions in 2002 were 1.17 tonnes, lower than the global average of 4.11 tonnes and than those of Brazil (1.80 tonnes), China (2.71 tonnes), and the Annex I country average (12.40 tonnes).

India needs energy consumption for growth and development: 300 million people in India do not have electricity and 650 million do not have access to the energy sources for modern cooking and lighting; thus India cannot promise to reduce fossil fuel use. Although GHG emissions in developing countries have risen, the focus should be on cumulative emissions or on per capita emissions. From either point of view, India should not be pressured to reduce emissions.

Table 13-1. *CO_2 Emissions, per Capita and Growth, Two Country Groups, 1991–2002*

Country group	Per capita (tonnes)		Growth (percent)
	1991	2002	1991–2002
Annex I countries	11.95	12.40	0.96
Populous developing countries			
(Brazil, China, India)	1.59	2.01	3.48
Brazil	1.47	1.80	3.53
China	2.16	2.71	3.05
India	0.84	1.17	4.81
Remaining countries (excluding Russia)	2.55	2.77	3.19
Total[a]	3.59	3.88	2.07
Global	4.25	4.11	1.03

Source: Author's analysis from the data by International Energy Agency, *World Energy Outlook* (Paris: 2004).

a. Total includes Annex I countries, Brazil, China, India, and remaining countries.

Instead, India's focus must be on sustainable development, which consists of economic, environmental, and social goals: poverty eradication, a problem that, as the Parikh/Kiran model points out, persists to the end of the time period considered (2026). (But even though an adverse impact on long-run GDP and welfare for the scenarios where carbon emissions have been tightened was observed, it is still India's responsibility to avoid unnecessary emissions.)

Parties to the UNFCCC agreed that their commitments would not be sufficient to meet the convention's stabilization objective, and they launched a new round of talks that led to the negotiation of the 1997 Kyoto Protocol. The protocol established legally binding targets for the industrialized countries that ratified the agreement. The point is that, with such a multilateral framework already set up, a few developing countries should not be pressured to reduce greenhouse gases just because they are large in size. The binding targets for the industrialized countries are justified on the grounds of accumulated emissions over the time of their development. Their current levels of emissions are also high in per capita terms. Since the scenarios for developing countries like Brazil, China, and India are different, they should not be made to aim for binding targets. There has to be some convincing criterion, based on a multilateral agreement, on the basis of which decisions should be made regarding what country should do what. As pointed out earlier, cumulative emissions or per capita emissions are potential measures to serve the purpose.

CO_2 Emissions and Developing Countries

Let us make a comparison among a few developing countries, shown in table 13-2. Among non–Annex I countries, 50 have per capita levels of GHG emissions above the global average, including OPEC countries, newly industrialized countries, South Africa, and others. Their per capita group average was 8.3 tonnes in 2002. On the other hand, the per capita average of 110 countries was 1.2 tonnes.

Table 13-2. CO_2 Emissions, per Capita, Three Country Groups

Country group	Per capita (tonnes)		Total (millions of tonnes)	
	1991	2002	1991	2002
50 countries above global average	6.46	8.30	2,219.07	2,762.1
110 countries below global average	1.08	1.23	1,736.29	2,501.71
Both groups	2.02	2.23	3,955.36	5,263.82
Brazil	1.47	1.8	214.15	313.47
China	2.16	2.71	2,520.99	3,509.91
India	0.84	1.17	727.82	1,219.81
Brazil, China, India	1.59	2.01	3,462.86	5,043.2

Source: See table 13-1.

In terms of total 2002 emissions, those of the 50 countries exceeded the emissions of the 110 countries (which include India, China, Brazil, and many other poor countries of Africa and Latin America).

The exclusion of India and China from the Annex I group and the inclusion of Netherlands, Belgium, and Luxembourg indicate that the UNFCCC implicitly recognizes the per capita principle, though it is not mentioned explicitly. Otherwise, why should countries like Netherlands and Belgium be in the Annex I group, when China and India are not?

This discussion reveals that there is a need for a third group of countries, perhaps using a global average for a specified year, such as 2000 or 2005. If a state exceeded the global average, it would be required to commit to reduce some of its emissions. China, although currently in the group below the global average, will reach the global average in a few years or may have reached it already, as there is a gap of three years before the data are available. Such a three-tier system, based on the per capita global average, would provide incentives for all countries to stay below the global average as long as they can.

Another way to limit greenhouse gas emissions is to stipulate sectoral global standards and make it possible for countries to attain their standards in critical sectors such as power, cement, and transport by including non–Annex I countries of all tiers. A separate carbon trading mechanism for these reductions could be introduced so that these countries could raise the required finance. The power sector is the most suitable for sectoral global standards, given that it produces the largest GHG emissions, where much can be done to improve efficiency standards to move toward the lowest use of coal possible. India could improve its efficiency (now 30 percent) toward that of the developed world (now 45 percent) in the coal-based power plant sector.

The UNFCCC provides that GHG-saving technologies could be transferred from Annex I countries to non–Annex I countries. Thus the former would have to find some way to fulfill their obligations through public-private partnership within their countries, in spite of saying that technology remains within the private sector.

Concluding Remarks

This chapter discusses the problem of climate change, mainly GHG emissions, and the ways to resolve it, especially from the Indian perspective. India's efforts to avoid and reduce GHG emissions include emphasis on energy conservation, promotion of renewable energy, abatement of air pollution, afforestation, wasteland development, economic reforms, fuel substitution, recycling, and more.

Climate change is a global problem and every country should take initiatives to resolve it. However, the UNFCCC rightly figured the very high contributions of the developed nations in GHG emissions and hence imposed binding targets on them. Their cumulative, as well as per capita, emissions are significantly higher than those of the developing nations.

Even though UNFCCC norms are not binding on developing nations like India, global pressure is being imposed not only on India but on China and Brazil as well. I find no justification for such pressure. In a multilateral framework, as provided by the UNFCCC, one cannot impose such blind requirements on these countries just because they are large in size. I also compare GHG emissions among countries based on whether their emissions are above or below the global average and find that the contribution by countries above the global average is much more than the contribution by the other group.

Two studies (referenced herein) emphasize that India is on its development path but that the country has a long way to go to reach the level where there should be binding commitments for GHG emission reduction. Nevertheless, India is willing to do its share toward sustainable development within the CDM framework.

Notes

1. Jyoti Parikh and Jyoti Prasad Painuly, "Population, Consumption Patterns and Global Warming," *AMBIO* 23, no. 7 (1994).
2. Gustav Speth, "Global Warming: Looking beyond Kyoto," talk given at Yale Center for the Study of Globalization, Yale University, October 21, 2005.
3. Jyoti Parikh and B. K. Chandra Kiran, "Economic Impact of Carbon Emission Restrictions: The Case of India," in *Energy Security, Climate Change, and Sustainable Development*, edited by J. Mathur, H. Wagner, and N. Bansal (New Delhi: Anamaya, 2007).

14

Correct Choices for China: Energy Conservation, a Cyclic Economy, and a Conservation-Minded Society

SHEN LONGHAI

The Kyoto Protocol to the United Nations Framework Convention on Climate Change (UNFCCC) took effect in February 2005, marking a substantial step toward reducing global greenhouse gases. It was the result of joint efforts made by many countries during the ten years after the UN treaty went into force in March 1994.

China is a developing nation with a huge population, most of low income and vulnerable to climate change. The country has always attached great importance to the problem and has been actively involved in international efforts to combat the greenhouse effect. It has also adopted effective countermeasures and honored its obligations under the convention. In recent years, China has taken the following measures in the global war on climate change.

—In 2002 the Ministry of Science and Technology published its *2001–2010 Program for Sustainable Development of Science and Technology*, initiated the compilation of the *National Assessment Report on Climate Change*, and launched China Climate Change Info Net, a web resource.[1]

—In 2003 (based on China's Agenda Twenty-One, the white paper on *China's Population, Environment, and Development in the Twenty-First Century*, published in 1994) the government promulgated the Program of Action for Sustainable Development in China in the Early Twenty-First Century.

—In 2004 China formally submitted *The People's Republic of China Initial National Communication on Climate Change to the Conference of the Parties to the Convention*. It also implemented the Interim Measures for Operation and Management of Clean Development Mechanism (CDM) Projects in China. In addition the government published *The China Medium- and Long-Term Energy Conservation Plan* and adopted a national energy development strategy aimed at optimizing energy conservation, improving energy structure, diversifying energy sources, strengthening environmental protection, and advancing technology and innovation.

—In 2005 China passed the Renewable Energy Law to promote the development of such new or renewable energy sources as wind, solar, geothermal, and biomass.

—In 2007 the government formulated China's National Climate Change Programme and devised a national strategy to tackle the impact of climate change in line with the principles embodied in the convention.

A Look Back

For more than two decades China has made active contributions to the ongoing global fight against climate change by adopting policies and measures for controlling population increase, improving energy efficiency, and expanding high-quality energy supply. A number of natural factors and human activities are responsible for climate change. Human activities cause greenhouse gas emissions as a result of energy use and farm-based methane production. From 1978 to 2004 China achieved an average increase of about 9 percent in its gross domestic product (GDP), underpinned by about an average annual 5 percent growth in energy consumption. In other words, with more than 900 million tons of coal equivalent saved, 50 percent of the energy needed to power China's economic growth was secured through production, while the remaining 50 percent was obtained via conservation.

During the same period China improved energy efficiency from 26 percent to 33 percent, reducing energy consumption per unit of output value. For example, it cut down on the energy consumption per ton of steel production by more than 30 percent. The energy conservation campaign resulted in a dramatic cut in the release of greenhouse gases, as exemplified by a reduction of nearly 600 million tons in carbon dioxide (CO_2) emissions from 1981 to 2000.

China's socioeconomic development has encountered deep-rooted contradictions and problems accumulated over long years; these problems—energy supply and security, greenhouse gas emissions, and environmental protection—constitute both opportunities and challenges for China and are expected to remain in existence in the first two decades of this century.

A Look Forward

China's extensive growth pattern has basically not changed since the policy of opening to the outside world was adopted in 1979. To realize its socioeconomic development goals, it is essential for the nation to replace its linear economy with a cyclic economy and build a society that is conservation-minded. In the future, as China continues its road to sustainable and rapid growth, both energy use and the resultant greenhouse gas emissions will tend to increase.

By 2020 China will have built a well-off society, with its GDP per capita quadrupled over that of the year 2000. By 2050 its people will have achieved living standards comparable to those of a midlevel developed country. To reach these goals, in the first twenty years of the century in particular, the Chinese government must address issues of energy supply and demand, energy security, and the deterioration of the energy environment, all of which have been increasingly the focus of concern around the world.

Most industrialized nations experienced a relatively fast increase in per capita energy consumption and rapid changes in energy structure with a rising proportion of oil needs, especially when their GDP per capita was between U.S.$3,000 and U.S.$10,000. The years leading up to 2020 will witness a phenomenal growth in China's heavy chemical industry and transportation, an imperative step toward realizing industrialization. Energy needs in the heavy chemical industry are usually four times those in light industry. Although China's urbanization rate is currently less than 40 percent, as the country develops, more cities will be born, and more energy will be consumed as a result of demand for air-conditioners and cars. At present, urban households use energy about three times that of their rural counterparts. In recent years, China's energy consumption coefficient of elasticity has exceeded 1, and in one recent summer electricity shortages were reported in ten provinces during peak hours. China's 2005 net crude oil imports totaled 142.75 million tons, accounting for some 43.9 percent of the nation's oil needs and 6.0 percent of the world's trade volume.

The Chinese economy is still following an extensive growth mode, featuring high investment, high consumption, and high pollution, as was experienced by some developed countries in the past. In 2005 China's primary energy production reached 2.06 billion tons of coal equivalent, while energy consumption amounted to 2.25 billion tons of coal equivalent, accounting for 13.7 percent and 14.8 percent of the world, respectively, both of which ranked second in the world. If the economy continues to grow in this pattern, without switching to an intensive growth mode, domestic energy resources and solutions alone will no longer be able to support it. Even with the use of foreign energy resources, this growth will be difficult to sustain. China's exploitable energy reserve per capita stands far below the world average. As of the end of 2002 proven reserves of coal, oil, and natural gas per capita were about 60 percent, 8 percent, and 5 percent, respectively, of the world average. In 2004 China's average primary energy consumption per capita was just 1.08 tons of oil equivalent, 66 percent of the world average (1.63 tons of oil equivalent) and only 13 percent that of the United States, which consumed 8.02 tons of oil equivalent per capita. In addition, China's installed power generation capacity stood at only 0.3 kilowatts per capita, merely a tenth of that of the United States.

How much energy is needed to achieve China's goals of social and economic development? Chinese analysts have designed three energy demand scenarios for 2020: a business-as-usual (BAU) case and two alternative scenarios. These scenarios are defined by sets of policies that reflect increased levels of national commitment to energy and environmental goals. In the BAU case the government basically maintains its current policy through 2020, and thus China's primary energy needs are expected to total 3.3 billion tons of coal equivalent. The first alternative scenario, the *moderate case,* is composed of relatively low-cost, moderate policy adjustments, cutting down energy demand to 2.9 billion tons of coal equivalent. The second alternative scenario, the *advanced case,* requires more vigorous policies and adjustments and would reduce energy consumption to 2.5 billion tons of coal equivalent.

In any case, China's energy needs are likely to more than double in two decades from the 2000 level. As the soaring demand for coal as the major source of energy continues, heavier atmospheric concentrations of greenhouse gases will be produced. By 2020 coal will remain the leading source of energy, accounting for 60–63 percent of the country's primary energy consumption, compared to 26–27 percent accounted for by oil and 7–9 percent accounted for by natural gas. Obviously, China's coal use will be at least 35 percentage points higher than the world average of 25 percent. Studies show that some 70 percent of overall carbon dioxide (CO_2) emissions come from coal burning. CO_2 emissions by China, which is already the second-largest emitter in the world, increased from 3.07 billion tons in 1994 to 5.07 billion tons in 2004, and the number will continue to rise by 2020.

Building a Cyclic Economy

A cyclic economy advocates the 3R concept: reduce, reuse, and recycle. A growth mode characterized by a balanced relationship among economic growth, social development, and environmental protection raises resource utilization efficiency through lower natural resources consumption, less waste processing, and higher resources productivity. These outcomes maximize economic and environmental benefits with minimum resources and environmental costs. Such an economy, one that seeks harmony with the ecosystem, is in line with the concept of sustainable growth. China is striving for a cyclic economy suited to its national conditions. The government is placing a priority on reducing resources consumption in a bid to gradually create a conservation-oriented growth pattern featuring low investment, low consumption, and high efficiency.

Developing a cyclic economy is a long-term task. According to present Chinese plans, by 2010 a fully functioning legal system will be built, and comprehensive measures will be taken in terms of policies, mechanisms, technologies, and management to step up the efforts of driving a cyclic economy. Resource efficiency will eventually be greatly improved, waste dramatically reduced, model enterprises created, and environment-friendly cities born.

Changing Energy Consumption

China, with a population of 1.3 billion, is poor in natural resources per capita. Its per capita water resources are less than a quarter of the world average, arable land less than half, forest less than a seventh, and most mineral resources less than half. Energy demand rises when the economy grows and people's living standards improve, but population growth, technology innovation, and energy use also affect how fast energy needs increase. Given the country's limited energy resources, it is difficult to imagine a China consuming energy in the same fashion that the United States does.

China is working toward a resource-saving growth mode suited to the Chinese situation, in an effort to foster a conservation-minded society that encourages not only thrift by producers but also reasonable and proper behavior by consumers. The country is trying to improve its consumption structure by introducing and promoting conservation-oriented technologies and resource-saving products.

To double energy consumption and quadruple GDP per capita between 2000 and 2020, China worked out a sustainable energy development strategy that calls for prioritizing conservation, improving efficiency, diversifying structure, protecting the environment, and promoting markets. Specifically, the draft of the Medium- and Long-Term Energy Development Program (2004–20), approved in principle by the Chinese government on June 30, 2004, urges the following:

—Make energy conservation the top priority. Energy conservation systems should be established and measures implemented in a comprehensive and strict manner so that the efficiency of energy use will be improved significantly.

—Adjust and optimize the nation's energy structure. Pursue an energy development strategy, with coal forming the mainstay and electricity the center of the energy structure, while promoting comprehensive development of oil, gas, and new forms of energy.

—Work for a rational geographic distribution of energy development projects, taking into account the needs of all areas and the factors of production, transport, and consumption. Energy and communication projects should develop in a coordinated way.

—Fully tap both domestic and overseas resources and markets. While making domestic energy exploration, with exploitation and construction projects as the basis, China should also actively participate in energy resource cooperation and development projects around the world.

—Rely on scientific and technological progress and innovation. Advanced technology should be employed and scientific management should be strengthened.

—Enhance environmental protection and strive to reduce the impact of energy production and consumption on the environment.

—Attach a high degree of importance to energy security. Energy supply should be diversified, construction of oil reserves should be accelerated, and energy security prewarning and rapid response mechanisms should be improved.

—Institute safeguard measures for energy development. Policies regarding energy resources and energy development should be improved, the market mechanism should be brought into full play, and input in the energy sector should be increased.

Prioritizing Energy Conservation

There is no doubt that providing domestic solutions and exploring overseas energy resources help ease the constraints on China's energy development, but to fundamentally solve the problems, it is paramount to conserve energy. In 2004 the Chinese government laid out its medium- and long-term energy saving objectives, projects, and measures. By 2010 energy consumption per 10,000 yuan GDP (constant price in 1990) is expected to drop from 2.68 tons of coal equivalent in 2002 to 2.25 tons, with an annual energy saving rate of 2.2 percent between 2003 and 2010. The nation's energy conservation capacity is expected to reach 400 million tons of coal equivalent.

As the government continues to speed up its efforts at energy conservation, the number is projected to go down to 1.54 tons of coal equivalent in 2020, with an annual average energy conservation rate of 3 percent from 2003 to 2020. Meanwhile, the energy saving capacity is expected to hit 1.4 billion tons of coal equivalent, 111 percent as much as the total planned, newly increased energy production of 1.26 billion tons of coal equivalent during the same period. This will lead to a cut in sulfur dioxide by 21 million tons. Achievement of objectives will be measured by energy consumption indicators per unit of major products, or amount of output. By 2010 China's products as a whole are expected to reach or approach the advanced international level of the early 1990s in terms of the indicators, of which large and medium-sized enterprises are expected to attain a level comparable to that of developed countries at the beginning of the twenty-first century. By 2020 China is expected to reach or approach the international advanced level.

The energy conservation plan highlights the electric power industry, the iron and steel industry, the nonferrous metals industry, the oil and petrochemical

industry, the chemical industry, the building material industry, the coal industry, the machinery building industry, in addition to transportation, construction, and commercial and residential buildings. The plan lists the following ten projects:
  —Coal-burning industrial boiler (kiln) retrofit,
  —District cogeneration,
  —Residual heat and pressure utilization,
  —Petroleum saving and substitution,
  —Motor system energy savings,
  —Energy system optimization,
  —Building energy conservation,
  —Green lighting,
  —Government agency energy conservation,
  —Energy saving monitoring and testing, and technology service system building.

Diversifying Energy Sources

China has been trying to gradually reduce the proportion of coal as the nation's primary energy consumption. Coal use decreased from 76 percent in 1990 to 68 percent in 2004 and is expected to stabilize at around 60 percent by 2020. Consumption of oil and natural gas increased from 17 percent to 23 percent in the same period. As China's crude oil production is projected to reach 180–200 million tons by 2020, oil needs will be satisfied largely through imports. From 2000 to 2020 China will see an average 9 percent rise in natural gas consumption each year: by 2020 overall natural gas demand will exceed 160 billion cubic meters, of which some 50 billion to 60 billion cubic meters, or 34 percent of total consumption, will come from imports.

China is also exerting itself to develop hydropower, nuclear power, and renewable energy. By 2020 the country's installed capacity of hydropower will reach 200 million to 240 million kilowatts, accounting for 19–22 percent of total electricity generation, an increase from 16.4 percent in 2000. In addition, the installed capacity of nuclear power will attain 40 million kilowatts, with an annualized 15.9 percent increase on average. By 2020 nuclear power is expected to generate 7 percent of total electricity, rising from a little over 1 percent in 2000.

Within the mix of primary energy consumption, the proportion of renewable energy is expected to increase from the present 7 percent to 15 percent by 2020. As a result, it will substitute consumption of fossil energy by 400 million tons of coal equivalent and reduce the emission of CO_2 by 1 billion tons and sulfur dioxide by over 7 million tons.

As energy use is the major cause for environmental deterioration, environmental protection has been an internal factor in China's policymaking toward energy strategy. The environment sets down constraints for China's future growth because energy development is constrained by environmental capacity, greenhouse gas emissions, and environmental requirements.

2020 and Beyond

As the amount of CO_2 release is to be limited, marginal costs of cutting CO_2 will go up. China will have to deal with the pressure from global environmental protection when developing energy. Higher economic input due to the limits set on greenhouse gas emissions will also force China to rethink its energy strategy.

The Kyoto Protocol has begun to shape world climate policies, but because the United States and Australia have refused to sign it, the effectiveness of its implementation will be discounted, and the treaty is unlikely to lead the world to where it wants to go. Also, whether signatory countries such as Russia and some EU members will live up to the pact remains to be seen. What should we do after 2012, or post-Kyoto? While scholars and analysts from various countries have put forward suggestions and plans, any of which need to be further discussed and studied, I believe that the following six steps should be considered when post-Kyoto actions are contemplated.

First, the relationship among economy, society, energy, and environment must be handled correctly. Climate change is the great challenge that humankind faces today, and understanding how to tackle the issue is a major task for both developed and developing countries, requiring overall planning and coordination. Developing nations need to concentrate on developing their economies and eradicating poverty. But at the same time, they must protect resources and energy to achieve sustainable growth. Rich nations should do their best to help poor countries avoid treading the beaten track of developing their economies first and then dealing with pollution afterward.

Second, the relationship between developing economies and cutting greenhouse gas emissions should be understood. Industrialized countries are obliged to limit emissions because the greenhouse effect was mainly caused by their activities, resulting in the long-time release of CO_2 and other greenhouse gases. Developing nations, which are not legally bound to emissions restrictions under the protocol, should nevertheless continue to carry out the principle of "common but differentiated responsibilities." China is unlikely to have any emissions targets by 2020, but it should try to cut greenhouse gas emissions in a manner suited to its national conditions and to contribute to global efforts to alleviate climate change.

Third, advanced countries should take concrete actions to provide more assistance to developing nations in terms of technology, funding, and capacity building. This way, developing countries will be able to use energy-saving and low-consumption technologies and equipment in a timely manner, to help avoid taking the same road toward modernization that rich countries did in the past.

Fourth, the importance of technology development and transfer needs to be recognized. The technology does exist, but the mechanisms for its dissemination and transfer are lacking. Technology development and transfer must be approached with an innovative and reformist mind. Industrialized nations should help set up more international cooperation mechanisms suited to the national conditions of various countries. Furthermore, government and private sectors should be encouraged to fully participate in projects tackling climate change, particularly with respect to CDM cooperation.

Fifth, adaptation to and mitigation of climate change must be balanced. To mitigate is to soften the effects of climate change, but adapting to climate change is equally important. Mitigation and adaptation are two indispensable paths for the convention to follow. The post-Kyoto negotiation process on adaptation should be accelerated to help improve developing countries' capabilities to adapt to climate change.

Sixth, public knowledge of climate change and research into climate change must be expanded. China will continue to encourage research and development of energy conservation technologies for clean coal and for reasonable use of natural gas within the framework of countering climate change. It welcomes developed nations to facilitate the transfer of energy conservation and renewable energy technology and the localization of equipment manufacturing. China, in line with the framework of sustainable growth, is ready to contribute to the alleviation of climate change by seeking effective means in a manner suited to its national conditions and capabilities.

Note

1. *2001–2010 Program for Sustainable Development of Science and Technology* (Beijing: Ministry of Science and Technology, 2002); *National Assessment Report on Climate Change* (Beijing: Ministry of Science and Technology, 2002); China Climate Change Info Net (www.ccchina.gov.cn).

Contributors

Sir Howard Dalton was the chief scientific adviser in the Department of the Environment, Food, and Rural Affairs (United Kingdom) until 2007. He is a professor of microbiology at the University of Warwick. His research interests include biochemistry and genetics, protein science, and the modification of organic compounds by bacteria and yeasts.

Alexander Golub has more than 25 years of experience in the field of environmental and natural resource economics and nearly 20 years of experience in energy economics and the economics of climate change, including applied analysis in climate change mitigation policy. He has been a leading adviser to the Russian government on climate policy, and his economic assessment of the Kyoto Protocol provided an important analysis that led to its ratification by the Russian Federation. Dr. Golub is with Environmental Defense in Washington, D.C.

Thomas Heller is the Shelton Professor of International Legal Studies at Stanford Law School and senior fellow at the Woods Institute for the Environment and at the Freeman Spogli Institute for International Studies. He was one of the lead authors on the Intergovernmental Panel on Climate Change's Working Group III report and, therefore, one of the scholars who shared the 2007 Nobel Peace Prize awarded to the IPCC. He teaches law and international political economy, with a particular focus on comparative economic law in Europe, the United States, and Japan and on strategies for investment or other business transactions in developing economies with weak legal systems and problematic governance. At the Stanford Program in Energy and Sustainable Development, his current research focuses on the political economy of energy sector reform in China, India, Brazil, South Africa, and Mexico, the evolution of natural gas markets, the changing organization of national oil companies, and the relation of energy futures to problems of environment and governance.

Gernot Klepper is policy coordinator for the Environment and Natural Resources program at the Kiel Institute for the World Economy in Germany. His research is focused on international and European climate policies, renewable energy, and transition to sustainable economic structures. Since 2001 he has served as co-chair of the German National Committee on Global Change Research of the German Research Foundation and the Federal Ministry of Education and Research. Dr. Klepper is a member of the High-Level Network of Leading Economists of the EU's Environment Directorate, of the European Environment Agency, and of the Scientific Committee of the International Human Dimensions Programme.

Richard S. Lindzen is Alfred P. Sloan Professor of Atmospheric Science at the Massachusetts Institute of Technology and has worked on the dynamics and physics of the atmosphere since the early 1960s. His work has ranged over topics such as tides on the Earth and other planets, the generation of large-scale flows by wave absorption, the instabilities that lead to phenomena ranging from turbulence and storms, the interactions of convection and storms in the tropics, and the cloud properties that determine the sensitivity of climate to increasing greenhouse gases. He is a member of numerous organizations including the National Academy of Sciences, the American Academy of Arts and Sciences, and the Norwegian Academy of Sciences and Letters.

Robert Mendelsohn is an environmental resource economist who concentrates his work on valuing the environment. He teaches at Yale University where he is the Edwin Weyerhaeuser Davis Professor in the School of Forestry and Environmental Studies. His early work included an integrated assessment model of air pollution that could measure the damages of emissions. This work has been extended to greenhouse gases, and he has returned to studying air pollution in the hope of measuring the marginal damages of emissions across the country. He has also worked on valuing natural ecosystems.

William D. Nordhaus is Sterling Professor of Economics at Yale University. He is a member of the National Academy of Sciences and a Fellow of the American Academy of Arts and Sciences. He is the author of many books, among them *Invention, Growth and Welfare, Is Growth Obsolete?, The Efficient Use of Energy Resources, Reforming Federal Regulation, Managing the Global Commons, Warming the World,* and (with Paul Samuelson) the classic textbook, *Economics,* with the 18th edition published in 2004. He has served on several committees of the National Academy of Sciences including the Committee on Nuclear and Alternative Energy Systems, the Panel on Policy Implications of Greenhouse Warming, and the Committee on the Implications for Science and Society of Abrupt Climate Change.

R. K. Pachauri is the director general of the Energy and Resources Institute in New Delhi. He has been chairman of the IPCC, which was awarded the 2007 Nobel Peace Prize, since April 2002. He has held positions at the World Bank, United Nations Development Program, the Resource Systems Institute of the East-West Center, and the Yale School of Forestry and Environmental Studies. In 2001, in recognition of his immense contribution to the field of environment, he was awarded the Padma Bhushan, one of India's highest civilian awards recognizing distinguished service to the nation in any field. Also in 2001 he was appointed to the Economic Advisory Council to the prime minister of India.

Jyoti Parikh is executive director of Integrated Research and Action for Development (IRADe). She is active in climate change modeling, mitigation, and adaptation issues. She has served as an energy consultant for the World Bank, the U.S. Department of Energy, the European Economic Community, and UN agencies such as UNIDO, FAO, UNU, and UNESCO. She has also served on numerous government committees in India. She was previously a senior professor at Indira Gandhi Institute of Development Research.

Sonja Peterson is a researcher with the Kiel Institute for the World Economy in Germany. She heads the Research Group on Climate and Energy and has written numerous papers on climate policy and related issues.

Stefan Rahmstorf is a professor of physics of the oceans at Potsdam University and a scientist at the Potsdam Institute for Climate Impact Research, where he has been since 1996. His research focuses on the role of ocean currents in climate change. He has held positions at the New Zealand Oceanographic Institute and the Institute of Marine Science at Kiel. In 1999 Dr. Rahmstorf was awarded the prestigious Centennial Fellowship Award of the U.S.-based James S. McDonnell Foundation. He is a member of the Panel on Abrupt Climate Change and of the German Advisory Council on Global Change.

Stephen H. Schneider is the Melvin and Joan Lane Professor for Interdisciplinary Environmental Sciences, professor of biological sciences, and a senior fellow in the Woods Institute for the Environment, Stanford University. In 1975 Dr. Schneider founded the interdisciplinary journal, *Climatic Change,* and continues to serve as its editor. He was honored in 1992 with a MacArthur Fellowship for his ability to integrate and interpret the results of global climate research. In 2002 he was elected to the U.S. National Academy of Sciences. Dr. Schneider contributed to all four IPCC Assessment Reports. In the most recent assessment, he served as a coordinating lead author for Working Group II and a member of the Synthesis Report writing team. In 2007, with four generations of IPCC authors, he received a collective Nobel Peace Prize.

Shen Longhai is director of the China Energy Conservation Association and senior adviser to the Energy Research Institute under the National Development and Reform Commission. He has held many government positions in the People's Republic of China, including director general for energy in the State Economic Commission and for Resource Conservation in the State Planning Commission. He has served as vice chairman of the China Energy Research Society and was economic counselor at the Chinese Embassy in Washington, D.C. For more than twenty years, he worked at the Ministry of Petroleum Industry, State Economy Commission and State Planning Commission in China. He was a participant in the establishment of the strategy documents, "China's Agenda 21" and "China's Issues and Options in Greenhouse Gas Emission Control," the latter supported by the United Nations and the World Bank.

Robert N. Stavins is Albert Pratt Professor of Business and Government at the John F. Kennedy School of Government of Harvard University, director of the Environmental Economics Program, and chairman of the Environment and Natural Resources Faculty Group. He is the former chair of the U.S. Environmental Protection Agency's Environmental Economics Advisory Board. His scholarship has focused on environmental economics and policy. He is the author of *Environmental Economics and Public Policy: Selected Papers of Robert N. Stavins* (2001) and has contributed to several other collections and academic journals.

John Stone is an adjunct research professor in the Department of Geography and Environmental Studies at Carleton University and is affiliated with the Canadian Meteorological and Oceanographic Society. His experiences since 2005 include senior sabbaticant, International Development Research Council, and senior consultant, SENES Consultants Ltd. Before this he served as executive director (climate change) for the Meteorological Service of Canada, Environment Canada; director-general, Atmospheric Environment Service, Environment Canada; director (Meteorological Research Branch), Atmospheric Environment Service, Environment Canada; and coordinator for the Second World Climate Conference Atmospheric Environment Service, Environment Canada.

Ernesto Zedillo is the director of the Yale Center for the Study of Globalization, professor in the field of international economics and politics, and adjunct professor of forestry and environmental studies at Yale University. He was the president of Mexico from 1994 to 2000. He was the chairman of the High Level Panel on Financing for Development in 2001, the co-coordinator of the Trade Task Force of the Millennium Development Project, co-chairman of the Commission on the Private Sector and Development, and the UN secretary general's special envoy for the 2005 World Summit. He currently serves on the High Level Commission on Legal Empowerment of the Poor, the World Bank's Commission on Growth and Development, and the High Level Task Force on Climate Change organized by the Club de Madrid and the United Nations Foundation. He was the recipient of the 2006 Sustainable Development Leadership Award presented by the Energy Resources Institute (TERI) in New Delhi.

Index

Kyoto framework proposals, 7–8, 126, 147–48, 222–23

Dion, Stephane, 197, 199

The Discovery of Global Warming (Weart), 34

Distributional effects: lifestyle changes, 19; post-Kyoto discussions, 119, 147–48; as significance marker, 76–79; in UNFCCC negotiations, 14

Distributional impact criteria, key vulnerabilities, 60

Economic Consequences of Possible Ratification . . . by the Russian Federation, 161–62

Economic damages, 83–85, 86. *See also* Cost *entries;* GDP patterns

Electricity: Canada, 195, 196–97, 198; China, 217, 220, 221; European Emissions Trading Scheme, 133; India, 211; United Kingdom, 187. *See also* Energy resources/consumption

Eleventh Conference of the Parties (COP-*11*), 115–16, 121, 183, 197–98, 199–200, 207

El Niño, 42, 48

Emissions levels: accumulation statistics, 207; in anti-alarmist arguments, 22–24; Canada, 6, 194–97, 200, 201; China, 109, 216, 218, 220, 221; in climate sensitivity models, 37–42, 48–49; EU reduction pledge, 3; fingerprint studies, 48; increase in, 35–37; India, 208–10; IPCC's reports, 68–73, 123–24, 178; Kyoto Protocol coverage, 92, 109, 145–46; Kyoto Protocol estimations, 92–93; per capita comparisons, 211–13; in probability analysis models, 73–77, 181; stabilization scenarios, 15, 18–19, 74, 179–80; United Kingdom, 176, 179, 184–85. *See also* Kyoto Protocol, architectural framework; Russia, CO_2 emissions; Tax-based approach; Trading systems

Energy resources/consumption: Canada, 195–97, 198; China, 216, 217–22; India, 206–07, 208*f,* 213; and international organizational behaviors, 125–26; projected demand, 180; Russia, 158,

159, 160–61, 166–68; in stabilization scenarios, 18–19; United Kingdom, 185–87

Equity issues. *See* Distributional *entries*

Equ scenario, European Emissions Trading Scheme, 104–07, 108

ETS. *See* European Emissions Trading Scheme (ETS)

European Emissions Trading Scheme (ETS): overview, 101–02, 109–11; coverage, 92; impact potential, 6, 104–09, 121; operating policies, 102–04, 126, 133–34; price fluctuations, 96, 122; United Kingdom participation, 186, 188–89

European Union (EU): CDM credit negotiations, 133; emissions reduction pledge, 3; G-*8* discussions, 181–82, 183; in international relations negotiations example, 125, 130–31, 139; Kyoto Protocol negotiations, 120, 158, 160, 172; stabilization proposal, 179. *See also* United Kingdom, climate policy

Fingerprint studies, 48

Finland, 103, 105

First Assessment Report, IPCC's, 14

First Russian National Communication to the UNFCCC, 159, 162

Flexible mechanisms. *See* Clean Development Mechanism (CDM)

Fourth Assessment Report, IPCC's, 3, 13–15, 59

France, 103

Fuel consumption. *See* Energy resources/consumption

G-*8,* climate change focus, 180–83

Gap scenario, European Emissions Trading Scheme, 104–07

GDP patterns: change impact, 4, 83, 84; China, 216, 217; in CO_2 stabilization model, 18; India, 209–10, 211–12; in post-Kyoto framework proposal, 8, 148–49; Russia, 163–66, 169–73; United Kingdom, 185

Germany, 102, 103, 161

GHG emissions. *See* Emissions levels

Glaciers. *See* Ice mass, losses